CONCISE

CHINESE-ENGLISH
DICTIONARY

ROMANIZED

CONCISE

CHINESE-ENGLISH DICTIONARY

ROMANIZED

---

*Containing nearly 10,000
romanized Chinese words
and expressions, Chinese
characters, and English
equivalents.*

James C. Quo

CHARLES E. TUTTLE CO.
Rutland, Vermont
Tokyo, Japan

Representatives

Continental Europe:
BOXERBOOKS, INC.
Zurich

British Isles:
PRENTICE-HALL INTERNATIONAL, INC.
London

Australasia:
PAUL FLESCH & CO., PTY. LTD.
Melbourne

Canada:
M. G. HURTIG LTD.
Edmonton

Published by the Charles E. Tuttle Co., Inc.
of Rutland, Vermont and Tokyo, Japan
with editorial offices at
Suido 1-chome, 2-6, Bunkyo-ku
Tokyo, Japan

Library of Congress
Catalog Card No. 60-14372

Standard Book No. 8048 0116-9

First edition, 1960
Eighth printing, 1970

PRINTED IN JAPAN

INTRODUCTION

This dictionary has been prepared for the purpose of providing the Western student of modern Chinese with a handy, portable, and useful guide to the Chinese language. More than that, it has specifically been designed to serve as a companion volume to my *Concise English-Chinese Dictionary Romanized* published earlier.

Every effort has been expended to make the two dictionaries parallel each other as closely as possible so that they can easily be used for cross reference. Chinese terms are romanized, and include the proper tone readings, followed by characters and English equivalents. Abbreviations used are shown on page vi.

Special emphasis has been given to military and political terms and expressions which have recently come into use.

Extensive tables and charts are included in the English-Chinese dictionary and have not been repeated in this volume.

It is the fervent hope of the author that this dictionary will serve as a useful aid to students of the Chinese language who heretofore have had to rely mainly on dictionaries designed for use by Chinese students of English, which contained no romanized readings.

April, 1960

James C. Quo

ABBREVIATIONS

a.	adjective
adv.	adverb
art.	article
conj.	conjunction
int.	interjection
n.	noun
prep.	preposition
pron.	pronoun
v.	verb
v. aux.	auxiliary verb
*	indicates a Republic of China term
**	indicates a Chinese Communist term

chem.	chemistry	*med.*	medical
elec.	electrical	*mil.*	military
engin.	engineering	*off.*	official
math.	mathematics	*U.S.*	United States

A

A¹ 啊 [a final particle, an exclamation]
AI² 挨 *v.* suffer. ~¹ *a.* near
AI¹ tz'u⁴ ~次 *a.* orderly
  ~² ~e⁴ ~餓 *v.* suffer from hunger
  ~ma⁴ ~罵 *v.* be blamed
  ~ta³ ~打 *v.* be beaten
AI⁴ 愛 *a.* fond; *v.* love, like; *n.* love, affection
  ~ch'ing² ~情 *n.* love
  ~jen² ~人 *n.* sweetheart, lover
  ~kuo² ~國 *n.* patriotism
  ~kuo² che³ ~國者 *n.* patriot
  ~kuo² ssu¹ hsiang³ ~國思想 *n.* patriotism
  ~kuo² tseng¹ ch'an³ yün⁴ tung⁴ ~國增產運動
  n. patriotic production campaign**
  ~lien⁴ ~戀 *v.* love
  ~shen² ~神 *n.* Venus, Cupid
AI⁴ 礙 *n.* obstacle; *v.* hinder, obstruct
AN¹ 安 *a.* quiet, calm, safe; *v.* tranquilize
  ~chih⁴ ~置 *v.* settle, lay down
  ~ching⁴ ~静 *a.* quiet, peaceful; *v.* keep quiet
  ~ch'üan² ~全 *n.* safety; *a.* safe
  ~ch'üan² chieh⁴ ~全界 *n.* safety zone
  ~ch'üan² yin¹ su⁴ ~全因素 *n.* factor of safety
  (*engin.*)
  ~hsi² jih⁴ ~息日 *n.* sabbath
  ~hsien² ~閒 *n.* leisure; *adv.* leisurely
  ~i⁴ ~逸 *n.* comfort, easy
  ~le⁴ ~樂 *a.* comfortable
  ~mien² yao⁴ ~眠藥 *n.* hypnotic (drug)
  ~p'ai² ~排 *v.* arrange
  ~shih⁴ ~適 *a.* comfortable
  ~ting⁴ ~定 *n.* tranquillity
  ~tsang⁴ ~葬 *v.* inter, bury
  ~wei⁴ ~慰 *v.* comfort
  ~wen³ ~穩 *a.* firm, stable, steady, safe
  ~wo⁴ ~臥 *v.* sleep

1

AN⁴ 岸 *n.* bank, shore

AN⁴ 按 *v.* press down, massage, hold, stop; *prep.* according to

~chao⁴ ~照 *prep.* according to

~shih² ~時 *v.* keep time

AN⁴ 案 *n.* table, record, case

~chien⁴ ~件 *n.* law case

~cho¹ ~桌 *n.* desk

~chüan⁴ ~卷 *n.* record (*off.*)

AN⁴ 暗 *a.* dark, gloomy; *adv.* secretly

~ch'i¹ ~漆 *n.* lusterless paint

~hao⁴ ~號 *n.* secret sign, secret mark

~kou¹ ~溝 *n.* culvert

~ma³ ~碼 *n.* cipher

~sha¹ ~殺 *n.* murder

~shih⁴ ~示 *v.* hint

~shih⁴ ~室 *n.* darkroom

~ti⁴ ~地 *adv.* secretly

~t'an⁴ ~探 *n.* detective

CH

CHA⁴ 炸 *v.* explode. ~² *v.* fry

~ch'en² ~沉 *v.* sink (by bombing)

~hui³ ~毀 *v.* blow up

~kao¹ ~高 *n.* height of burst

~lieh⁴ ~裂 *n.* burst (explosion)

~tan⁴ ~彈 *n.* bomb

~yao⁴ ~藥 *n.* explosive

CHAN¹ 粘 *v.* paste up, stick. NIEN² *a.* glutinous

~¹ t'ieh¹ ~貼 *v.* paste

t'u³ ~土 *n.* clay

CHAN³ 展 *v.* unfold, open

~ch'i¹ ~期 *v.* postpone

~hsien⁴ ~限 *v.* extend

~k'ai¹ ~開 *v.* deploy

~lan³ hui⁴ ~覽會 *n.* exhibition

~wang⁴ k'ung³ ~望孔 *n.* vision slit

CHAN⁴ 佔 *v.* occupy

2

~chü⁴ ~攄 *v.* occupy; *n.* occupation
~ling³ chen⁴ ti⁴ ~領陣地 *v.* occupy a position
~ling³ chün¹ ~領軍 *n.* occupation forces
~ling³ ch'ü¹ ~領區 *n.* occupied area (by our own forces)
CHAN⁴ 站 *v.* stand; *n.* station
~chang³ ~長 *n.* station master
~chu⁴ ~住 *v.* halt
~kang³ ~崗 *v.* post
~li⁴ ~立 *v.* stand up
~wen³ ~穩 *v.* stand firmly
CHAN⁴ 暫 *n.* a short time; *adv.* temporarily, briefly
~shih² ~時 *a.* temporary; *adv.* temporarily
~t'ing² ~停 *n.* suspension
CHAN⁴ 戰 *v.* fight, fear, tremble; *n.* fight, battle, war
~cheng¹ ~爭 *n.* war
~chien⁴ ~艦 *n.* battleship, warship
~ch'ang³ ~場 *n.* battlefield, field
~ch'ü¹ ~區 *n.* theater of operations
~fei⁴ ~費 *n.* military expenditure
~hao² ~壕 *n.* trench
~hsien⁴ ~線 *n.* battle front
~i⁴ ~役 *n.* campaign
~kung¹ ~功 *n.* exploit
~k'uang⁴ ~況 *n.* tactical situation
~li⁴ ~慄 *v.* tremble
~li⁴ p'in³ ~利品 *n.* trophy
~lüeh⁴ ~略 *n.* strategy; *a.* strategic
~lüeh⁴ chi⁴ hua⁴ wei³ yüan² hui⁴ ~略計劃委員會 *n.* Strategy Planning and Research Committee*
~pai⁴ ~敗 *v.* defeat
~sheng⁴ ~勝 *v.* win (a battle); *n.* victory
~shih² ~時 *n.* wartime
~shih³ ~史 *n.* war history
~shih⁴ ~士 *n.* warrior
~shu⁴ ~術 *n.* tactics
~ti⁴ chi⁴ che³ ~地記者 *n.* war correspondent
~tou⁴ chi¹ ~鬪機 *n.* combat airplane

3

~tou⁴ li⁴ ~鬭力 *n.* battle efficiency
~tou⁴ ying¹ hsiung² ~鬭英雄 *n.* combat hero**
CHANG¹ 張 *n.* sheet; *v.* display, open, expand
~kung¹ ~弓 *v.* draw a bow
~k'ai¹ ~開 *v.* open
~lo² ~羅 *v.* raise money
CHANG¹ 章 *a.* elegant; *n.* essay, rule, chapter; *v.* manifest
~ch'eng² ~程 *n.* regulation, rule
~fa³ ~法 *n.* phraseology
CHANG³ 掌 *n.* palm, sole; *v.* control
~kuei⁴ ~櫃 *n.* accountant, shop-owner
~kung¹ ~工 *n.* blacksmith
~li³ ~理 *v.* manage
~wo⁴ ~握 *v.* control
CHANG³ 長 *a.* older; *n.* head, chief, commander, length. CH'ANG² *a.* long
~³ chin⁴ ~進 *n.* progress
~hsiung¹ ~兄 *n.* oldest brother
~lao³ hui⁴ ~老會 *n.* rectory
~tzu³ ~子 *n.* oldest son
~² teng⁴ ~凳 *n.* bench
~tuan³ ~短 *n.* length
~t'u² tien⁴ hua⁴ ~途電話 *n.* long-distance telephone
CHANG⁴ 漲 *v.* overflow, expand
~chia⁴ ~價 *v.* raise the price
~ch'ao² ~潮 *n.* flood-tide
~shui³ ~水 *n.* tide
CHANG⁴ 丈 *n.* Chinese linear measure for 11.75 feet
~fu¹ ~夫 *n.* husband
~jen² ~人 *n.* father of one's wife (father-in-law)
~mu³ ~母 *n.* mother of one's wife (mother-in-law)
CHANG⁴ 仗 *n.* weapon; *v.* rely on, depend on
CHANG⁴ 帳 *n.* curtain, tent. [Same as 賬] account
~fang² ~房 *n.* cashier's department
~mu⁴ ~目 *n.* account
~p'eng² ~蓬 *n.* tent
~tan¹ ~單 *n.* bill

4

CHAO¹ 招 *v.* beckon, confess, invite
~**chi²** ~集 *v.* muster
~**chih⁴** ~致 *v.* invite attack
~**hu¹** ~呼 *v.* beckon
~**je³** ~惹 *v.* incur
~**ping¹** ~兵 *v.* recruit
~**p'ai²** ~牌 *n.* signboard (store)
~**tai⁴** ~待 *v.* entertain
~**tai⁴ yüan²** ~待員 *n.* usher
~**t'ieh¹** ~貼 *n.* poster
~**tsu¹** ~租 *v.* be let for rent
~**yao²** ~搖 *v.* exaggerate
CHAO¹ 朝 *see* **CH'AO²**
CHAO² 着 *v.* cause, send, put on; [a prep.] **CHE¹** [a suffix]
CHAO³ 找 *v.* seek, look for
~**ch'iao⁴ men²** ~竅門 *v.* find a secret technical contrivance**
~**hsün²** ~尋 *v.* find
~**t'ou²** ~頭 *n.* change (money)
CHAO⁴ 召 *v.* call, summon
~**chi²** ~集 *v.* assemble
CHAO⁴ 照 *v.* enlighten, illuminate
~**ch'ang²** ~常 *adv.* as usual
~**hsiang⁴** ~相 *n.* photograph; *v.* take photograph of
~**hsiang⁴ chi¹** ~相機 *n.* camera
~**hsiang⁴ shu⁴** ~相術 *n.* photography
~**ku⁴** ~顧 *v.* patronize, take care of
~**liao⁴** ~料 *v.* take care of, look after
~**ming² tan⁴** ~明彈 *n.* flare bomb
~**ming² teng¹** ~明燈 *n.* illuminating light
~**yao⁴** ~耀 *v.* shine on
CHE¹ 遮 *v.* screen, intercept, hide
~**hu⁴** ~護 *v.* shelter
~**man²** ~瞞 *v.* conceal
~**pi⁴** ~庇 *v.* protect
~**pi⁴** ~避 *v.* screen, blind, mask
~**pi⁴ ting³** ~避頂 *n.* grazing point
CHE¹ 着 *see* **CHAO²**
CHE² 折 *v.* bend, discount

5

~k'ou⁴ ~扣 *n.* discount
~shih² chia⁴ ~實價 *n.* net price
~shih² kung¹ chai⁴ ~實公債 *n.* parity bond**
~shih² tan¹ wei⁴ ~實單位 *n.* parity unit**
CHE³ 者 [a final particle, a suffix]
CHE⁴ 這 *a.* & *pron.* this; *adv.* here. [Also read CHEI⁴]
~hsieh¹ ~些 *a.* & *pron.* these
~ko⁴ ~個 *a.* & *pron.* this
~li³ ~裏 *adv.* here
~yang⁴ ~樣 *adv.* thus, so
CHEI⁴ 這 *see* CHE⁴
CHEN¹ 眞 *a.* real, true, genuine
~cheng⁴ ~正 *a.* real, true
~chu¹ ~珠 *n.* pearl
~hua⁴ ~話 *n.* truth
~k'ung¹ ~空 *n.* vacuum
~k'ung¹ kuan³ ~空管 *n.* vacuum tube
~li³ ~理 *n.* truth
CHEN¹ 針 *n.* needle, pin
~hsien⁴ ~線 *n.* needlework
~hsien⁴ pao¹ ~線包 *n.* sewing kit
~tz'u⁴ fa³ ~刺法 *n.* acupuncture
CHEN⁴ 振 *v.* arouse, stimulate
~chiu⁴ ~救 *v.* save from danger
~hsing¹ ~興 *v.* develop
~tung⁴ ~動 *v.* vibrate; *n.* vibration
~tso⁴ ~作 *v.* stimulate, encourage
CHIH³ 紙 *n.* paper
~pi⁴ ~幣 *n.* paper money
~san³ ~傘 *n.* paper umbrella
~shan⁴ ~扇 *n.* paper fan
~yen¹ ~煙 *n.* cigarette
~yüan¹ ~鳶 *n.* kite
CHEN⁴ 鎭 *n.* town; *v.* keep, protect
~shou³ ~守 *v.* guard
~ya¹ ~壓 *v.* suppress
CHEN⁴ 陣 *n.* tactics, array, moment
~chung¹ jih⁴ chi⁴ ~中日記 *n.* war diary
~hsien⁴ ~綫 *n.* line of battle
~ti⁴ ~地 *n.* fire position (*mil.*)

6

~wang² ~亡 *v.* be killed in action

~yü³ ~雨 *n.* shower

CHENG¹ 爭 *v.* quarrel, dispute, debate

~lun⁴ ~論 *n.* & *v.* quarrel

~to² ~奪 *v.* contest (for a position)

~tou⁴ ~鬥 *v.* fight

CHENG¹ 征 *v.* invade, attack, levy

~chan⁴ ~戰 *v.* fight a battle

~fa² ~伐 *v.* invade, attack

~fu² ~服 *v.* conquer

~ping¹ ~兵 *v.* conscript

~shou¹ ~收 *v.* levy, collect

~shui⁴ ~稅 *v.* levy taxes

CHENG³ 整 *v.* adjust, arrange ; *a.* entire, whole

~ch'i² hsien⁴ ~齊線 *n.* alignment

~ko⁴ ~個 *a.* integral, whole, entire

~li³ ~理 *v.* reorganize

~tun⁴ ~頓 *v.* reorganize

CHENG⁴ 正 *a.* upright, proper ; *v.* make right, correct

~¹ yüeh⁴ ~月 *n.* January

~⁴ chih² ~直 *a.* righteous, upright

~fang¹ ~方 *n.* square

~i⁴ ~義 *n.* justice

~mien⁴ ~面 *n.* positive

~shih⁴ ~式 *a.* formal ; *adv.* formerly

CHENG⁴ 政 *n.* government, administration, executive, politics

~chieh⁴ ~界 *n.* political circle

~chih⁴ ~治 *n.* politics

~chih⁴ chia¹ ~治家 *n.* statesman

~chih⁴ chü² ~治局 *n.* politburo

~chih⁴ fa³ lü⁴ wei³ yüan² hui⁴ ~治法律委員會 *n.* Committee of Political and Legal Affairs**

~chih⁴ fan⁴ ~治犯 *n.* political prisoner

~chih⁴ hui⁴ i⁴ ~治會議 *n.* political conference

~chih⁴ huo² tung⁴ ~治活動 *n.* political activity

~chih⁴ hsüeh² ~治學 *n.* political science

~chih⁴ kung¹ tso⁴ ~治工作 *n.* political work

~chih⁴ pu⁴ ~治部 *n.* political department

~chih⁴ sheng¹ huo² ~治生活 *n.* political life

7

~chih⁴ wang² ming⁴ ~治亡命 *n.* political refugee

~ch'üan² ~權 *n.* political power

~fa³ ~法 *n.* politics and law

~fu³ ~府 *n.* government

~k'o⁴ ~客 *n.* politician

~pien⁴ ~變 *n.* revolution, coup d'etat

~tang³ ~黨 *n.* political party

~t'i³ ~體 *n.* form of government

~ts'e⁴ ~策 *n.* policy

~wu⁴ yüan⁴ ~務院 *n.* Government Administrative Council**

CHENG⁴ 證 *n.* evidence, legal testimony, proof; *v.* prove, testify, verify

~chü⁴ ~據 *n.* evidence

~jen² ~人 *n.* witness

~ming² ~明 *v.* prove

~shu¹ ~書 *n.* certificate

CHI¹ 機 *n.* machine; *a.* opportune, motive

~ch'i⁴ chiao³ t'a⁴ ch'e¹ ~器脚踏車 *n.* motorcycle

~ch'iao³ ~巧 *a.* skillful

~hui⁴ ~會 *n.* opportunity, chance

~hsieh⁴ ~械 *n.* machinery; *a.* mechanical

~hsieh⁴ hua⁴ ~械化 *v.* mechanize

~hsieh⁴ kung¹ ch'eng² ~械工程 *n.* mechanical engineering

~hsieh⁴ shih¹ ~械師 *n.* mechanist

~hsieh⁴ wei² wu⁴ lun⁴ ~械唯物論 *n.* mechanistic materialism**

~i² ~宜 *n.* policy, line of action

~kuan¹ ~關 *n.* organ, organization

~kuan¹ ch'iang¹ ~關鎗 *n.* machine gun

~mi⁴ ~密 *a.* secret, confidential (security classification)

~mou² ~謀 *n.* stratagem

~tung⁴ ~動 *a.* mobile

~yao⁴ ~要 *a.* confidential, classified

~yu² ~油 *n.* oil

CHI¹ 激 *n.* rush; *v.* rouse, excite; *a.* indignant

~ang² ~昂 *a.* spirited, passionate

8

~li⁴ ~勵 *v.* encourage
~lieh⁴ ~烈 *a.* bitter, violent (combat)
~nu⁴ ~怒 *v.* enrage
~tung⁴ ~動 *v.* rouse, excite
CHI¹ 積 *v.* gather, store up, accumulate
  ~chi² ~極 *a.* positive, constructive
  ~hsü⁴ ~蓄 *n. & v.* deposit
CHI¹ 績 *n.* meritorious service; *v.* spin, twist
CHI¹ 饑 *n.* famine, dearth; *a.* hungry
  ~chin⁸ ~饉 *n.* famine
  ~e⁴ ~餓 *n.* hunger
  ~min² ~民 *n.* starving person
CHI¹ 鶏 *n.* chicken, hen, cock
  ~chiao⁴ ~叫 *v.* crow (cock)
  ~kuan¹ ~冠 *n.* cock's comb
  ~tan⁴ ~蛋 *n.* hen's egg
CHI¹ 基 *n.* foundation, base, land, property
  ~ch'u³ ~礎 *n.* foundation, base
  ~hsien⁴ ~線 *n.* base line
  ~pen³ chin¹ ~本金 *n.* reserve fund
  ~pen³ tan¹ wei⁴ ~本單位 *n.* basic unit
  ~pen³ te¹ ~本的 *a.* fundamental
  ~ti⁴ ~地 *n.* base (of operations)
  ~tu¹ chiao⁴ ~督教 *n.* Christianity
CHI¹ 擊 *v.* strike, beat, attack, whip
  ~fa¹ ~發 *v.* firing mechanism
  ~k'uei⁴ ~潰 *v.* rout
  ~lo⁴ ~落 *v.* bring down (aircraft)
  ~pai⁴ ~敗 *v.* defeat
  ~p'o⁴ ~破 *v.* break (by striking)
  ~t'ui⁴ ~退 *v.* repel, repulse
CHI² 吉 *a.* lucky, fortunate
  ~chao⁴ ~兆 *a.* lucky
  ~li⁴ ~利 *n.* good luck
  ~p'u³ ch'e¹ ~普車 *n.* jeep
CHI² 急 *a.* urgent, hasty; *n.* urgent message
  ~chin⁴ chu⁸ i⁴ ~進主義 *n.* radicalism
  ~chin⁴ p'ai⁴ ~進派 *n.* radical party
  ~chiu⁴ ~救 *n.* first aid
  ~hsing² chün¹ ~行軍 *n.* rapid march
  ~hsing² ch'e¹ ~行車 *n.* express (train, bus)

~**mang²** ~忙 *a.* hasty
~**su²** ~速 *a.* quick, fast, swift
~**tien⁴** ~電 *n.* urgent telegram
~**tsao⁴** ~躁 *a.* passionate
~**ts'u⁴** ~促 *n. & v.* hurry
~**yü³** ~雨 *n.* shower
CHI² 及 *v.* reach to; *prep. & conj.* till
CHI² 即 *adv.* immediately, now
~**k'o⁴** ~刻 *adv.* immediately, at once
~**shih³** ~使 *adv.* even if, though
CHI² 籍 *n.* record, register, list
~**kuan⁴** ~貫 *n.* birthplace
~**mo⁴** ~沒 *v.* confiscate
CHI² 集 *v.* collect; *n.* market
~**chieh¹** ~結 *n.* troop concentration
~**chung¹** ~中 *v.* focus, concentrate
~**chung¹ ying²** ~中營 *n.* concentration camp
~**ch'üan²** ~權 *n.* centralized control
~**ho²** ~合 *v.* assemble, rally
~**ho² ti⁴** ~合地 *n.* assembly area
~**hui⁴** ~會 *v.* hold a meeting
~**t'i³ nung² ch'ang³** ~體農場 *n.* collective farm**
CHI² 極 *n.* zenith, end; *adv.* very, extremely
~**chia¹** ~佳 *a.* best
~**e⁴** ~惡 *a.* worst
~**hsing²** ~刑 *n.* capital punishment
~**ta⁴** ~大 *a.* greatest, largest
~**tuan¹** ~端 *n.* extremity, extreme
CHI² 級 *n.* class, grade, step
CHI³ 己 *pron.* I, myself
CHI³ 幾 *v.* be near, approximate; *adv.* almost
~**ho²** ~何 *n.* geometry
CHI³ 擠 *v.* crowd, press, milk
~**ju³** ~乳 *v.* milk
CHI³ 給 *see* KEI³
CHI⁴ 計 *v.* count, calculate, compute; *n.* calculation, plot
~**hua⁴** ~劃 *n.* plan, scheme
~**hua⁴ kuan³ li³** ~劃管理 *n.* planned management**

10

~i⁴ ~議 *v.* discuss
~mou² ~謀 *n.* plot, trick
~suan⁴ ~算 *v.* calculate
~suan⁴ ch'i⁴ ~算器 *n.* calculating machine
~suan⁴ ch'ih³ ~算尺 *n.* slide rule
CHI⁴ 季 *n.* season
~hou⁴ feng¹ ~候風 *n.* monsoon
~k'an¹ ~刊 *n.* quarterly
~p'iao⁴ ~票 *n.* season ticket
CHI⁴ 既 *conj.* since, whereas
CHI⁴ 寄 *v.* send, lodge at, deliver to
~su⁴ ~宿 *v.* lodge at
~su⁴ she⁴ ~宿舍 *n.* dormitory
~sheng¹ wu⁴ ~生物 *n.* parasite
~shou⁴ ~售 *n.* consignment
~t'o¹ ~託 *v.* entrust
~ts'un² ~存 *v.* deposit
~wang⁴ ~望 *v.* expect
CHI⁴ 記 *v.* record, remember, write down
~chang⁴ pu⁴ ~帳簿 *n.* cashbook
~hao⁴ ~號 *n.* sign, mark, symbol
~hsing⁴ ~性 *n.* memory
~i⁴ ~憶 *v.* recollect
~i⁴ li⁴ ~憶力 *n.* memory
~nien⁴ ~念 *n.* remembrance
~shih⁴ pu⁴ ~事簿 *n.* notebook
~shou² ~熟 *v.* memorize
~te² ~得 *v.* remember
CHI⁴ 紀 *n.* century, record
~lu⁴ ~錄 *n.* record
~lü⁴ ~律 *n.* discipline
~nien⁴ ~念 *v.* commemorate
~nien⁴ hui⁴ ~念會 *n.* memorial meeting
~nien⁴ jih⁴ ~念日 *n.* anniversary
~nien⁴ pei¹ ~念碑 *n.* stone monument
~nien⁴ p'in³ ~念品 *n.* souvenir, memorial
~shih⁴ ~事 *n.* memorandum
~yüan² ~元 *n.* epoch, era
~yüan² ch'ien² ~元前 *n.* before Christ (B.C.)
~yüan² hou⁴ ~元後 *n.* after Christ (A.D.)
CHI⁴ 際 *n.* limit, juncture, occasion, time

11

CHI⁴ 濟 *v.* aid, relieve

CHI⁴ 繼 *n.* adoption; *v.* continue, succeed
~**ch'eng²** ~承 *v.* inherit; *n.* inheritance
~**fu⁴** ~父 *n.* stepfather
~**hsü⁴** ~續 *v.* continue; *n.* continuation
~**mu³** ~母 *n.* stepmother
~**nü³** ~女 *n.* stepdaughter
~**tzu³** ~子 *n.* stepson

CHI⁴ 技 *n.* art, skill, talent
~**ch'iao³** ~巧 *a.* skillful
~**i⁴** ~藝 *n.* art
~**neng²** ~能 *n.* skill, talent, ability
~**shu⁴** ~術 *n.* technique; *a.* technical
~**shu⁴ ho² tso⁴** ~術合作 *n.* technical cooperation

CHIA¹ 家 *n.* home, family, house
~**chang³** ~長 *n.* head of a family
~**cheng⁴** ~政 *n.* household affairs
~**cheng⁴ fu⁴** ~政婦 *n.* housekeeper
~**chü⁴** ~具 *n.* furniture
~**hsiang¹** ~鄉 *n.* native place
~**t'ing²** ~庭 *n.* home, family
~**yung⁴** ~用 *n.* family expenditure

CHIA¹ 加 *v.* add; *n.* addition; *a.* additional; *prep.* plus
~**pei⁴** ~倍 *v.* double
~**su²** ~速 *v.* speed, accelerate
~**yu²** ~油 *v.* lubricate, oil, fuel

CHIA¹ 夾 *n.* pincers, clip, wallet; *v.* hold tight
~**chiao³** ~角 *n.* offset angle
~**ch'a¹** ~叉 *n.* gunnery bracket
~**kung¹** ~攻 *n.* converging attack
~**pan³** ~板 *n.* splint
~**tsa²** ~雜 *a.* mixed

CHIA³ 甲 *n.* armor; *a.* first
~**chou⁴** ~胄 *n.* armor
~**pan³** ~板 *n.* deck
~**teng³** ~等 *n.* first class

CHIA³ 假 *a.* false. ~⁴ *n.* leave
~³**chuang¹** ~裝 *v.* disguise, pretend
~**fa³** ~髮 *n.* wig
~**hua⁴** ~話 *n.* lie

12

~hsiang³ ti² ~想敵 *n.* imaginary enemy
~hsiao⁴ ~笑 *v.* smirk
~mei⁴ ~寐 *n.* nap
~mien⁴ chü⁴ ~面具 *n.* mask
~shih³ ~使 *conj.* if; *prep.* in case of
~shih⁴ ~釋 *n.* parole
~ting⁴ ~定 *v.* suppose
~wu⁴ ~物 *n.* counterfeit
~⁴ jih⁴ ~日 *n.* holiday
CHIA⁴ 價 *n.* price, cost, value
~ang² ~昂 *a.* expensive
~chih² ~值 *n.* value
~ko² ~格 *n.* price
~lien² ~廉 *a.* cheap
~mu⁴ piao³ ~目表 *n.* price list
CHIA⁴ 架 *n.* shelf, stand, rack, frame; *v.* kidnap
~ch'iao² ~橋 *v.* build a bridge over
~ch'iao² tso⁴ yeh⁴ tui⁴ ~橋作業隊 *n.* bridging party
~hsien⁴ ~線 *n.* wire laying
CHIA⁴ 稼 *n.* crops
CHIA⁴ 嫁 *v.* marry
~chuang¹ ~妝 *n.* dowry, portion
CHIANG¹ 將 *v.aux.* shall, will; *v.* be ready to.
~⁴ *v.* command; *n.* side, general, marshal
~¹ chin⁴ ~近 *adv.* nearly, presently
~lai² ~來 *a.* & n. future
~⁴ chün¹ ~軍 *n.* general
~kuan¹ ~官 *n.* general officer
CHIANG¹ 江 *n.* river
CHIANG³ 講 *v.* explain, talk
~chieh³ ~解 *v.* explain; *n.* explanation
~ho² ~和 *v.* negotiate
~hua⁴ ~話 *v.* talk, speak
~tao⁴ ~道 *v.* preach
~t'ai² ~台 *n.* platform, pulpit
~shih¹ ~師 *n.* lecturer, instructor
~yen³ ~演 *n.* & *v.* lecture
CHIANG³ 奬 *v.* praise, encourage, reward
~chang¹ ~章 *n.* meritorious medal
~li⁴ ~勵 *v.* encourage

13

~p'in³ ~品 *n.* prize, reward

CHIANG⁴ 醬 *n.* soy sauce, jam

~ts'ai⁴ ~菜 *n.* vegetables (pickled)

~yu² ~油 *n.* sauce

CHIANG⁴ 匠 *n.* workman, craftsman, mechanic

CHIANG⁴ 降 *v.* drop, reduce, descend. HSIANG²
   v. surrender

~chi² ~級 *v.* reduce in rank, demote

~hsüeh³ ~雪 *v.* snow

~lao⁴ ~落 *v.* descend, land (from the air)

~lao⁴ san³ ~落傘 *n.* parachute

~yü³ ~雨 *v.* rain

hsiang² fu² ~服 *v.* surrender

CHIANG⁴ 疘 *see* MA²

CHIAO¹ 交 *v.* associate, pay, deliver, give

~chan⁴ ~戰 *v.* fight; *n.* hostilities

~chieh² ~結 *v.* associate with

~chieh⁴ ~界 *n.* boundary, border

~ch'ing² ~情 *n.* friendship

~fu⁴ ~付 *v.* pay, deliver

~huan² ~還 *v.* return

~huan⁴ ~換 *v.* exchange

~hsiang³ ch'ü³ ~響曲 *n.* symphony

~i⁴ ~易 *n.* trade, bargain, business deal

~i⁴ so³ ~易所 *n.* stock exchange

~kou⁴ ~媾 *v.* copulate; *n.* coition

~liu² tien⁴ ~流電 *n.* alternative current

~she⁴ ~涉 *v.* negotiate

~tai⁴ ~代 *v.* hand over

~tai⁴ cheng⁴ ts'e⁴ ~代政策 *v.* explain policy to
   one's immediate subordinate**

~t'i⁴ ~替 *v.* substitute

~t'ung¹ ~通 *v.* communicate; *n.* traffic

~t'ung¹ pu⁴ ~通部 *n.* Ministry of Communications

~yu³ ~友 *v.* make friends with

CHIAO¹ 焦 *a.* burned, anxious; *v.* scorch

~chi² ~急 *a.* anxious

~tien³ ~點 *n.* focus

~t'an⁴ ~炭 *n.* coke (coal)

CHIAO¹ 膠 *n.* glue; *a.* sticky

~chih² ~質 *n.* glue, gum
~chu⁴ ~住 *n.* stick fast
~chüan³ ~卷 *n.* photographic film
~p'i² ~皮 *n.* rubber
~shui³ ~水 *n.* glue, mucilage
~wan² ~丸 *n.* capsule
CHIAO³ 角 *n.* horn, corner, angle
~chu² ~逐 *v.* compete
~li⁴ ~力 *n.* wrestling
~tu⁴ ~度 *n.* angle
~t'ieh³ ~鐵 *n.* angle iron
CHIAO³ 脚 *n.* foot
~ch'i⁴ ping⁴ ~氣病 *n.* beriberi
~t'a⁴ ch'e¹ ~踏車 *n.* bicycle
CHIAO⁴ 叫 *v.* cry, call, shout
~han³ ~喊 *v.* shout
~hua⁴ tzu¹ ~化子 *n.* begger
CHIAO⁴ 教 *n.* doctrine, sect, school; *v.* cause, make. ~¹ *v.* teach
~¹ yang³ ~養 *n.* breeding (manners)
~⁴ huang² ~皇 *n.* The Pope, pontiff
~hui⁴ ~會 *n.* religious mission
~hsün⁴ ~訓 *n.* instruction
~i⁴ ~義 *n.* doctrine
~kuan¹ ~官 *n.* instructor, officer
~k'o¹ shu¹ ~科書 *n.* textbook
~lien⁴ ~練 *v.* train
~shih⁴ ~室 *n.* classroom
~shou⁴ ~授 *n.* professor
~t'ang² ~堂 *n.* church
~t'iao² chu³ i⁴ che³ ~條主義者 *n.* doctrinaires**
~t'iao² chu³ i⁴ ssu¹ hsiang³ ~條主義思想 *n.* doctrinaire ways of thought**
~t'u² ~徒 *n.* disciple
~yü⁴ ~育 *v.* educate; *n.* education
~yü⁴ chi¹ chin¹ ~育基金 *n.* educational fund
~yü⁴ pu⁴ ~育部 *n.* Ministry of Education
~yü⁴ ying³ p'ien⁴ ~育影片 *n.* training film
~yüan² ~員 *n.* teacher, professor
CHIAO⁴ 較 *v.* compare, examine, compete; *n.* comparison

15

~ch'a¹ ~差 *a.* worse
~hao³ ~好 *a.* better
~hsiao³ ~小 *a.* smaller
~kao¹ ~高 *a.* higher, taller
~kuei⁴ ~貴 *a.* dearer
~lien² ~廉 *a.* cheaper
~shao³ ~少 *a.* less
~ta⁴ ~大 *a.* bigger
~ti¹ ~低 *a.* lower
~to¹ ~多 *a.* more
~tuan³ ~短 *a.* shorter

CHIAO⁴ 校 *v.* revise. **HSIAO⁴** *n.* school
~kao³ ~稿 *v.* proofread
~ting⁴ ~訂 *v.* revise
~tui⁴ ~對 *v.* proofread
~tui⁴ che³ ~對者 *n.* proofreader
hsiao⁴ chang³ ~長 *n.* school principal, college president

CHIEH¹ 街 *n.* street
~shih⁴ ~市 *n.* city street
~tao⁴ ~道 *n.* avenue

CHIEH¹ 接 *v.* receive, connect, follow, succeed to
~chi⁴ ~濟 *v.* supply
~chin⁴ ~近 *prep.* near, by; *v.* approach
~ch'u⁴ ~觸 *v.* contact
~ho² ~合 *v.* join, assemble
~hsien⁴ sheng¹ ~線生 *n.* telephone operator
~hsü⁴ ~續 *v.* continue
~shou¹ ~收 *v.* take office
~tai⁴ ~待 *v.* receive friends
~tai⁴ shih⁴ ~待室 *n.* drawing room, parlor
~wen³ ~吻 *v.* kiss

CHIEH¹ 階 *n.* rank, step, degree
~chi² ~級 *n.* rank, grade
~chi² tou⁴ cheng¹ ~級鬥爭 *n.* class struggle**
~t'i¹ ~梯 *n.* step

CHIEH² 節 *n.* joint, knot, verse
~chih⁴ ~制 *v.* control (restrain)
~jih⁴ ~日 *n.* holiday, festival
~ts'ao¹ ~操 *a.* chaste
~yü⁴ ~育 *n.* birth control

16

~yüeh¹ ~約 *a.* frugal
CHIEH² 結 *v.* tie
  ~chang⁴ ~賬 *v.* settle an account
  ~chiao¹ ~交 *v.* make friends, associate
  ~ching¹ ~晶 *n.* crystal
  ~chü² ~局 *n.* end, conclusion
  ~ho² ~合 *v.* assemble weapons
  ~ho² ~核 *n.* tuberculosis
  ~hun¹ ~婚 *n.* wedding
  ~kou⁴ ~構 *n.* structure
  ~kuo³ ~果 *n.* result, consequence
  ~lun⁴ ~論 *n.* conclusion
  ~ping¹ ~冰 *v.* freeze
  ~shu⁴ ~束 *v.* close, end, finish
CHIEH² 潔 *a.* pure, clean, neat, chaste
CHIEH³ 姐 *n.* older sister
  ~fu¹ ~夫 *n.* older sister's husband (brother-in-law)
CHIEH³ 解 *v.* undo, loosen, explain. ~⁴ *v.* convey
  ~chüeh² ~決 *v.* solve
  ~ch'u² ching³ pao⁴ hsin⁴ hao⁴ ~除警報信號 *v.* all clear signal
  ~ch'u² ch'i⁴ yüeh¹ ~除契約 *n.* termination of contract
  ~ch'u² wu³ chuang¹ ~除武裝 *v.* disarm
  ~fang⁴ chün¹ ~放軍 *n.* liberation army**
  ~fang⁴ ch'ü¹ ~放區 *n.* liberated area**
  ~fang⁴ pao⁴ ~放報 *n.* Liberty Daily** (newspaper)
  ~hsi¹ ~析 *n.* analysis
  ~hsi¹ chi³ ho² ~析幾何 *n.* analytic geometry
  ~k'ai¹ ~開 *v.* untie
  ~san⁴ ~散 *v.* disband a unit
  ~shih⁴ ~釋 *v.* explain
  ~tu² chi⁴ ~毒劑 *n.* antidote
CHIEH⁴ 界 *n.* border, boundary, circle (group)
  ~hsien⁴ ~限 *n.* limitation
  ~shuo¹ ~說 *n.* definition
CHIEH⁴ 介 *prep.* between
  ~hsi⁴ tz'u² ~系詞 *n.* preposition
  ~i⁴ ~意 *v.* care

17

~shao⁴ ~紹 *v.* introduce
~yü² ~於 *prep.* between
CHIEH⁴ 借 *v.* borrow, lend
~chü⁴ ~據 *n.* promissory note
~k'uan³ ~款 *v.* make a loan
CHIEH⁴ 戒 *v.* refrain
~chih³ ~指 *n.* finger ring
~ch'ih³ ~尺 *n.* ferule
~yen² ~嚴 *n.* martial law, curfew
CHIEN¹ 間 *n.* room, space. ~⁴ *v.* separate
~⁴ chieh¹ ~接 *a.* indirect
~chieh¹ ching¹ yen⁴ ~接經驗 *n.* indirect experience**
~huo⁴ ~或 *adv.* occasionally
~hsi⁴ ~隙 *n.* gap (in line of battle)
~ko² ~隔 *n.* interval
~tieh² ~諜 *n.* spy
~tieh² huo² tung⁴ ~諜活動 *n.* espionage
~tuan⁴ ~斷 *v.* interrupt
CHIEN¹ 漸 *v.* soak. ~⁴ *adv.* gradually
CHIEN¹ 堅 *a.* strong, durable, firm, hard
~ch'iang² ~强 *a.* vigorous
~ch'ih² ~持 *v.* insist
~ku⁴ ~固 *a.* hard
~ting⁴ ~定 *a.* firm
~ying⁴ ~硬 *n.* rigid
CHIEN¹ 肩 *n.* shoulder
~chang¹ ~章 *n.* epaulet
CHIEN¹ 監 *v.* oversee; *n.* jail. ~⁴ *n.* college
~ch'a² yüan⁴ ~察院 *n.* control yuan*
~fan⁴ ~犯 *n.* criminal
~shih⁴ ~視 *v.* overlook
~tu¹ ~督 *v.* supervise; *n.* supervision, supervi-
sor
~yü⁴ ~獄 *n.* jail, prison
CHIEN¹ 尖 *n.* point; *a.* sharp
~li⁴ ~利 *a.* sharp
CHIEN¹ 艱 *n.* difficulty, suffering, distress; *a.*
malicious
~hsien³ ~險 *a.* difficult and dangerous
~k'u³ ~苦 *n.* trouble

18

~nan² ~難 *a.* difficult; *n.* difficulty
CHIEN¹ 奸 *a.* crafty, tricky, villainous
~cha⁴ ~詐 *a.* deceitful
~hua² ~滑 *a.* tricky, knavish
~hsi⁴ ~細 *n.* traitor, spy
CHIEN³ 簡 *n.* letter, document, record; *v.* a-bridge; *a.* simple, easy
~lüeh⁴ ~略 *a.* abridged
~pien⁴ ~便 *a.* convenient
~tan¹ ~單 *a.* simple; *n.* simplicity
~tuan³ ~短 *a.* short, brief
~yao⁴ ~要 *a.* terse
CHIEN³ 檢 *v.* arrange, collate, gather; *n.* label, envelope
~ch'a² ~查 *v.* examine, check, inspect, censor
~ch'a² kuan¹ ~察官 *n.* inspector
~ting⁴ ~定 *a.* authorized
~yüeh⁴ ~閱 *v.* inspect troops
CHIEN³ 儉 *a.* frugal, economical
~p'u² ~僕 *n.* frugality, thrift
~sheng³ ~省 *a.* frugal
CHIEN³ 減 *v.* decrease, reduce, subtract; *n.* reduction
~ch'ing¹ ~輕 *v.* relieve
~fa³ ~法 *n.* subtraction
~hao⁴ ~號 *n.* minus, minus sign
~hsin¹ ~薪 *n.* reduction in pay
~shao³ ~少 *v.* reduce, decrease
CHIEN³ 剪 *v.* cut
~fa³ ~髮 *n.* haircut
~fa³ chü⁴ ~髮具 *n.* clippers (tool)
~tao¹ ~刀 *n.* scissors
~tuan³ ~短 *v.* cut short, clip
~tuan⁴ ~斷 *v.* cut
CHIEN⁴ 見 *v.* see
~cheng⁴ ~證 *n.* witness
~hsiao⁴ ~效 *a.* effective
~mien⁴ ~面 *n.* interview
~shih⁴ ~識 *n.* experience, knowledge
CHIEN⁴ 件 *n.* article, item
CHIEN⁴ 建 *v.* establish, build, construct

19

~chu⁴ shih¹ ~築師 *n.* architect

~i⁴ ~議 *v.* suggest; *n.* suggestion

~kuo² fang¹ lüeh⁴ ~國方略 *n.* plans for national reconstruction*

~kuo² ta⁴ kang¹ ~國大綱 *n.* fundamentals of national reconstruction*

~li⁴ ~立 *v.* establish

~she⁴ ~設 *n.* construction

~she⁴ kung¹ tso⁴ ~設工作 *n.* construction work

~tsao⁴ ~造 *v.* build, construct

CHIEN⁴ 賤 *a.* mean, cheap, low, worthless

~chia⁴ ~價 *n.* low price

~jen² ~人 *n.* worthless, good-for-nothing

CHIEN⁴ 健 *a.* strong, vigorous

~chuang⁴ ~壯 *a.* strong

~k'ang¹ ~康 *a.* healthy; *n.* health

~k'ang¹ cheng⁴ ming² shu¹ ~康證明書 *n.* health certificate

~mei³ ~美 *n.* physical beauty

~wang⁴ ~忘 *a.* absent-minded

CHIH¹ 知 *v.* know, understand

~chiao¹ ~交 *a.* intimacy

~chüeh² ~覺 *n.* sensation

~ch'ih³ ~恥 *v.* feel ashamed

~shih⁴ ~識 *n.* knowledge

~shih⁴ chieh¹ chi² ~識階級 *n.* intelligentsia, intellectual

~shih⁴ li³ shou³ ~識裏手 *n.* wiseacre**

~tao⁴ ~道 *v.* known

~tsu² ~足 *a.* satisfied

CHIH¹ 支 *n.* branch; *v.* draw

~ch'ih² ~持 *v.* support, hold up

~ch'u¹ ~出 *v.* disburse, pay out

~fu⁴ ~付 *v.* pay, defray

~liu² ~流 *n.* & *a.* tributary

~pu⁴ ~部 *n.* branch office

~p'ei⁴ ~配 *v.* manage, control, conduct, handle, direct

~p'iao⁴ ~票 *n.* check

~p'iao⁴ pen³ ~票本 *n.* checkbook

~tien⁴ ~店 *n.* branch store

20

CHIH¹ 隻 *a.* one, single
CHIH¹ 織 *v.* weave, spin
  ~chi¹ ~機 *n.* loom
  ~kung¹ ~工 *n.* weaver
  ~pu⁴ ~布 *v.* weave cloth
  ~wu⁴ ~物 *n.* fabric, textile
CHIH¹ 之 *v.* go to, arrive at; *pron.* he, she, it, this, that; *prep.* of, for; *a.* possessive
CHIH² 職 *n.* duty
  ~ch'üan² ~權 *n.* authority
  ~tse² ~責 *n.* duty
  ~wu⁴ ~務 *n.* duty, service, work
  ~yeh⁴ ~業 *n.* occupation, vocation, profession
  ~yüan² ~員 *n.* staff employee
CHIH² 植 *n. & v.* plant
  ~shu⁴ chieh² ~樹節 *n.* Arbor Day (U.S.), Tree Planting Day
  ~wu⁴ ~物 *n.* plant
  ~wu⁴ hsüeh² ~物學 *n.* botany
  ~wu⁴ hsüeh² chia¹ ~物學家 *n.* botanist
CHIH² 直 *a.* straight, direct, frank
  ~chiao³ ~角 *n.* right angle
  ~chieh¹ ~接 *a.* direct
  ~chieh¹ ching¹ yen⁴ ~接經驗 *n.* direct experience**
  ~ching⁴ ~徑 *n.* diameter
  ~chüeh² ~覺 *n.* intuition
  ~te¹ ~的 *a.* straight
  ~yen² ~言 *v.* speak frankly
CHIH² 值 *v.* cost; *n.* worth, price; *a.* worthy
  ~ch'ien² ~錢 *a.* valuable
  ~jih⁴ ~日 *v.* be on duty for the day
  ~jih⁴ kuan¹ ~日官 *n.* officer of the day
  ~pan¹ ~班 *v.* be on duty
  ~te² ~得 *a.* worthy
CHIH² 質 *n.* substance, matter, material. ~⁴ *n.* pledge; *v.* pawn
  ~liang⁴ ~量 *n.* quality
  ~p'u² te¹ ~樸的 *a.* plain, simple
  ~wen⁴ ~問 *v.* complain
  ~⁴ tang⁴ ~當 *n.* pawnshop

21

~wu⁴ ~物 *n.* security pledge

~ya¹ ~押 *v.* pledge security

CHIH² 執 *v.* hold, grasp, seize, arrest

~chao⁴ ~照 *n.* license (document)

~cheng⁴ ~政 *v.* manage the government

~hsing² ~行 *v.* execute, carry out; *n.* performance of duty

~hsing² wei³ yüan² hui⁴ ~行委員會 *n.* executive committee

~niu⁴ ~拗 *a.* obstinate

~wen⁴ ~問 *n.* inquiry

CHIH³ 指 *n.* finger; *v.* point.   ~¹ chia³ ~甲 *n.* fingernail

~³ chai¹ ~摘 *v.* denounce

~chiao⁴ ~教 *v.* ask for advice

~huan² ~環 *n.* ring finger

~hui¹ ~揮 *v.* command, order

~hui¹ kuan¹ ~揮官 *n.* commander

~nan² ~南 *n.* guidebook

~nan² chen¹ ~南針 *n.* compass

~piao¹ ~標 *n.* target

~shih⁴ ~示 *v.* indicate, show

~tao⁴ ~導 *v.* direct, lead, instruct

~ting⁴ ~定 *v.* appoint, designate

CHIH³ 只 *adv.* only, merely, just

CHIH³ 止 *v.* stop, cease; *n.* cessation

~hsüeh⁴ yao⁴ ~血藥 *n.* styptic

~pu⁴ ~步 *v.* halt

~t'ung⁴ yao⁴ ~痛藥 *n.* anodyne

CHIH⁴ 至 *v.* reach, arrive at; *prep.* to, until; *conj.* until

~chin¹ ~今 *adv.* up to the present time

~ch'eng² ~誠 *a.* most sincere

~ch'in¹ ~親 *a.* most intimate

~shao³ ~少 *adv.* at least

~to¹ ~多 *adv.* at most

CHIH⁴ 致 *v.* cause

CHIH⁴ 製 *v.* manufacture

~tsao⁴ ~造 *v.* manufacture

~tsao⁴ ch'ang³ ~造廠 *n.* factory

~tsao⁴ p'in³ ~造品 *n.* manufacture goods

22

CHIH⁴ 制 *n.* rule, system; *v.* control, regulate
~e⁴ ~扼 *v.* pin down
~fu² ~服 *n.* uniform
~k'ung¹ ch'uan² ~空權 *n.* air superiority
~shih⁴ chiao⁴ lien⁴ ~式敎練 *n.* drill
~ting⁴ ~定 *v.* regulate, enact
~tu⁴ ~度 *n.* system
~t'u² ch'ih³ ~圖尺 *n.* pantograph
~ya¹ ~壓 *v.* neutralize by fire
CHIH⁴ 治 *v.* govern, regulate, cure; *a.* peaceful
~an¹ ~安 *n.* public safety
~li³ ~理 *v.* manage
~liao² ~療 *v.* cure
~wai⁴ fa³ ch'üan² ~外法權 *n.* extraterritoriality
CHIH⁴ 置 *v.* let go, put aside, arrange
CHIH⁴ 志 *n.* ambition, aim, intention
~hsiang⁴ ~向 *n.* ambition
~shih⁴ ~士 *n.* patriot
~yüan⁴ ~願 *n.* will
~yüan⁴ ping¹ ~願兵 *n.* volunteer
~yüan⁴ shu¹ ~願書 *n.* written agreement
CHIN¹ 今 *adv.* now; *n.* present, modern
~hou⁴ ~後 *adv.* henceforth, hereafter
~nien² ~年 *n.* this year
~t'ien¹ ~天 *n.* today
~tsao³ ~早 *n.* this morning
~yeh⁴ ~夜 *n.* tonight
CHIN¹ 巾 *n.* towel, napkin, handkerchief
~kuo¹ ~幗 *n.* womankind
~kuo¹ ying¹ hsiung² ~幗英雄 *n.* heroine
CHIN¹ 金 *n.* gold, metal; *a.* golden
~chi¹ na⁴ shuang¹ ~鷄納霜 *n.* quinine
~jung² ~融 *n.* finance
~kang¹ tsuan⁴ ~剛鑽 *n.* diamond
~pen³ wei⁴ ~本位 *n.* gold standard
~pi⁴ ~幣 *n.* gold coin
~se⁴ ~色 *a.* golden
~tzu⁴ t'a³ ~字塔 *n.* pyramid
~t'iao² ~條 *n.* gold bar
~yin² hua¹ ~銀花 *n.* woodbine
~yü² ~魚 *n.* goldfish

23

CHIN¹ 津 *n.* ferry, ford, saliva

~t'ieh¹ ~貼 *n.* allowance

CHIN¹ 斤 *n.* Chinese weight for 604.79 grams

~liang³ ~兩 *n.* weight

CHIN¹ 筋 *n.* sinew

~jou⁴ ~肉 *n.* muscle

~li⁴ ~力 *n.* sinew (strength)

CHIN³ 緊 *a.* urgent, important; *v.* bind tight

~chang¹ ~張 *n.* physical tension

~chi² ~急 *a.* urgent; *n.* emergency

~chi² ching³ pao⁴ hsin⁴ hao⁴ ~急警報信號 *n.* air raid danger signal

~chi² shih² ch'i¹ ~急時期 *n.* state of emergency

~ts'ou⁴ ~湊 *a.* close tight

CHIN³ 僅 *adv.* only, merely, hardly, scarcely

CHIN⁴ 近 *a.* near, close

~chan⁴ ~戰 *n.* close combat

~chiao¹ ~郊 *n.* suburb

~chü⁴ li² sou¹ so³ ~距離搜索 *n.* close reconnaissance

~hu¹ ~乎 *adv.* approximately

~lai² ~來 *adv.* recently

~lin² ~鄰 *n.* neighborhood

~p'o⁴ ~迫 *v.* make ready to sap

~shih⁴ ~世 *a.* modern

~shih⁴ ~視 *a.* near-sighted

~shih⁴ yen³ ~視眼 *n.* near-sighted

~tai⁴ shih³ ~代史 *n.* modern history

~tan⁴ ~彈 *n.* short-sighted

~ti⁴ ~地 *n.* vicinity

~tung¹ ~東 *n.* Near East

CHIN⁴ 進 *v.* enter, advance

~chan³ ~展 *n.* progress, gain

~ch'ang³ teng¹ ~場燈 *n.* approach light

~hua⁴ ~化 *n.* evolution

~hua⁴ lun⁴ ~化論 *n.* theory of evolution

~hsing² ~行 *v.* proceed

~hsing² chien⁴ she⁴ ~行建設 *v.* proceed with construction**

~hsing² ch'ü³ ~行曲 *n.* march music

~hsing² hsüan¹ ch'uan² ~行宣傳 *v.* conduct

24

propaganda**

~hsing² tzu⁴ wo³ p'i¹ p'ing² ～行自我批評 *v.* make self-criticism**

~ju⁴ chen⁴ ti⁴ ～入陣地 *v.* enter a position

~kung¹ ～攻 *v.* attack

~kung⁴ ～貢 *v.* send tribute

~k'ou³ huo⁴ ～口貨 *n.* import

~k'ou³ shui⁴ ～口稅 *n.* import duty

~k'uan³ ～款 *n.* income

~lu⁴ ～路 *n.* avenues of approach

~pu⁴ ～步 *v.* progress

CHIN⁴ 盡 *a.* all, finished; *adv.* entirely; *v.* exhaust, end; *n.* the last

~hsin¹ ～心 *v.* devote

~li⁴ ～力 *v.* try one's best

~t'ou² ～頭 *n.* end

CHIN⁴ 禁 *v.* forbid, prohibit, restrain, keep off

~chih³ ～止 *v.* forbid, prohibit

~chih³ ju⁴ nei⁴ ～止入內 *v.* keep out

~ling⁴ ～令 *n.* prohibition order

~yen¹ ～煙 *n.* no smoking

CHING¹ 京 *n.* capital

~ch'eng² ～城 *n.* national capital

CHING¹ 經 *n.* classics; *v.* pass through

~chi⁴ ～濟 *a.* economical; *n.* economy

~chi⁴ chu³ i⁴ ～濟主義 *n.* economism

~chi⁴ feng¹ so³ ～濟封鎖 *n.* economic blockade

~chi⁴ ho² suan⁴ chih⁴ ～濟核算制 *n.* economic accounting system**

~chi⁴ hsüeh² ～濟學 *n.* economics

~chi⁴ hsüeh² chia¹ ～濟學家 *n.* economist

~chi⁴ jen² ～紀人 *n.* broker, agent

~chi⁴ k'ung³ huang¹ ～濟恐慌 *n.* economic horror

~chi⁴ pu⁴ ～濟部 *n.* Ministry of Economics*

~ch'ang² ～常 *a.* constant; *adv.* usually

~fei⁴ ～費 *n.* fund

~hsien⁴ ～線 *n.* meridian of longitude

~kuo⁴ ～過 *v.* pass

~li³ ～理 *n.* logistics, manager

~shang¹ ～商 *v.* trade

25

~shih³ fa³ ~始法 *n.* lay-out method (*engin.*)

~tien³ ~典 *n.* classics

~tu⁴ ~度 *n.* longitude

~wei³ tu⁴ ~緯度 *n.* map coordinates

~yen⁴ ~驗 *n.* experience

~yen⁴ lun⁴ ~驗論 *n.* "empiricism"**

~yu² ~由 *prep.* via

CHING¹ 精 *a.* skillful, fine, delicate

~chi'ao³ ~巧 *a.* skillful

~ch'ung² ~蟲 *n.* sperm cell

~ch'üeh⁴ ~確 *a.* accurate

~hua² ~華 *n.* essence

~jui⁴ pu⁴ tui⁴ ~銳部隊 *n.* crack units

~li⁴ ~力 *n.* energy, vigor

~shen² ~神 *a.* spiritual; *n.* spirit

~shen² ping⁴ ~神病 *n.* insanity

~tu⁴ ~度 *n.* accuracy

~yeh⁴ ~液 *n.* semen, sperm, seminal fluid

CHING¹ 驚 *v.* fear; *a.* afraid, frightened, terrified

~ch'i² ~奇 *a.* surprised, marvelous

~hsia⁴ ~嚇 *v.* scare

~hsien³ ~險 *a.* dangerous, adventurous

~jen² ~人 *a.* surprising, astonishing, amazing

~tung⁴ ~動 *v.* disturb

CHING³ 景 *n.* view, scenery

~chih⁴ ~緻 *n.* scenery

~hsiang⁴ ~象 *n.* sight

~k'uang⁴ ~況 *n.* condition, circumstance

~se⁴ ~色 *n.* landscape

~yang³ ~仰 *v.* admire

CHING³ 井 *n.* well

~jan² ~然 *a.* orderly

CHING³ 警 *n.* police; *v.* warn, stimulate

~chieh⁴ ~戒 *n.* defensive security

~chieh⁴ ~界 *n.* police circles

~chung¹ ~鐘 *n.* alarm bell

~ch'a² ~察 *n.* police

~ch'a² chü² ~察局 *n.* police bureau

~kao⁴ ~告 *v.* warn; *n.* admonition

~pao⁴ ~報 *n.* alarm, air raid alarm

~pei⁴ ~備 *v.* alert

26

CHING⁴ 覓 v. search; adv. finally

CHING⁴ 境 n. frontier, boundary, region, district, condition

~chieh⁴ ~界 n. boundary

~k'uang⁴ ~況 n. condition

CHING⁴ 敬 v. respect, honor

~ai⁴ ~愛 v. love and respect deeply, revere

~chung⁴ ~重 v. respect

~ch'i³ ~啓 v. inform

~feng⁴ ~奉 v. worship

~li³ ~禮 v. salute

CHING⁴ 競 v. struggle, quarrel

~cheng¹ ~爭 n. competition

~chi⁴ ~技 n. game

~sai⁴ ~賽 n. match (contest)

CHING⁴ 靜 a. quiet, still, repose, silent

~chih³ ~止 n. rest (absence of motion)

~mo⁴ ~脈 n. vein

~tien⁴ ~電 n. static electricity

~yang³ ~養 v. rest

CHING⁴ 淨 a. pure, spotless, neat; v. wash; adv. only

~k'uei¹ ~虧 n. net loss

~li⁴ ~利 n. net profit

~liang⁴ ~量 n. net weight

CHING⁴ 勁 a. strong, unyielding

~lü³ ~旅 n. crack units

CHIU¹ 究 v. investigate, inquire

~ching⁴ ~竟 adv. finally, at last

~ch'a² ~查 v. examine, investigate

~fa² ~罰 v. punish

~pan⁴ ~辦 v. prosecute

~wen⁴ ~問 v. investigate; n. investigation

CHIU¹ 糾 v. impeach, collect, correct

~cheng⁴ ~正 v. correct; n. correction

~fen¹ ~紛 n. quarrel

CHIU³ 久 a. lasting, permanent, long; adv. lastingly, permanently, long

~liu² ~留 v. stay long

~pieh² ~別 a. long separated

~yüan³ ~遠 adv. forever

27

CHIU³ 酒 *n.* wine, liquor, spirits
~ching¹ ~精 *n.* alcohol
~lou² ~樓 *n.* restaurant
~pa¹ chien¹ ~吧間 *n.* bar room
~pei¹ ~杯 *n.* wine glass
~tien⁴ ~店 *n.* bar room, tavern, saloon
~tsui⁴ ~醉 *a.* drunk, intoxicated

CHIU³ 九 *n.* & *a.* nine
~che² ~折 *n.* ten-per cent discount
~san¹ hsüeh² she⁴ ~三學社 *n.* Chiu San Society**
~yüeh⁴ ~月 *n.* September

CHIU⁴ 就 *v.* go to, follow; *adv.* immediately
~chih² ~職 *n.* inauguration
~ch'in³ ~寢 *v.* go to bed
~shih⁴ ~是 *adv.* namely
~ti⁴ shen³ p'an⁴ ~地審判 *n.* on-the-spot trial**

CHIU⁴ 救 *v.* rescue, save
~chi² ~急 *n.* first aid
~chi² yao⁴ pao¹ ~急藥包 *n.* first-aid packet
~hu⁴ ch'e¹ ~護車 *n.* ambulance
~huo³ chi¹ ~火機 *n.* fire engine
~sheng¹ ch'uan² ~生船 *n.* lifeboat
~sheng¹ tai⁴ ~生帶 *n.* life belt

CHIU⁴ 舊 *a.* old, ancient; *adv.* formerly
~chi⁴ ~跡 *n.* ruins
~li⁴ ~例 *n.* precedent
~shih⁴ ~式 *n.* old style; *a.* old-fashioned
~yüeh¹ ~約 *n.* Old Testament

CHO¹ 桌 *n.* table, desk
~pu⁴ ~布 *n.* tablecloth
~tzu¹ ~子 *n.* table

CHO¹ 捉 *v.* catch, arrest
~mi² ts'ang² ~迷藏 *n.* hide-and-seek
~pu³ ~捕 *v.* arrest, catch

CHOU¹ 周 *n.* revolutionary movement, circumference
~chi⁴ ~濟 *v.* bestow
~ch'üan² ~全 *adv.* completely
~tao⁴ ~到 *adv.* completely
~wei² ~圍 *n.* surroundings

28

CHOU¹ 週 *n.* week, cycle; *adv.* weekly
~ch'i¹ hsing⁴ ~期性 *a.* periodic
~k'an¹ ~刊 *n.* weekly magazine
~nien² ~年 *n.* anniversary
~wei² ~圍 *n.* surroundings
~yu² ~遊 *v.* travel
CHOU¹ 州 *n.* prefecture, State (U.S.)
CHU¹ 豬 *n.* pig
~jou⁴ ~肉 *n.* pork
CHU¹ 朱 *n.* red, vermilion; *a.* scarlet
~hung² ~紅 *a.* scarlet
~sha¹ ~砂 *n.* cinnabar
CHU¹ 珠 *n.* pearl
~pao³ ~寶 *n.* jewel, gem
~pao³ shang¹ ~寶商 *n.* jeweler
~suan⁴ ~算 *n.* abacus
CHU² 竹 *n.* bamboo
~kan¹ ~竿 *n.* bamboo cane
~mu⁴ ~幕 *n.* bamboo curtain
CHU² 築 *v.* build
CHU³ 主 *n.* lord, master, owner, host; *a.* principal, main
~chang¹ ~張 *n.* assertion, advocacy; *v.* advocate
~chiao⁴ ~教 *n.* bishop
~ch'ih² ~持 *v.* have charge of
~ch'üan² ~權 *n.* sovereignty
~fan⁴ ~犯 *n.* law principal
~fu⁴ ~婦 *n.* housewife
~hsi² ~席 *n.* chairman
~i⁴ ~義 *n.* principle, doctrine, theory
~jen² ~人 *n.* master, owner, employer, host
~jen⁴ ~任 *n.* director (of general office), committee chairman
~jen⁴ wei³ yüan² ~任委員 *n.* committee chairman
~jih⁴ hsüeh² hsiao⁴ ~日學校 *n.* Sunday school
~ku⁴ ~顧 *n.* customer
~kuan¹ ~觀 *n.* subjectivity
~kuan¹ hsing⁴ ~觀性 *n.* subjectivism**
~li⁴ chien⁴ ~力艦 *n.* capital ship
~pi³ ~筆 *n.* chief editor

29

~wei⁴ ~位 *n.* host's seat, subjective case

~yao⁴ ~要 *n.* importance, essence

CHU³ 煮 *v.* boil

~fu² ~沸 *v.* boil

CHU⁴ 住 *v.* dwell, live

~chai² ~宅 *n.* home, residence, house

~chih³ ~址 *n.* mail address

~so³ ~所 *n.* dwelling

CHU⁴ 注 *v.* pour, instill

~chung⁴ ~重 *v.* emphasize

~i⁴ ~意 *n.* attention; *v.* pay attention

~ju⁴ ~入 *v.* pour

~mu⁴ ~目 *v.* gaze

~she⁴ ~射 *n.* injection

~she⁴ ch'i⁴ ~射器 *n.* injector

~shih⁴ ~視 *v.* gaze

CHU⁴ 柱 *n.* pillar

CHU⁴ 祝 *v.* pray, celebrate

~fu² ~福 *v.* bless

~ho⁴ ~賀 *v.* congratulate

CHU⁴ 助 *v.* help, assist; *n.* help

~chiao⁴ ~教 *n.* assistant professor

~kung¹ ~攻 *n.* secondary attack

~li³ ~理 *n.* assistant

~shou³ ~手 *n.* assistant

~tung⁴ tz'u² ~動詞 *n.* auxiliary verb

CHUA¹ 抓 *v.* scratch

~ch'ü³ ~取 *v.* choose, select

~yang³ ~癢 *v.* scratch an itchy place

CHUAN¹ 專 *a.* single, particular

~chia¹ ~家 *n.* expert

~chih⁴ ~制 *n.* absolutism, despotism

~hsin¹ ~心 *v.* pay attention

~k'o¹ ~科 *n.* academy

~mai⁴ ch'üan² ~賣權 *n.* monopoly

~mai⁴ p'in³ ~賣品 *n.* commercial monopoly

~men² ~門 *n.* specialty

~shih³ ~使 *n.* special representative

CHUAN¹ 磚 *n.* brick, tile

CHUAN³ 轉 *v.* transmit, forward. ~⁴ *v.* turn around; *n.* motor revolutions

30

~³ chi¹ ~機 *n.* turning point
~chiao¹ ~交 *adv.* in care of
~chin⁴ ~進 *v.* make a retrograde movement
~shun⁴ ~瞬 *v.* wink
~t'a³ ~塔 *n.* turret
~yün⁴ ~運 *v.* transport
CHUAN⁴ 賺 *v.* gain, earn
~ch'ien² ~錢 *v.* earn money
CHUAN⁴ 傳 *see* CH'UAN²
CHUANG¹ 裝 *v.* pack, contain, decorate
~chia³ ~甲 *a.* armor plated, armored
~chia³ ch'e¹ ~甲車 *n.* armored car
~chia³ ping¹ hsüeh² hsiao⁴ ~甲兵學校 *n.* Armored Force School*
~chia³ ping¹ lü³ ~甲兵旅 *n.* armored brigade
~chia³ pu⁴ tui⁴ ~甲部隊 *n.* armored force
~huang² ~璜 *n.* decoration
~hsiang¹ ~箱 *v.* pack; *n.* packing
~pei⁴ ~備 *n.* equipment, kit
~ping⁴ ~病 *v.* malinger
~p'ei⁴ ~配 *v.* assembly
~shih⁴ ~飾 *v.* adorn, decorate
~shih⁴ p'in³ ~飾品 *n.* ornament
~shu⁴ ~束 *v.* dress
~ting⁴ ~訂 *v.* bind sheets of paper
~t'ien² ~填 *v.* load ammunition
~tsai⁴ ~載 *v.* load
~yang² ~佯 *v.* pretend
~yao⁴ ~藥 *n.* powder charge
~yün⁴ ~運 *v.* transport
CHUANG¹ 莊 *n.* village, farm, agriculture, store
~hu⁴ ~戶 *n.* farmer
~yen² ~嚴 *a.* stately
CHUANG⁴ 壯 *a.* strong, healthy
~chien⁴ ~健 *a.* able-bodied, strong and healthy
~chih⁴ ~志 *a.* strong-minded
~li⁴ ~麗 *a.* magnificent, grand, stately
~nien² ~年 *n.* manhood
~ting¹ ~丁 *n.* able-bodied man
CHUANG⁴ 狀 *n.* shape, form, petition, warrant
~k'uang⁴ p'an⁴ tuan⁴ ~況判斷 *n.* estimate of

31

the situation
~t'ai⁴ ~態 *n.* condition, state
CHUI¹ 追 *v.* follow, chase, pursuit
~chiu¹ ~究 *v.* investigate
~ch'iu² ~求 *v.* chase, hunt
~hui³ ~悔 *v.* repent
~kan³ ~趕 *v.* pursuit
~ssu¹ ~思 *v.* recall
~tao⁴ hui⁴ ~悼會 *n.* memorial service
CHUN³ 準 *n.* standard, accuracy; *a.* right, accurate
~ch'üeh⁴ ~確 *a.* accurate, exact; *n.* accuracy
~pei⁴ ~備 *v.* prepare; *n.* preparation
~pei⁴ chin¹ ~備金 *n.* reserve funds
~shih² ~時 *a.* punctual
~tu⁴ ~度 *n.* accuracy
CHUN³ 准 *v.* allow, permit, grant, approve
~chiang⁴ ~將 *n.* brigadier general, commodore
~hsü³ ~許 *v.* authorize
~ju⁴ ~入 *v.* let in
CHUNG¹ 鐘 *n.* bell, clock
~lou² ~樓 *n.* bell-tower
~pai³ ~擺 *n.* pendulum
~piao³ chiang⁴ ~錶匠 *n.* watchmaker
~tien³ ~點 *n.* hour
CHUNG¹ 中 *a.* middle, central; *n.* center; *prep.* between, among, within, in. ~⁴ *v.* hit
~chiang⁴ ~將 *n.* lieutenant general, vice admiral
~chien¹ ~間 *a.* middle, central; *prep.* between, among
~chih³ ~止 *n.* cessation
~hua² ch'üan² kuo² hsüeh² sheng¹ lien² ho² hui⁴ ~華全國學生聯合會 *n.* All-China Students' Federation**
~hua² ch'üan² kuo² min² chu³ ch'ing¹ nien² lien² ho² tsung³ hui⁴ ~華全國民主青年聯合總會 *n.* All-China Federation of Democratic Youth**
~hua² ch'üan² kuo² min² chu³ fu⁴ nü³ lien² ho² hui⁴ ~華全國民主婦女聯合會 *n.* All-China Democratic Women's Federation**

32

~hua² ch'üan² kuo² tsung³ kung¹ hui⁴ ~華全國總公會 *n.* All-China Federation of Labor**

~hua² ch'üan² kuo² wen² hsüeh² i⁴ shu⁴ chieh⁴ lien² ho² hui⁴ ~華全國文學藝術界聯合會 *n.* All-China Federation of Literary and Art Circles**

~hua² min² kuo² ~華民國 *n.* Republic of China

~hua² min² kuo² hsien⁴ fa³ ~華民國憲法 *n.* Constitution of the Republic of China*

~hsiao⁴ ~校 *n.* lieutenant colonel, commander

~hsin¹ ~心 *n.* center

~hsing⁴ ~性 *n.* neuter

~hsüeh² hsiao⁴ ~學校 *n.* high school

~ku³ ~古 *n.* Middle Ages

~kung⁴ ~共 *n.* Chinese Communist Party**

~kung⁴ chung¹ yang¹ ~共中央 *n.* Central Committee of the Chinese Communist Party**

~kung⁴ ch'i¹ chieh⁴ san¹ chung¹ ch'üan² hui⁴ ~共七屆三中全會 *n.* Third Plenary Session of the Central Committee elected by the Seventh Party Congress**

~kuo² ~國 *n.* China

~kuo² chih⁴ kung¹ tang³ ~國致公黨 *n.* China Chih Kung Tang**

~kuo² ch'ing¹ nien² fan³ kung⁴ chiu⁴ kuo² t'uan² ~國青年反共救國團 *n.* China Youth Anti-Communist National Salvation Corps*

~kuo² fu² li⁴ hui⁴ ~國福利會 *n.* China Welfare Institute**

~kuo² hua⁴ ~國話 *n.* Chinese, spoken Chinese

~kuo² hung² shih² tzu⁴ hui⁴ ~國紅十字會 *n.* Red Cross Society of China**

~kuo² hsin¹ min² chu³ chu³ i⁴ ch'ing¹ nien² t'uan² ~國新民主主義青年團 *n.* China New Democratic Youth League**

~kuo² jen² ~國人 *n.* Chinese

~kuo² jen² min² cheng⁴ chih⁴ hsieh² shang¹ hui⁴ i⁴ ch'üan² kuo² wei³ yüan² hui⁴ ~國人民政治協商會議全國委員會 *n.* National Committee of Chinese People's Political Consultative Conference**

33

~kuo² jen² min² cheng⁴ chih⁴ hsieh² shang¹ hui⁴ i⁴ ch'üan² t'i³ hui⁴ i⁴ ~國人民政治協商會議全體會議 *n.* Plenary Session of Chinese People's Political Consultative Conference**

~kuo² jen² min² chieh³ fang⁴ chün¹ ~國人民解放軍 *n.* Chinese People's Volunteers**

~kuo² jen² min² hang² k'ung¹ kung¹ ssu¹ ~國人民航空公司 *n.* National Civil Aviation Company**

~kuo² jen² min² pao³ wei⁴ shih⁴ chieh⁴ ho² p'ing² fan³ tui⁴ mei³ kuo² ch'in¹ lüeh⁴ wei³ yüan² hui⁴ ~國人民保衛世界和平反對美國侵略委員會 *n.* Chinese People's Committee for World Peace and Against American Aggression**

~kuo² jen² min² wai⁴ chiao¹ hsüeh² hui⁴ ~國人民外交學會 *n.* Chinese People's Institute of Foreign Affairs**

~kuo² kung⁴ ch'an³ tang³ ~國共産黨 *n.* Chinese Communist Party**

~kuo² kuo² min² tang³ ko² ming⁴ wei³ yüan² hui⁴ ~國國民黨革命委員會 *n.* Revolutionary Committee of the Kuomintang**

~kuo² min² chu³ t'ung² meng² ~國民主同盟 *n.* China Democratic League**

~kuo² min² chu³ ts'u⁴ chin⁴ hui⁴ ~國民主促進會 *n.* China Association for Promoting Democracy**

~kuo² nung² kung¹ min² chu³ tang³ ~國農工民主黨 *n.* Chinese Peasants and Workers Democratic Party**

~kuo² yin² hang² ~國銀行 *n.* Bank of China

~li⁴ ~立 *n.* neutrality

~su¹ yu³ hao³ hsieh² hui⁴ ~蘇友好協會 *n.* Sino-Soviet Friendship Association**

~su¹ yu³ hao³ t'ung² meng² hu⁴ chu⁴ t'iao² yüeh¹ ~蘇友好同盟互助條約 *n.* Sino-Soviet Treaty of Friendship, Alliance and Mutual Assistance**

~shan¹ fu² ~山服 *n.* Sun Yat-Sen Uniform

~shih⁴ ~士 *n.* sergeant first class (army)

~teng³ ~等 *n.* average

~teng³ chiao⁴ yü⁴ ~等敎育 n. secondary education

~tuan⁴ ~斷 v. discontinue

~t'u² ~途 n. midway, halfway

~wei⁴ ~尉 n. first lieutenant, lieutenant junior grade

~wen² ~文 n. Chinese language

~yang¹ ~央 a. central, middle

~yang¹ cheng⁴ fu³ ~央政府 n. Central Government

~yang¹ jen² min² cheng⁴ fu³ wei³ yüan² hui⁴ ~央人民政府委員會 n. Central People's Government Council**

~yang¹ jih⁴ pao⁴ ~央日報 n. Central Daily News*

~yang¹ she⁴ ~央社 n. Central News Agency*

~yang¹ tang³ pu⁴ ~央黨部 n. Central Kuomintang Headquarters

~yang¹ yin² hang² ~央銀行 n. Central Bank of China

~yung¹ ~庸 n. mean

~⁴ feng¹ ~風 n. apoplexy

~shu³ ~暑 v. suffer a heat stroke; n. sunstroke

~tu² ~毒 n. infection

CHUNG¹ 忠 a. loyal, faithful; n. loyalty

~hou⁴ ~厚 a. trustworthy, reliable

~hsiao⁴ ~孝 a. loyal

~hsin⁴ ~信 a. faithful

~i⁴ ~義 a. honest and righteous

~kao⁴ ~告 v. advise; n. advice

~shih² ~實 a. honest; n. honesty

CHUNG¹ 終 n. end; adv. finally; v. die

~chieh² ~結 n. conclusion

~chü² ~局 n. conclusion

CHUNG³ 種 n. seed, kind. ~⁴ v. plant, cultivate

~³ lei⁴ ~類 n. kind, class, sort, variety

~tsu² ~族 n. race, tribe

~tzu³ ~子 n. seed

~⁴ chih² ~植 v. plant

~tou⁴ ~痘 v. vaccinate; n. vaccination

CHUNG⁴ 重 a. heavy, severe; n. weight. CH'-

35

UNG² *n.* fold, repetition
~hsin¹ ~心 *n.* center of gravity
~shui⁴ ~税 *n.* heavy tax
~yao⁴ ~要 *a.* important
~yin¹ ~音 *n.* accent
`ch'ung² fu⁴ ~複 *n.* repetition
~hun¹ ~婚 *n.* bigamy
~hsiu¹ ~修 *v.* repair
~ting⁴ te¹ ~訂的 *a.* revised
CHUNG⁴ 衆 *a.* all, many, numerous
CHÜ¹ 居 *n.* dwelling, abode; *v.* dwell, live
~chu⁴ ~住 *v.* live, dwell
~ch'u⁴ ~処 *n.* residence, abode
~liu² ~留 *v.* sojourn
~min² ~民 *n.* inhabitant, resident
CHÜ² 局 *n.* bureau (office)
~chang³ ~長 *n.* chief of a bureau
~mien⁴ ~面 *n.* situation
~pu⁴ ~部 *a.* local
~shih⁴ ~勢 *n.* situation, condition
~wai⁴ jen² ~外人 *n.* outsider
CHÜ³ 舉 *v.* raise, lift up, begin
~chien⁴ ~薦 *v.* recommend personnel
~chung⁴ ~重 *n.* weight lifting
~kuo² ~國 *n.* whole country
~shou³ ~手 *v.* raise a hand
~shou³ li³ ~手禮 *n.* hand salute
~tung⁴ ~動 *n.* behavior
CHÜ⁴ 句 *n.* sentence
~fa³ ~法 *n.* syntax
~tien³ ~點 *n.* punctuation
CHÜ⁴ 據 *n.* evidence; *v.* rely upon; *adv.* according to
~cheng⁴ ~證 *n.* proof, evidence
~ling³ ~領 *v.* occupy
~tien³ ~點 *n.* key point
CHÜ⁴ 聚 *v.* collect, gather, assemble
~ho² ~合 *v.* unite
~tu³ ~賭 *v.* assemble for gambling
~ts'an¹ ~餐 *v.* dine together
CHÜ⁴ 具 *n.* tool

36

~ch'eng² ~呈 v. submit a petition
~ling³ ~領 v. receive
~pao⁴ ~報 v. submit a report
~t'i³ te¹ ~體的 a. concrete
CHÜ⁴ 劇 n. play; v. add; a. severe, strong; adv. very, more
~chung¹ jen² ~中人 n. cast (actors)
~lieh⁴ ~烈 a. violent; n. violence
~pen³ ~本 n. drama
~tao⁴ ~盜 n. highwayman
~yüan⁴ ~院 n. theater
CHÜ⁴ 拒 v. oppose, refuse
~chüeh² ~絕 v. reject, refuse
~pu³ ~捕 v. resist arrest
~ti² ~敵 v. resist an enemy
CHÜAN¹ 捐 v. contribute
~ch'i⁴ ~棄 v. abandon
~ch'ü¹ ~軀 v. sacrifice one's life
~k'uan³ ~款 n. contribution
~shui⁴ ~稅 n. taxation
CHÜAN³ 捲 v. curl, roll up, pack up
~hsin¹ ts'ai⁴ ~心菜 n. cabbage
~t'ao² ~逃 v. abscond
~yen¹ ~煙 n. cigarette
CHÜEH² 決 v. decide, sentence; adv. decidedly
~lieh⁴ ~裂 n. breach (quarrel)
~pu⁴ ~不 adv. never, by no means
~ting⁴ ~定 v. decide, determine; n. decision, determination; a. decided, determined
~tou⁴ ~鬥 n. duel; v. fight a duel
~tuan⁴ ~斷 n. decision
CHÜEH² 絕 v. break off, sever; adv. extremely, very
~chi⁴ ~跡 v. cease
~chiao¹ ~交 v. sever friendship
~pi⁴ ~壁 n. precipice, cliff
~ting³ ~頂 n. summit
~tui⁴ ~對 a. absolute
~wang⁴ ~望 v. despair
~yüan² ~緣 n. insulation
~yüan² t'i³ ~緣體 n. insulator

37

CHÜEH² 覺 *v.* feel, understand, discover
~t'ung⁴ ~痛 *v.* feel pain
~wu⁴ ~悟 *v.* understand

CHÜN¹ 均 *a.* equal, even, uniform, all
~i¹ ~一 *a.* same, equal
~shih⁴ ~勢 *n.* balance of power
~t'an¹ ~攤 *v.* share equally

CHÜN¹ 軍 *n.* army, troop, soldier; *v.* station, banish (units)
~chang³ ~長 *n.* army commander
~cheng⁴ wei³ yüan² hui⁴ ~政委員會 *n.* Military and Administrative Committee**
~chi⁴ ~紀 *n.* military discipline
~chieh⁴ ~界 *n.* military circles
~chien⁴ ~艦 *n.* warship
~chuang¹ ~裝 *n.* uniform
~fa² ~閥 n. warlord
~fa³ ~法 *n.* military law
~fa³ chü² ~法局 *n.* Judge Advocate General*
~fei⁴ ~費 *n.* military expenditure
~hao⁴ ~號 *n.* army bugle
~huo³ ~火 *n.* munitions, ordnance materiel
~hsiang³ ~餉 *n.* army pay
~hsieh⁴ pao³ yang³ hsün⁴ lien⁴ pan¹ ~械保養訓練班 *n.* Ordnance Maintenance Training Class*
~hsü¹ ~需 *n.* military supplies, quartermaster
~hsü¹ hsün⁴ lien⁴ pan¹ ~需訓練班 *n.* Quartermaster Training Class*
~i¹ ~醫 *n.* medical officer
~jen² ~人 *n.* soldier, military personnel
~kuan¹ ~官 *n.* line officer
~liang² ~糧 *n.* military provisions
~pei⁴ ~備 *n.* armament
~tui⁴ ~隊 *n.* troop
~ying² ~營 *n.* military camp
~yu² chü² ~郵局 *n.* army post officer
~yung⁴ chi¹ ~用機 *n.* military plane
~yung⁴ p'iao⁴ ~用票 *n.* Military Payment Certificate (MPC)
~yung⁴ tien⁴ hua⁴ ~用電話 *n.* army telephone

38

~yüeh⁴ tui⁴ ~樂隊 *n.* military band
CHÜN⁴ 菌 *n.* bacteria

CH'

CH'A¹ 差 *n.* difference, distinction. CH'AĪ¹ *n.*
  legate; *v.* send
~pieh² ~別 *n.* difference; *v.* differ
~pu⁴ to¹ ~不多 *adv.* almost
~wu⁴ ~誤 *n.* error, mistake
ch'ai¹ ch'ien³ ~遣 *v.* send, dispatch
~i⁴ ~役 *n.* public servant
~shih⁴ ~事 *n.* business, employment
CH'A¹ 插 *v.* stick in, insert, pierce
~ch'ü³ ~曲 *n.* musical interlude
~ju⁴ ~入 *v.* insert
~k'ou³ ~口 *v.* interrupt
CH'A² 茶 *n.* tea
~ch'ih² ~匙 *n.* teaspoon
~fang² ~房 *n.* restaurant waiter
~hu² ~壺 *n.* tea kettle, teapot
~hua¹ ~花 *n.* camellia
~hua⁴ hui⁴ ~話會 *n.* tea party
~kuan³ ~館 *n.* tea shop
~pei¹ ~杯 *n.* teacup
~tien³ ~點 *n.* refreshment
~tien⁴ ~店 *n.* tea shop
CH'A² 查 *v.* examine, search
~chang⁴ ~帳 *v.* audit
~chiu¹ ~究 *v.* investigate
~wen⁴ ~問 *v.* question, examine
~yen⁴ ~驗 *v.* examine
CH'A² 察 *v.* examine, investigate
~chiu¹ ~究 *v.* investigate, examine
CH'AI¹ 差 *see* CH'A¹
CH'AI² 柴 *n.* firewood
CH'AN³ 產 *v.* produce, bear; *n.* production
~ch'u¹ liang⁴ ~出量 *n.* output
~fu⁴ ~婦 *n.* confined woman
~k'o¹ ~科 *n.* midwifery

~k'o¹ hu⁴ shih⁴ ~科護士 *n.* maternity nurse
~k'o¹ i¹ yüan⁴ ~科醫院 *n.* maternity hospital
~sheng¹ ~生 *v.* produce, bear
~wu⁴ ~物 *n.* product
~yeh⁴ ~業 *n.* estate
CH'ANG¹ 倡 *v.* promote; *n.* promotion
~tao³ ~導 *v.* promote
CH'ANG² 常 *a.* constant, regular, frequent; *adv.* always, usually
~ch'ang² ~常 *adv.* always, often
~kuei¹ ~規 *n.* routine
~pei⁴ chün¹ ~備軍 *n.* standing army
~shih⁴ ~識 *n.* common sense
~wu⁴ wei³ yüan² ~務委員 *n.* standing committee member
~wu⁴ wei³ yüan² hui⁴ ~務委員會 *n.* standing committee
CH'ANG² 腸 *n.* intestines
~ping⁴ ~病 *n.* intestinal malady
CH'ANG² 長 *see* CHANG³
CH'ANG³ 場 *n.* yard, open place
CH'ANG³ 廠 *n.* factory, manufacturing, workshop
CH'ANG⁴ 唱 *v.* sing
~ko¹ ~歌 *v.* sing songs
~ko¹ pan¹ ~歌班 *n.* choir
CH'AO¹ 吵 *n.* bawl, quarrel, uproar
~nao⁴ ~鬧 *v.* quarrel
CH'AO¹ 超 *v.* step over, surpass
~e² wan² ch'eng² ~額完成 *n.* over-fulfillment**
~fan²~凡 *a.* unusual
~jen² ~人 *a.* superhuman
~kuo⁴ ~過 *v.* surpass, exceed, excel
~teng³ ~等 *a.* excellent
CH'AO² 朝 *n.* court, dynasty, Korea; *v.* face; *prep.* toward. CHAO¹ *n.* morning
~tai⁴ ~代 *n.* dynasty
~t'ing² ~廷 *n.* court
CH'E¹ 車 *n.* automobile, carriage, vehicle
~chan⁴ ~站 *n.* station (railroad, bus)
~chang³ ~掌 *n.* streetcar conductor
~chia⁴ ~架 *n.* vehicle chassis

40

~chou² ~軸 *n.* vehicle axle
~ch'uang² ~床 *n.* lathe
~fu¹ ~夫 *n.* chauffeur, driver, coachman
~liang⁴ ~輛 *n.* vehicle
~lun² ~輪 *n.* vehicle wheel
~p'iao⁴ ~票 *n.* transportation ticket
~t'ai¹ ~胎 *n.* tire
CH'EN² 陳 *a.* ancient, old; *v.* arrange, exhibit, state
~chiu⁴ ~舊 *a.* old, out-of-date
~fu³ ~腐 *a.* old-fashioned
~lieh⁴ ~列 *v.* display
~lieh⁴ p'in³ ~列品 *n.* exhibit objects
~she⁴ ~設 *v.* arrange
~shu⁴ ~述 *v.* state, explain
CH'EN² 晨 *n.* morning, dawn
~pao⁴ ~報 *n.* morning paper
CH'EN⁴ 趁 *v.* go to, avail of
~shih⁴ ~勢 *v.* take advantage
CH'ENG¹ 稱 *v.* weigh, call, praise. ~⁴ *a.* fit; *n.* balance
~¹ hu¹ ~呼 *v.* call, style, name
~hsieh⁴ ~謝 *v.* thank
~yang² ~揚 *v.* praise
~⁴ hsin¹ ~心 *a.* satisfied
CH'ENG² 成 *v.* finish, succeed
~chi¹ ~績 *n.* efficiency, school record
~jen² ~仁 *v.* die for a noble cause
~kung¹ ~功 *n.* success, achievement
~li⁴ ~立 *v.* establish, constitute (a new unit)
~pen³ ~本 *n.* cost
CH'ENG² 城 *n.* city
~ch'iang² ~牆 *n.* city wall
~pao³ ~堡 *n.* castle
~shih⁴ ~市 *n.* city, town
~shih⁴ mai³ pan⁴ chieh¹ chi² ~市買辦階級 *n.* comprador class in the cities**
CH'ENG² 程 *n.* measure, route, rule, journey
~hsü⁴ ~序 *n.* procedure, order
~tu⁴ ~度 *n.* standard
CH'ENG² 誠 *a.* sincere, true, real

41

~i⁴ ~意 *a.* sincere

~k'en³ ~懇 *a.* sincere

~shih² ~實 *a.* honest

CH'ENG² 乘 *v.* ride, multiply. ~⁴ *n.* chariot, annals

~chi¹ ~機 *v.* take advantage of

~ch'uan² ~船 *v.* board a ship

~fa³ ~法 *n.* multiplication

~huo³ ch'e¹ ~火車 *v.* board a train

~k'o⁴ ~客 *n.* passenger

~liang² ~涼 *v.* enjoy the cool air

~ma³ ~馬 *v.* ride a horse; *n.* riding horse

~yüan² ~員 *n.* crew

CH'ENG² 承 *v.* support, uphold, receive, consent

~chi⁴ ~繼 *v.* adopt

~chi⁴ jen² ~繼人 *n.* successor

~jen⁴ ~認 *v.* acknowledge, recognize

~lan³ ~攬 *v.* contract

~no⁴ ~諾 *v.* promise

~shou⁴ ~受 *v.* receive

~tsu¹ ~租 *v.* rent from

CH'ENG² 盛 *see* SHENG⁴

CH'I¹ 七 *n.* & *a.* seven

~hsien² ch'in² ~絃琴 *n.* lyre

~yüeh⁴ ~月 *n.* July

CH'I¹ 期 *v.* expect; *n.* period

~chien¹ ~間 *n.* duration

~hsien⁴ ~限 *n.* a limit of time

~p'iao⁴ ~票 *n.* promissory note

~wang⁴ ~望 *v.* expect, hope

CH'I¹ 妻 *n.* wife, better-half

CH'I¹ 欺 *v.* cheat

~meng² ~朦 *v.* fool

~p'ien⁴ ~騙 *v.* cheat

~wu³ ~侮 *v.* insult

CH'I² 齊 *n.* harmony, order; *v.* equalize; *a.* even, uniform

~cheng³ ~整 *a.* orderly, neat

~chi² ~集 *v.* gather, collect

~ch'üan² ~全 *a.* complete

~hsin¹ ~心 *adv.* unanimously

42

~pei⁴ ~備 *a.* all ready
~she⁴ ~射 *n.* salvo fire
CH'I² 騎 *v.* ride, sit astride
~ma³ ~馬 *v.* mount a horse
~ping¹ ~兵 *n.* cavalry
~shih¹ ~師 *n.* skilled horseman
~shih⁴ ~士 *n.* knight
~shu⁴ ~術 *n.* horsemanship
CH'I² 奇 *a.* strange, wonderful, marvelous
~chen¹ ~珍 *n.* rare treasure
~chi⁴ ~跡 *n.* miracle
~ch'iao³ ~巧 *a.* wonderful
~i⁴ ~異 *a.* remarkable
~shu⁴ ~數 *n.* odd number
~t'an² ~談 *n.* strange talk
~ts'ai² ~才 *n.* remarkable talents
CH'I² 其 *pron.* they, he, she, it ; *a.* this, that
~shih² ~實 *adv.* in fact
~yü² ~餘 *n.* rest
CH'I² 旗 *n.* flag, banner
~chien⁴ ~艦 *n.* flagship
~chih⁴ ~幟 *n.* flag
~kan¹ ~竿 *n.* flagpole
~yü³ ~語 *n.* flag semaphore
CH'I³ 起 *v.* stand up, rise, start
~chung⁴ chi¹ ~重機 *n.* crane, jack, hoist
~ch'uang² hao⁴ ~床號 *n.* reveille
~fei¹ ~飛 *v.* take off (airplane)
~fu² ti⁴ ~伏地 *n.* rolling terrain
~huo³ ~火 *v.* catch fire
~huo⁴ tan¹ ~貨單 *n.* bill of lading
~kao³ ~稿 *v.* draft
~lai² ~來 *v.* get up, arise
~li⁴ ~立 *v.* stand up
~mao² ~錨 *v.* weigh anchor
~su⁴ ~訴 *v.* accuse
~su⁴ jen² ~訴人 *n.* suitor (lawsuit)
~shen¹ ~身 *v.* arise
~tien³ ~點 *n.* starting point
~ts'ao³ ~草 *v.* draft
CH'I³ 啓 *v.* open, begin, announce, notice, explain

~**fa**¹ ～發 *v.* instruct
~**meng**² ～蒙 *a.* elementary; *n.* beginning
~**shih**⁴ ～事 *n.* notice
CH'I⁴ 器 *n.* utensil, vessel
~**chü**⁴ ～具 *n.* apparatus, furniture
~**kuan**¹ ～官 *n.* organ
~**min**³ ～皿 *n.* utensil, vessel
~**ts'ai**² ～材 *n.* materiel (weapons and equipment)
CH'I⁴ 汽 *n.* steam
~**ch'e**¹ ～車 *n.* automobile, motor car
~**ch'uan**² ～船 *n.* steamboat, steamship
~**ti**² ～笛 *n.* steam whistle
~**yu**² ～油 *n.* gasoline
CH'I⁴ 氣 n. steam, air, breath
~**ch'iu**² ～球 *n.* balloon
~**ch'uan**³ ～喘 *n.* asthma; *a.* asthmatic
~**hou**⁴ ～候 *n.* climate
~**hsiang**⁴ **hsüeh**² ～象學 *n.* meteorology
~**hsiang**⁴ **t'ai**² ～象臺 *n.* observatory
~**kuan**³ ～管 *n.* windpipe, trachea
~**li**⁴ ～力 *n.* energy, strength
~**se**⁴ ～色 *n.* complexion
~**t'i**³ ～體 *n.* gas
~**ya**¹ ～壓 *n.* air pressure
~**wei**⁴ ～味 *n.* smell, odor
~**yen**⁴ ～焰 *n.* flame
CH'IA⁴ 恰 *adv.* just, exactly
~**ch'iao**³ ～巧 *adv.* fortunately
CH'IANG¹ 槍 *n.* lance. [Same as 鎗] gun, rifle
~**liu**² **tan**⁴ ～榴彈 *n.* rifle grenade
~**shang**¹ ～傷 *n.* bullet wound
~**shen**¹ ～身 *n.* gun barrel
~**tan**⁴ ～彈 *n.* bullet, cartridge
~**t'ang**² ～膛 *n.* barrel bore
CH'IANG² 強 *a.* strong. ～³ *v.* force
~² **tao**⁴ ～盜 *n.* robber
~**ying**⁴ ～硬 *a.* unyielding
~³ **to**² ～奪 *v.* seize (by force)
CH'IANG² 牆 *n.* wall
CH'IANG³ 搶 *v.* rob, plunder

44

~chieh² ~劫 *n.* plunder
~chieh² che³ ~劫者 *n.* robber
~to² tsui⁴ ~奪罪 *n.* burglary
CH'IAO² 瞧 *v.* look on, consider
CH'IAO² 橋 *n.* bridge
~liang² ~樑 *n.* bridge
~p'ai² hsi⁴ ~牌戲 *n.* bridge (card game)
~tung⁴ ~洞 *n.* arch of bridge
~t'ou² pao³ ~頭堡 *n.* bridgehead
CH'IAO³ 巧 *a.* cunning, clever, ingenious
~chi⁴ ~計 *n.* ingenuity
~miao⁴ ~妙 *a.* ingenious, skillful
~yü⁴ ~遇 *v.* meet by chance
CH'IEH¹ 切 *v.* cut
~¹ hsien⁴ ~線 *n.* tangent
~k'ai¹ ~開 *v.* cut apart, mince, slice
~⁴ chi⁴ ~忌 *a.* prohibitive, prohibitory
~shih² ~實 *a.* real, true; *adv.* really, truly
~wang⁴ ~望 *a.* eager
CH'IEH³ 且 *adv.* also, moreover, besides
CH'IEN¹ 千 *n.* & *a.* thousand
CH'IEN¹ 牽 *v.* pull, haul, connect
~chih⁴ ~制 *v.* hold (the enemy)
~ch'iang² ~强 *n.* halter, tie rope
~lien² ~連 *v.* involve
CH'IEN¹ 簽 *n.* paper slip, signature; *v.* sign, endorse
~cheng⁴ ~證 *n.* visa
~ming² ~名 *n.* signature
~t'iao² ~條 *n.* paper slip, label
~tzu⁴ ~字 *n.* signature
CH'IEN² 前 *n.* *prep.* before, in front of, in advance of, ahead of; *adv.* formerly, previously; *a.* previous, front
~chih⁴ tz'u² ~置詞 *n.* preposition
~chin⁴ ~進 *v.* move forward, advance
~fang¹ ~方 *n.* front (opposite of rear)
~feng¹ ~鋒 *n.* vanguard
~hsien⁴ ~綫 *n.* front (line of battle)
~jen⁴ ~任 *n.* predecessor
~men² ~門 *n.* front door

45

~mien⁴ ~面 n. front

~shao⁴ ~哨 n. outpost

~t'u² ~途 n. chance of future success

~wei⁴ ~衛 n. advance guard

~yüan² ~緣 n. leading edge

CH'IEN² 錢 n. money, current coin, wealth

~hsiang¹ ~箱 n. till

~pi⁴ ~幣 n. money, current coin, currency

~tai⁴ ~袋 n. purse

CH'IEN³ 淺 a. shallow, superficial; v. run a-
ground

~hsüeh² ~學 a. shallow, superficial

~i⁴ ~易 a. easy

~po² ~薄 a. shallow

CH'IEN⁴ 欠 v. owe

~chai⁴ ~債 v. owe debt

~ch'üeh¹ ~缺 a. insufficient

~shen¹ ~伸 v. yawn

CH'IH¹ 吃 v. eat

~chin³ ~緊 a. critical, dangerous

~ching¹ ~驚 v. be frightened

~fan⁴ ~飯 v. take meals

~k'uei¹ ~虧 v. suffer a loss

~li⁴ ~力 a. difficult

~ts'u⁴ ~醋 v. be jealous

CH'IH² 池 n. pool, pond

~t'ang² ~塘 n. pond

CH'IH² 持 v. hold, maintain

~chiu³ chan⁴ ~久戰 n. delaying resistance

~chiu³ hsing⁴ ~久性 a. persistent

~chiu³ li⁴ ~久力 n. endurance

CH'IH² 遲 n. delay; v. defer; a. slow, late

~tao⁴ ~到 a. late

~yen² ~延 v. delay

CH'IH³ 尺 n. Chinese linear measure for 14.1
inches

~² ts'un⁴ ~寸 n. size

~³ tu² ~牘 n. letter writing

CH'IH³ 恥 a. ashamed

~hsiao⁴ ~笑 v. ridicule

~ju⁴ ~辱 n. shame, disgrace

46

CH'IH³ 齒 *n.* teeth, age
　~lun² ~輪 *n.* gear (mechanical)
CH'IN¹ 親 *n.* relation; *v.* love, approach, kiss; *a.* dear, close, own
　~ai⁴ te¹ ~愛的 *a.* dear
　~ch'i¹ ~戚 *n.* relative
　~mi⁴ ~密 *a.* intimate; *n.* intimacy
　~shan⁴ ~善 *a.* kind, close
　~tsui³ ~嘴 *n.* & *v.* kiss
　~tzu⁴ ~自 *adv.* personally
CH'IN¹ 侵 *v.* invade
　~chan⁴ ~佔 *v.* occupy
　~ch'e⁴ li⁴ ~徹力 *n.* force of penetration
　~lüeh⁴ ~略 *v.* invade; *n.* invasion
　~shih² ~蝕 *n.* erosion
　~t'un¹ ~吞 *v.* squeeze
CH'IN² 勤 *a.* diligent, industrious; *n.* diligence
　~chien³ ~儉 *a.* diligent and frugal
　~hsüeh² ~學 *v.* study hard
　~k'u³ ~苦 *a.* toilsome, laborious
　~lao² ~勞 *a.* toilsome, laborious
CH'ING¹ 輕 *a.* light, easy, low, unimportant
　~chi¹ kuan¹ ch'iang¹ ~機關槍 *n.* light machine gun
　~chien⁴ ~賤 *a.* low, mean
　~ch'i⁴ ch'iu² ~氣球 *n.* hydrogen balloon
　~fu² ~浮 *a.* unsteady, flimsy
　~hsin⁴ ~信 *v.* believe recklessly
　~i⁴ ~易 *a.* easy
　~kung¹ yeh⁴ pu⁴ ~工業部 *n.* Ministry of Light Industry**
　~k'uai⁴ ~快 *a.* nimble
　~k'uang² ~狂 *a.* frivolous
　~ping¹ ch'i⁴ ~兵器 *n.* light arms
　~po² ~薄 *a.* disrespectful
　~shang¹ che³ ~傷者 *n.* walking wounded
　~shih⁴ ~視 *v.* despise
　~yin¹ yüeh⁴ ~音樂 *n.* light music
CH'ING¹ 清 *v.* purify, pure; *a.* pure, clear
　~chieh² ~潔 *n.* cleanness
　~ching⁴ ~淨 *a.* clean

47

~ch'u³ ~楚 *a.* clear
~hsiang¹ ~香 *a.* fragrant
~hsien² ~閒 *adv.* leisurely
~hsiu⁴ ~秀 *a.* pretty
~lang³ ~朗 *a.* clear
~li³ ~理 *v.* settle
~lien² ~廉 *n.* integrity
~po² ~白 *n.* innocence
~sao³ ~掃 *v.* clear (field of fire)
~suan⁴ ~算 *v.* liquidate; *n.* liquidation
~tang³ ~黨 *n.* purge (from a party)
CH'ING¹ 青 *a.* green
~ch'un¹ ~春 *n.* youth; *a.* juvenile, youthful
~ch'un¹ ch'i¹ ~春期 *n.* adolescence
~nien² ~年 *n.* youth, young man
~nien² hui⁴ ~年會 *n.* Young Men's Christian Association
~wa¹ ~蛙 *n.* frog
CH'ING² 情 *n.* passion, affection, emotion, circumstance, fact
~ai⁴ ~愛 *n.* affection, love
~chieh² ~節 *n.* plot (of a play)
~hsing² ~形 *n.* condition, situation, state
~hsü⁴ ~緒 *n.* emotion
~i² ~誼 *n.* friendship
~jen² ~人 *n.* lover, sweetheart
~kan³ ~感 *n.* emotion; *a.* sentimental, emotional
~li³ ~理 *n.* reason
~pao⁴ ~報 *n.* intelligence, information (*mil.*)
~pao⁴ tsung³ shu³ ~報總署 *n.* Information Administration**
~shu¹ ~書 *n.* love letter
~yüan⁴ ~願 *a.* willing
CH'ING² 晴 *n.* a clear sky
~t'ien¹ ~天 *n.* fine weather
~yü³ piao³ ~雨表 *n.* barometer
CH'ING³ 請 *v.* beg, request, invite
~chin⁴ ~進 *v.* come in (please)
~ch'iu² ~求 *n.* & *v.* request
~k'o⁴ ~客 *v.* invite guests

48

~t'ieh³ ~帖 *n.* invitation card
~tso⁴ ~坐 *v.* sit down (please)
~yüan⁴ ~願 *n.* petition
CH'ING⁴ 慶 *v.* congratulate
 ~chu⁴ ~祝 *v.* celebrate; *n.* celebration
 ~ho⁴ ~賀 *v.* congratulate; *n.* congratulations
CH'IU¹ 秋 *n.* autumn, fall
 ~chi⁴ ~季 *n.* autumn, fall
 ~shou¹ ~收 *n.* harvest
CH'IU² 求 *v.* beg, ask, request
 ~chien⁴ ~見 *v.* request an interview
 ~chu⁴ ~助 *v.* ask for help
 ~ch'ing² ~情 *v.* ask a favor
 ~hun¹ ~婚 *v.* woo, court
 ~hsüeh² ~學 *v.* learn, study
CH'IU² 球 *n.* ball, globe
 ~ch'ang³ ~場 *n.* playground
 ~hsing² ~形 *n.* sphere, globe
 ~men² ~門 *n.* goal (sports)
CH'IUNG² 窮 *a.* poor, exhausted
 ~jen² ~人 *n.* poor people
 ~k'un⁴ ~困 *a.* impoverished
CH'OU¹ 抽 *v.* draw
 ~chin¹ ~筋 *n.* spasm
 ~ch'ien¹ ~籤 *v.* draw lots
 ~hsiang⁴ ~象 *n.* abstraction
 ~hsien² ~閒 *v.* take a little leisure
 ~shui⁴ ~稅 *v.* levy taxes
 ~shui³ t'ung³ ~水筒 *n.* water pump
 ~t'i⁴ ~屜 *n.* drawer (furniture)
CH'OU² 酬 *v.* entertain, repay
 ~hsieh⁴ ~謝 *v.* return thanks
 ~lao² ~勞 *n. & v.* reward
 ~pao⁴ ~報 *v.* remunerate; *n.* remuneration
 ~wu⁴ ~物 *n.* gratuity
CH'OU² 籌 *n.* lot, ticket; *v.* calculate
 ~chieh⁴ ~借 *v.* raise money
 ~hua⁴ ~劃 *v.* plan
 ~pei⁴ ~備 *v.* prepare
CH'OU² 綢 *n.* silk cloth
 ~i¹ ~衣 *n.* silk garment

49

CH'OU² 仇 *n.* enmity, hate
~**hen⁴** ~恨 *n.* enmity, hate
~**jen²** ~人 *n.* enemy
~**ti²** ~敵 *n.* enemy
CH'OU² 愁 *a.* sad; *n.* sorrow
~**men⁴** ~悶 *a.* sorry, sad
CH'OU⁴ 臭 *a.* stench, stink
~**ch'i⁴** ~氣 *n.* stink
~**ch'ung²** ~蟲 *n.* bedbug
~**ming²** ~名 *n.* bad reputation
~**shui³** ~水 *n.* carbonic acid
CH'U¹ 出 *v.* go out, produce, pay
~**chung⁴** ~衆 *a.* noteworthy
~**ch'an³** ~產 *v.* produce, bear; *n.* product
~**fa¹** ~發 *v.* start, begin a journey
~**han⁴** ~汗 *v.* perspire, sweat
~**hsi²** ~席 *v.* attend
~**hsien⁴** ~現 *v.* appear; *n.* appearance
~**hsün²** ~巡 *v.* go in a circuit; *n.* circuit
~**k'ou³** ~口 *n.* exit
~**ming²** ~名 *a.* celebrated, famous, well-known
~**pan³** ~版 *v.* publish
~**p'in³** ~品 *n.* manufacture, product
~**tsu¹** ~租 *adv.* for rent
~**ya²** ~芽 *v.* put forth buds
~**yu²** ~遊 *v.* travel; *n.* excursion, pleasure trip
CH'U¹ 初 *a.* original, beginning
~**chi²** ~級 *a.* primary, elementary
~**chi² chiao⁴ lien⁴ chi¹** ~級教練機 *n.* primary trainer
~**hsüeh² che³** ~學者 *n.* beginner
~**liao²** ~療 *n.* first aid
~**pan³** ~版 *n.* first edition
~**pu⁴ te¹** ~步的 *a.* elementary
~**su⁴** ~速 *n.* muzzle velocity
~**teng³ chiao⁴ yü⁴** ~等教育 *n.* elementary education
~**teng³ hsüeh² hsiao⁴** ~等學校 *n.* elementary school
~**tz'u⁴** ~次 *n.* first time
CH'U² 除 *v.* exclude, divide, remove

50

~ch'ü⁴ ~去 v. remove
~fa³ ~法 n. division (mathematics)
~fei¹ ~非 conj. unless
~hsi¹ ~夕 n. New Year's Eve
~ken¹ ~根 v. eradicate
~ming² ~名 v. dismiss; n. dismissal
~tz'u³ i³ wai⁴ ~此以外 adv. besides
CH'U² 鋤 n. & v. hoe
CH'U³ 處 v. stay, rest, dwell, arrange, punish.
　~⁴ n. place, matter, condition
~³ fa² ~罰 v. punish
~li³ ~理 v. manage
~nü³ ~女 n. virgin, maiden
~nü³ mo⁴ ~女膜 n. hymen
~⁴ chang³ ~長 n. director
~ch'u⁴ ~處 adv. everywhere
CH'U³ 楚 a. woody; n. pain
CH'U⁴ 畜 n. animal; v. rear, raise
~mu⁴ ~牧 n. pasturage
~sheng¹ ~牲 n. brute
~yang³ ~養 v. rear, raise, feed
CH'UAN¹ 川 n. stream
~tzu¹ ~資 n. traveling expenses
CH'UAN¹ 穿 v. penetrate, put on, pass
~chen¹ ~針 v. thread a needle
~chia³ ~甲 n. armor-piercing
~hsieh² ~鞋 v. put on shoes
~i¹ ~衣 v. wear, put on
CH'UAN² 船 n. ship, boat
~chu³ ~主 n. ship captain
~fu¹ ~夫 n. boatman
~ku³ ~骨 n. keel
~ts'ang¹ ~艙 n. hold of a ship
~wei² ~桅 n. mast
~wei³ ~尾 n. stern
CH'UAN² 傳 v. transmit, summon, pass. CHUAN⁴
　n. biography
~chiao⁴ ~教 v. preach
~chiao⁴ shih⁴ ~教士 n. priest
~jan³ ~染 v. infect; n. infection
~jan³ ping⁴ ~染病 n. infectious diseases

51

~pu⁴ ~佈 *v.* spread
~p'iao⁴ ~票 *n.* summons
~ta² ~達 *n.* transmission
~tan¹ ~單 *n.* leaflet, handbill
~ti⁴ ~遞 *v.* transmit; *n.* transmission
chuan⁴ chi⁴ ~記 *n.* biography
CH'UANG¹ 窗 *n.* window
~hu⁴ ~戶 *n.* window
~lien² ~簾 *n.* window curtain
CH'UANG¹ 創 *v.* cut. ~⁴ *v.* create, begin
~¹ shang¹ chi⁴ ~傷劑 *n.* vulnerary medicine
~⁴ chih⁴ ch'üan² ~制權 *n.* initiative
~li⁴ ~立 *v.* establish
~pan⁴ jen² ~辦人 *n.* founder
~shih³ ~始 *v.* begin, start
~tsao⁴ ~造 *v.* create; *n.* creation
~yeh⁴ ~業 *n.* set up a foundation
CH'UANG² 牀 *n.* bed
~chia⁴ ~架 *n.* bedstead
~ju⁴ ~褥 *n.* mattress
~pien¹ ~邊 *n.* bedside
~p'u⁴ ~舖 *n.* bed, bedding
~tan¹ ~單 *n.* bedspread
CH'UI¹ 吹 *v.* blow
~hsü¹ ~噓 *v.* recommend; *n.* recommendation
~k'ou³ shao⁴ ~口哨 *v.* whistle
~niu² ~牛 *v.* boast
CH'UI² 錘 *n.* counterweight
CH'UN¹ 春 *n.* spring
~chi⁴ ~季 *n.* spring
~chia⁴ ~假 *n.* spring vacation
~ch'ing² ~情 *n.* passion (sexual love)
~ch'ing² fa¹ tung⁴ ch'i¹ ~情發動期 *n.* puberty
CH'UN² 純 *a.* pure, simple
~cheng⁴ ~正 *a.* righteous, upright
~chieh² ~潔 *n.* purity, cleanness
~hsiao⁴ ~孝 *a.* filial
~jan² ~然 *adv.* purely
~li⁴ ~利 *n.* net profit
~liang² ~良 *a.* good
~se⁴ ~色 *n.* pure color

52

~ts'ui⁴ ~粹 *a.* pure
CH'UNG¹ 充 *v.* fill
　~chün¹ ~軍 *v.* banish
　~fen⁴ te¹ ~分的 *a.* sufficient
　~kung¹ ~公 *v.* confiscate; *n.* confiscation
　~man³ ~滿 *v.* fill
　~shih² ~實 *n.* fulfillment
　~yü⁴ ~裕 *a.* abundant
CH'UNG¹ 衝 *v.* push forward
　~ch'u¹ ~出 *v.* break from encirclement
　~feng¹ ~鋒 *v.* assault
　~ju⁴ ~入 *v.* break in a defense
　~kuo⁴ ~過 *v.* overrun a position
　~p'o⁴ ~破 *v.* break in
　~t'u⁴ ~突 *v.* conflict
CH'UNG² 蟲 *n.* insect
CH'Ü¹ 曲 *a.* crooked, bent, twisted, curved. ~³
　n. song, aria, air
　~che² ~折 *adv.* zigzag; *a.* complicated
　~chieh³ ~解 *n.* misunderstanding, distortion
　~hsien⁴ ~綫 *n.* curve
　~hsien⁴ mei³ ~綫美 *n.* curve of beauty
CH'Ü¹ 區 *n.* place, district, zone
　~ch'ih⁴ wei⁴ ta⁴ tui⁴ ~赤衛大隊 *n.* district Com-
　munist guards**
　~ch'ü¹ ~區 *a.* small, petty, trifling
　~fen¹ ~分 *n.* partition
　~pieh² ~別 *v.* distinguish
　~yü⁴ ~域 *n.* region
CH'Ü³ 取 *v.* take
　~hsiao¹ ~消 *v.* nullify
　~nuan³ ~暖 *v.* make warm
CH'Ü³ 娶 *v.* marry a wife
　~ch'i¹ ~妻 *v.* marry a wife
CH'Ü⁴ 去 *v.* go
　~nien² ~年 *n.* last year
CH'Ü⁴ 趣 *a.* pleasant; *v.* hasten to
　~hua⁴ ~話 *n.* joke
　~shih⁴ ~事 *n.* interesting story
　~wei⁴ ~味 *n.* interest, taste
CH'ÜAN¹ 圈 *n.* circle, ring, snare, dot

~t'ao⁴ ~套 *n.* snare (trap)
CH'ÜAN² 全 *a.* whole, complete, entire, perfect
~ch'üan² ~權 *n.* plenipotentiary
~kuo² te¹ ~國的 *a.* national
~mien⁴ te¹ ~面的 *a.* overall (everything)
~neng² ~能 *a.* almighty
~t'i³ ~體 *pron.* all
~wu² ~無 *pron.* none
CH'ÜAN² 泉 *n.* fountain, spring, source
~shui³ ~水 *n.* spring water
~yüan² ~源 *n.* fountain
CH'ÜAN² 權 *n.* power, authority
~heng² ~衡 *v.* weigh (consider)
~hsien⁴ ~限 *n.* authority
~li⁴ ~利 *n.* right (privilege)
~li⁴ ~力 *n.* power (authority)
~ping³ ~柄 *n.* power
~shih⁴ ~勢 *n.* authority, influence
~wei¹ ~威 *n.* expert authority
CH'ÜAN⁴ 勸 *v.* advise, exhort, admonish
~chieh³ ~解 *v.* compromise
~chieh⁴ ~戒 *v.* advise
~mien³ ~勉 *v.* admonish
~tao³ ~導 *v.* exhort
~wei⁴ ~慰 *v.* condole
CH'ÜEH¹ 缺 *n.* defect, imperfection, lack, shortage; *a.* defective; *prep.* less
~fa² ~乏 *n.* lack, shortage
~han⁴ ~憾 *v.* disappoint
~huo⁴ ~貨 *n.* out of stock
~hsi² ~席 *a.* absent
~hsien⁴ ~陷 *n.* deficiency
~k'ou³ ~口 *n.* breach, gap
~tien³ ~點 *n.* weak point, defect
CH'ÜEH⁴ 卻 *v.* withdraw, reject, decline; *adv.* still, yet
CH'ÜEH⁴ 確 *adv.* really, truly, accurate
~cheng⁴ ~證 *n.* evidence
~chih¹ ~知 *v.* be sure
~shih² ~實 *a.* real, actual, true; *adv.* really, actually, truly

54

~ting⁴ ～定 *a.* certain

CH'ÜN² 群 *n.* flock, herd, crowd, group

~chung⁴ ～衆 *n.* masses

~chung⁴ lu⁴ hsien⁴ ～衆路線 *n.* mass line**

E

E² 俄 *a.* momentary; *adv.* suddenly, momentarily.

~⁴ *n.* Russia

E⁴ 餓 *a.* hungry; *n.* hunger

~ssu³ ～死 *v.* starve; *n.* starvation

E⁴ 惡 *a.* bad, evil

~hsi² ～習 *n.* bad habits

~i⁴ ～意 *n.* malignity

~kan³ ～感 *n.* bad feeling

~kuei³ ～鬼 *n.* devil

~tu² ～毒 *a.* vicious

EN¹ 恩 *n.* favor, mercy, kindness

~ai⁴ ～愛 *n.* affection

~ch'ing² ～情 *n.* kindness

~feng⁴ ～俸 *n.* pension

~hui⁴ ～惠 *n.* favor, beneficence

~jen² ～人 *n.* benefactor

ERH² 兒 *n.* son. ~¹ -son [a suffix]

~hsi⁴ ～戲 *n.* puerility

~nü³ ～女 *n.* children (your own)

~t'ung² ～童 *n.* children (other's)

~t'ung² chieh² ～童節 *n.* Children's Day

~tzu³ ～子 *n.* son

ERH² 而 *conj.* but, also, and, yet, nevertheless, however

~chin¹ ～今 *adv.* now

~ch'ieh³ ～且 *adv.* moreover, also

ERH³ 耳 *n.* ear

~lung² ～聾 *a.* deaf

~wen² ～聞 *v.* hear

~yü³ ～語 *v.* whisper

ERH⁴ 二 *n.* & *a.* two

~yüeh⁴ ～月 *n.* February

55

F

FA¹ 發 v. start, issue, dispatch (documents); n. round of ammunition

~chan³ ~展 v. develop

~chi³ ~給 v. issue supplies

~chiao⁴ ~酵 v. ferment; n. fermentation

~ch'i³ ~起 v. promote (start)

~ch'i³ jen² ~起人 n. founder

~hun¹ ~昏 v. faint

~hsiang³ ~餉 v. pay

~hsien⁴ ~見 v. discover

~hsin⁴ che³ ~信者 n. sender of a message

~hsing² ~行 v. publish

~jo⁴ ~熱 v. have fever

~ming² ~明 v. invent

~ming² chia¹ ~明家 n. inventor

~nu⁴ ~怒 v. become angry

~piao³ ~表 v. announce

~p'iao⁴ ~票 n. invoice

~she⁴ ~射 v. fire (shoot)

~sheng¹ ~生 v. happen

~shih⁴ ~誓 v. swear

~tien⁴ chi¹ ~電機 n. generator, dynamo

~tung⁴ chi¹ ~動機 n. engine, motor

~ts'ai² ~財 become rich

~yen² ~言 v. speak

~yen² ~炎 n. inflammation

~yin¹ hsüeh² ~音學 n. phonetics

FA² 罰 n. punishment, penalty, fine; v. punish

~hsin¹ ~薪 n. forfeiture of pay

~k'uan³ ~款 n. & v. fine

~tse² ~則 n. penal regulations

FA³ 法 n. law, process, method; a. legal

~chih⁴ wei³ yüan² hui⁴ ~制委員會 n. Commission of Legislative Affairs**

~hsüeh² yüan⁴ ~學院 n. college of law

~kuan¹ ~官 n. judge

~ling⁴ ~令 n. law

56

~lü⁴ ~律 *n.* law
~t'ing² ~庭 *n.* court, tribunal (law)
~yüan⁴ ~院 *n.* law court
FA³ 髪 *n.* hair
~shua¹ ~刷 *n.* hair-brush
~yu² ~油 *n.* pomade, hair tonic
FAN¹ 翻 *v.* turn over, upset
~i⁴ ~譯 *v.* translate, interpret
~i⁴ yüan² ~譯員 *n.* translator, interpreter
~ken¹ tou³ ~筋斗 *n.* somersault
~shen¹ ~身 *v.* turn over to**
~yin⁴ ~印 *v.* reprint
FAN² 凡 *a.* all, every; *prep.* whatever
~jen² ~人 *n.* mankind, laity
~li⁴ ~例 *n.* example
~su² ~俗 *a.* vulgar
~shih⁴ ~事 *pron.* everything
FAN² 煩 *v.* trouble
~jao³ ~擾 *v.* annoy
~men⁴ ~悶 *a.* sad
~nan² ~難 *a.* difficult
~nao³ ~惱 *n.* worry
FAN³ 反 *v.* reverse, revolt, rebel
~fu⁴ ~復 *n.* repetition
~hui³ ~悔 *v.* repent
~hsiang³ ~響 *n.* response, reaction
~hsing² hui⁴ ~行賄 *n.* anti-bribery**
~hsing³ ~省 *n.* introspection
~kuan¹ liao² chu³ i⁴ ~官僚主義 *n.* anti-bu-
reaucracy**
~kung⁴ i⁴ shih⁴ ~共義士 *n.* anti-Communist
patriots
~kung⁴ k'ang⁴ e⁴ ~共抗俄 *v.* fight against the
Communists and Russians
~k'ang⁴ ~抗 *v.* oppose, resist
~lang⁴ fei⁴ ~浪費 *n.* anti-waste**
~pi³ li⁴ ~比例 *n.* inverse proportion
~p'an⁴ ~叛 *v.* rebel
~she⁴ ~射 *v.* reflect
~tao⁴ ch'ieh⁴ kuo² chia¹ ching¹ chi⁴ ch'ing²
pao⁴ ~盜竊國家經濟情報 *n.* anti-stealing of eco-

nomic information from government sources for private speculation**

~tao⁴ ch'ieh⁴ kuo² chia¹ tzu¹ ts'ai² ~盜竊國家資財 *n.* anti-theft of state property**

~tung⁴ ~動 *n.* reaction (political)

~t'an¹ wu¹ ~貪污 *n.* anti-corruption**

~t'ou¹ kung¹ chien³ liao⁴ ~偷工減料 *n.* anti-cheating on government contracts**

~t'ou¹ shui⁴ lou⁴ shui⁴ ~偷稅漏稅 *n.* anti-tax evasion**

~ying⁴ ~應 *n.* reaction (*chem.*)

FAN⁴ 飯 *n.* meal

~tien⁴ ~店 *n.* restaurant

FAN⁴ 犯 *n.* prisoner, criminal; *v.* offend, violate

~fa³ ~法 *v.* offend against the law

~jen² ~人 *n.* prisoner, criminal

~tsui⁴ ~罪 *n.* crime

~tsui⁴ hsüeh² ~罪學 *n.* criminology

FAN⁴ 範 *n.* pattern

~ch'ou² ~疇 *n.* category

~pen³ ~本 *n.* pattern, model

~wei² ~圍 *n.* limit, scope

FANG¹ 方 *n.* direction, square; *a.* square quad-rangular

~chang⁴ ~丈 *n.* abbot

~chen¹ ~針 *n.* aim, objective, direction

~ch'eng² shih⁴ ~程式 *n.* equation

~fa³ ~法 *n.* method, means, way

~hsiang⁴ ~向 *n.* direction

~pien⁴ ~便 *n.* convenience; *a.* convenient

~yen² ~言 *n.* dialect

FANG² 房 *n.* house, room, chamber

~chüan¹ ~捐 *n.* house rent

~ch'an³ ~產 *n.* estate, landed property

~k'o⁴ ~客 *n.* tenant

~shih⁴ ~事 *n.* venery (sexual)

~tung¹ ~東 *n.* landlord, landlady

~tsu¹ ~租 *n.* rent

~wu¹ ~屋 *n.* house

FANG² 防 *n.* defense, protection; *v.* defend, guard against

~k'ung¹ ~空 *n.* ground air defense
~k'ung¹ hsüeh² hsiao⁴ ~空學校 *n.* Anti-Air Raid School*
~k'ung¹ tung⁴ ~空洞 *n.* air-raid shelter
~k'ung¹ yen³ hsi² ~空演習 *n.* air-raid drill
~shou³ ~守 *v.* defend
~yü⁴ hsien⁴ ~禦線 *n.* line of defense
FANG² 妨 *v.* hinder, obstruct
~hai⁴ ~害 *v.* harass
FANG³ 訪 *v.* visit, search out, inquire into
~k'o⁴ ~客 *n.* visitor
~wen⁴ ~問 *v.* interview
FANG³ 紡 *v.* spin (material)
~chih¹ ~織 *v.* spin and weave
~ch'e¹ ~車 *n.* reel
~ch'ui² ~錘 *n.* spindle
~sha¹ ~紗 *n.* cotton spinning
~sha¹ ch'ang³ ~紗廠 *n.* spinning mill
FANG⁴ 放 *v.* set free, exile, place, put
~chang⁴ ~賑 *v.* give credit
~chia⁴ ~假 *n.* holiday, vacation
~chu² ~逐 *v.* exile
~ch'i⁴ ~棄 *v.* abandon
~ch'i⁴ ~氣 *n.* deflation (of object)
~huo³ tsui⁴ ~火罪 *n.* arson
~hsiang³ ~餉 *v.* hand out the pay
~hsüeh² ~學 *v.* let out school
~jen⁴ ~任 *n.* laissez faire
~sung¹ ~鬆 *v.* untie, loosen
~ssu⁴ ~肆 *a.* impudent, impolite
~ta⁴ ~大 *v.* enlarge
~ta⁴ ching⁴ ~大鏡 *n.* magnifying lens
~tang⁴ ~蕩 *a.* profligate, wanton
FEI¹ 飛 *v.* fly; *n.* flight
~chi¹ ~機 *n.* airplane, aircraft
~chi¹ chih⁴ tsao⁴ ch'ang³ ~機製造廠 *n.* airplane factory
~chi¹ ch'ang³ ~機場 *n.* airdrome, airport
~ch'in² ~禽 *n.* bird
~ch'uan² ~船 *n.* airship
~hsing² ~行 *n.* flight (flying)

59

~hsing² chia¹ ~行家 *n.* pilot, aviator

~hsing² shu⁴ ~行術 *n.* aviation

~hsing² yüan² ~行員 *n.* pilot, aviator

~pen¹ ~奔 *v.* gallop

~tan⁴ ~彈 *n.* wild shot

~yen⁴ ~雁 *n.* wild-goose

FEI¹ 非 *adv.* no, not, wrong; *a.* no, wrong

~chan⁴ chu³ i⁴ che³ ~戰主義者 *n.* conscientious objector

~cheng⁴ shih⁴ ~正式 *a.* informal

~chin¹ shu³ ~金屬 *n.* non-metal

~ch'ang² ~常 *adv.* exceedingly; *a.* extraordinary, unusual

~fa³ ~法 *a.* illegal

~li³ ~禮 *a.* indecent

~wu³ chuang¹ ch'ü¹ ~武裝區 *n.* demilitarized zone

FEI² 肥 *a.* fat, stout

~chuang⁴ ~壯 *a.* fat and strong

~jou⁴ ~肉 *n.* fat meat

~jun⁴ ~潤 *a.* glossy

~liao⁴ ~料 *n.* fertilizer, manure

~ni⁴ ~膩 *a.* greasy

~p'ang⁴ ~胖 *a.* fat

~ta⁴ ~大 *a.* stout

~tsao⁴ ~皂 *n.* soap

~wo⁴ ~沃 *a.* fertile

FEI³ 匪 *n.* bandit, highwayman, robber

~tang³ ~黨 *n.* bandit clique

~t'u² ~徒 *n.* bandit

FEI⁴ 費 *v.* use, spend, waste; *n.* fee, fare

~shih² ~時 *v.* waste time

~yung⁴ ~用 *n.* expenditure, expense

FEI⁴ 肺 *n.* lung

~chieh² ho² ping⁴ ~結核病 *n.* pulmonary tuberculosis

~yen² ~炎 *n.* pneumonia

FEI⁴ 廢 *a.* useless, wasteful, ruined; *v.* abandon

~chih³ ~紙 *n.* waste paper

~ch'i⁴ ~棄 *v.* abandon

~ch'u² ~除 *v.* abolish; *n.* abolition

60

~hua⁴ ~話 *n.* verbiage
~jen² ~人 *n.* cripple, disabled person
~wu⁴ ~物 *n.* trash
FEN¹ 分 *n.* cent, minute, division; *v.* divide, separate
　~chieh³ ~解 *v.* analyze; *n.* analysis
　~hua⁴ ~化 *n.* differentiation
　~hsi¹ ~析 *v.* analyze; *n.* analysis
　~ko¹ ~割 *n.* partition
　~kung¹ ~工 *n.* division of labor
　~lei⁴ ~類 *n. & v.* classify; *n.* classification
　~li² ~離 *n. & v.* separate, depart
　~pi⁴ ~泌 *v.* secrete; *n.* secretion
　~pieh² ~別 *v.* separate, distinguish
　~pu⁴ ~佈 *v.* spread, scatter, distribute
　~p'ai⁴ ~派 *v.* distribute
　~p'ei⁴ ~配 *n.* distribution
　~san⁴ ~散 *n. & v.* disperse, scatter
　~shu⁴ ~數 *n.* grade, rating, fraction
　~tien⁴ ~店 *n.* branch store
　~tzu³ ~子 *n.* molecule, member
　~wan³ ~娩 *n.* confinement
FEN¹ 紛 *a.* confused; *n.* disorder
　~ch'i² ~歧 *a.* different, discrepant
　~luan⁴ ~亂 *n.* disorder
FEN³ 粉 *n.* flour, powder
　~hung² ~紅 *n.* pink
　~pi³ ~筆 *n.* chalk
　~sui⁴ ~碎 *n.* smash
　~shih⁴ ~飾 *v.* paint, adorn
　~ssu¹ ~糸 *n.* vermicelli
FEN⁴ 奮 *v.* arouse, strike; *a.* zealous
　~mien³ ~勉 *v.* encourage
　~tou⁴ ~鬥 *n. & v.* struggle
　~yung³ ~勇 *a.* courageous, brave
FEN⁴ 糞 *n.* stool, excrement, dung
FENG¹ 封 *v.* seal, close, blockade
　~chien⁴ chih⁴ tu⁴ ~建制度 *n.* feudal system
　~chien⁴ she⁴ hui⁴ ~建社會 *n.* feudal society
　~chien⁴ shih⁴ li⁴ ~建勢力 *n.* feudal influence
　~chien⁴ ssu¹ hsiang³ ~建思想 *n.* feudalism

61

~**chien⁴ te¹** ~建的 *a.* feudal
~**pi⁴** ~閉 *v.* close
~**so³** ~鎖 *n.* & *v.* blockade
~**t'iao²** ~條 *n.* label
FENG¹ 風 *n.* wind, breeze
~**cheng¹** ~箏 *n.* kite
~**ching³** ~景 *n.* scenery, landscape
~**ch'in²** ~琴 *n.* musical organ
~**ch'ing²** ~情 *n.* climate
~**hsiang¹** ~箱 *n.* bellows
~**su²** ~俗 *n.* custom
~**shan⁴** ~扇 *n.* electric fan
~**shih¹ ping⁴** ~溼病 *n.* rheumatism
~**ya³** ~雅 *a.* refined
~**yü³ piao³** ~雨表 *n.* barometer
FENG¹ 豐 *a.* copious, plentiful, abundant
~**fu⁴** ~富 *a.* copious, rich
~**man³** ~滿 *a.* plentiful, rich
~**shou¹** ~收 *n.* ample harvest
FENG² 縫 *v.* sew, mend. ~⁴ *n.* crack, split
~² **chen¹** ~針 *n.* sewing needle
~**i¹** ~衣 *v.* stitch clothes
~**jen⁴** ~紉 *n.* needlework, sewing
~**jen⁴ chi¹** ~紉機 *n.* sewing machine
~**jen⁴ hsien⁴** ~紉線 *n.* sewing thread
FOU³ 否 *a.* negative ; *adv.* no, not
~**chüeh²** ~決 *v.* vote down
~**jen⁴** ~認 *v.* deny ; *n.* denial
~**tse²** ~則 *adv.* otherwise
FU¹ 夫 *n.* husband
~**fu⁴** ~婦 *n.* couple, husband and wife
~**jen²** ~人 *n.* madam, lady, wife
FU² 服 *n.* clothes, dress ; *v.* dress, obey, be submissive
~**shih⁴** ~飾 *n.* adornment
~**shih⁴** ~式 *n.* costume
~**shih⁴** ~侍 *v.* serve
~**tu²** ~毒 *v.* take poison purposely
~**ts'ung²** ~從 *v.* obey ; *n.* obedience ; *a.* obedient
~**wu⁴** ~務 *v.* serve ; *n.* service
~**yao⁴** ~藥 *v.* take medicine

62

FU² 伏 *v.* prostrate, surrender, ambush
  ~luan³ ~卵 *v.* hatch
  ~ping¹ ~兵 *n.* ambush
  ~wo⁴ ~臥 *v.* lie down flat
FU² ~扶 *v.* aid, help
  ~chu⁴ ~助 *v.* aid, assist
  ~ch'ih² ~持 *v.* support
  ~yang³ ~養 *v.* support, rear (family)
FU² 福 *n.* good fortune, felicity, blessing
  ~ch'i⁴ ~氣 *n.* good fortune
FU³ 府 *n.* prefecture, residence, mansion
FU³ 腐 *a.* rotten, spoiled, putrid; *n.* decay
  ~hua⁴ ~化 *a.* putrid (food)
  ~hua⁴ fen⁴ tzu³ ~化份子 *a.* corrupt elements
  ~lan⁴ ~爛 *a.* rotten, corrupt, decayed
  ~pai⁴ ~敗 *a.* corrupt
  ~shih² ~蝕 *n.* corrosion
FU³ 斧 *n.* hatchet, axe
  ~yüeh⁴ ~鉞 *n.* halberd
FU⁴ 父 *n.* father, daddy, papa, pop
  ~mu³ ~母 *n.* parent
FU⁴ 婦 *n.* woman, lady
  ~ju² ~孺 *n.* women and children
  ~nü³ ~女 *n.* woman, lady
  ~tao⁴ ~道 *n.* womanhood (character)
  ~te² ~德 *n.* woman's virtue
FU⁴ 富 *a.* rich, abundant, wealthy
  ~ch'iang² ~強 *a.* rich and strong
  ~li⁴ ~麗 *a.* splendid
  ~weng¹ ~翁 *n.* millionaire
FU⁴ 負 *n.* defeat, lose; *v.* fail, lose; *a.* negative
  ~chai⁴ ~債 *v.* owe money
  ~chung⁴ ~重 *n.* heavy burden
  ~hsin¹ ~心 *a.* ungrateful
  ~tan¹ ~擔 *n.* burden
  ~yüeh¹ ~約 *v.* break one's promise
FU⁴ 付 *v.* pay; *n.* payment
  ~ch'i⁴ ~訖 *a.* paid
  ~ch'ing¹ ~清 *v.* pay in full
  ~ch'u¹ ~出 *v.* pay
  ~huan² ~還 *v.* pay back

~hsien⁴ ~現 *v.* pay in cash

~k'an¹ ~刊 *v.* be published

FU⁴ 附 *v.* attach, subjoin, enclose

~chi⁴ ~記 *n.* remarks

~chia¹ shui⁴ ~加稅 *n.* surtax

~chin⁴ ~近 *a.* near, adjacent

~lu⁴~錄 *n.* appendix

~shu³ ~屬 *a.* dependent, accessory

~shu³ p'in³ ~屬品 *n.* accessory

~yung¹ kuo² ~庸國 *n.* satellite nation

FU⁴ 副 *v.* aid; *n.* assistant, second

~chien³ ch'a² chang³ ~檢察長 *n.* Deputy Procurator-General

~chu³ hsi² ~主席 *n.* vice-chairman

~chu³ jen⁴ ~主任 *n.* vice-chairman

~chu³ jen⁴ wei³ yüan² ~主任委員 *n.* vice-chairman

~fei¹ hsing² yüan² ~飛行員 *n.* co-pilot

~hang² chang³ ~行長 *n.* assistant managing director

~kuan¹ ~官 *n.* adjutant, personal aide

~ling³ shih⁴ ~領事 *n.* vice-consul

~mi⁴ shu¹ chang³ ~祕書長 *n.* assistant secretary-general

~pen³ ~本 *n.* duplicate copy

~pu⁴ chang³ ~部長 *n.* vice-minister

~shu³ chang³ ~署長 *n.* vice-pirector

~tsung³ li³ ~總理 *n.* vice-premier

~tsung³ t'ung³ ~總統 *n.* vice-president

~yüan⁴ chang³ ~院長 *n.* vice-president

FU⁴ 復 *v.* reply, restore, return; *adv.* again

~chih² ~職 *v.* rehabilitate (former rank)

~ch'ou² ~仇 *n.* revenge

~huo² chieh² ~活節 *n.* Easter

~hsing¹ ~興 *v.* revive

~sung⁴ ~誦 *v.* repeat a message

~yüan² ~元 *n.* recovery (health)

~yüan² ~原 *v.* recover from illness

~yüan² ~員 *n.* demobilization

FU⁴ 複 *a.* double

~hsüan³ ~選 *n.* indirect vote

64

~li⁴ ~利 *n.* compound interest
~shu⁴ ~數 *n.* plural number
~tsa² ~雜 *a.* complicated, complex

H

HA¹ 哈 [an exclamation]
HAI² 孩 *n.* child
 ~t'ung² ~童 *n.* child
HAI² 還 *see* HUAN²
HAI³ 海 *n.* sea
 ~an⁴ ~岸 *n.* coast
 ~an⁴ fang² yü⁴ ~岸防禦 *n.* coast defense
 ~an⁴ hsien⁴ ~岸線 *n.* coastline
 ~chün¹ ~軍 *n.* Navy
 ~chün¹ chi¹ hsieh⁴ hsüeh² hsiao⁴ ~軍機械學校 *n.* Navy Mechanics School*
 ~chün¹ chi¹ ti⁴~ ~軍基地 *n.* naval base
 ~chün¹ chih³ hui¹ ts'an¹ mou² hsüeh² hsiao⁴ ~軍指揮參謀學校 *n.* Navy Command and Staff College*
 ~chün¹ chün¹ kuan¹ hsüeh² hsiao⁴ ~軍軍官學校 *n.* Navy Academy*
 ~chün¹ lu⁴ chan⁴ tui⁴ ~軍陸戰隊 *n.* marines
 ~chün¹ pu⁴ ~軍部 *n.* Department of the Navy (*U.S.*)
 ~chün¹ shih⁴ ping¹ hsüeh² hsiao⁴ ~軍士兵學校 *n.* Navy Petty Officers and Seamen School*
 ~chün¹ tsao⁴ ch'uan² ch'ang³ ~軍造船廠 *n.* navy yard
 ~chün¹ tsung³ ssu¹ ling⁴ pu⁴ ~軍總司令部 *n.* Navy Headquarters*
 ~chün¹ wu³ kuan¹ ~軍武官 *n.* naval attache
 ~fang² ~防 *n.* coast guard
 ~hsia² ~峽 *n.* strait
 ~kang³ ~港 *n.* seaport, harbor
 ~kuan¹ ~關 *n.* custom house
 ~k'ou³ ~口 *n.* seaport, port, harbor
 ~li³ ~里 *n.* nautical mile
 ~pa² ~拔 *n.* above sea level (height)

~**pin¹** ~濱 *n.* seashore

~**p'ing²** **mien⁴** ~平面 *n.* sea level

~**shang⁴** **pao³** **hsien³** ~上保險 *n.* marine insurance

~**shui³** **yü⁴** ~水浴 *n.* swimming

~**tao³** ~島 *n.* island

~**tao⁴** ~盜 *n.* pirate

~**ti³** **tien⁴** **hsien⁴** ~底電線 n. cablegram

~**t'an¹** ~灘 *n.* beach

~**wai⁴** **yüan³** **cheng¹** ~外遠征 *n.* overseas expedition

~**wan¹** ~灣 *n.* bay

~**yang²** ~洋 *n.* ocean

~**yüan²** ~員 seaman

~**yün⁴** ~運 *n.* sea transportation

HAI⁴ 害 *v.* injure, hurt, harm; *n.* disadvantage

~**hsiu¹** ~羞 *a.* bashful, shy

~**ping⁴** ~病 *v.* suffer from sickness

~**p'a⁴** ~怕 *a.* afraid

HAN² 寒 *a.* cold, chilly, poor

~**leng³** ~冷 *a.* cold

~**shu³** **piao³** ~暑表 *n.* thermometer

~**tai⁴** ~帶 *n.* Frigid Zone

HAN² 含 *v.* contain, hold

~**hu²** ~糊 *a.* vague, ambiguous

~**hsiu¹** ~羞 *a.* bashful, shy

~**yüan¹** ~冤 *v.* have a grievance

HAN³ 喊 *v.* cry, call

HAN⁴ 汗 *n.* perspiration, sweat

~**hsien⁴** ~腺 *n.* sweat gland

~**shan¹** ~衫 *n.* undershirt

HAN⁴ 旱 *n.* drought; *a.* rainless, dry

~**tsai¹** ~災 *n.* drought

HAN⁴ 漢 *n.* ancient Chinese dynasty, Chinese

~**jen²** ~人 n. Chinese people

~**tsu²** ~族 *n.* Chinese race

~**wen²** ~文 *n.* Chinese writing

HANG² 航 *v.* navigate, sail

~**ch'eng²** ~程 *n.* course (way)

~**hai³** ~海 *n.* navigation

~**hai³** **chia¹** ~海家 *n.* navigator

66

~hsien⁴ ~線 *n.* sea route, air line route
~k'ung¹ ~空 *n.* aviation, air navigation
~k'ung¹ chan⁴ ~空站 *n.* airdrome
~k'ung¹ chi¹ ~空機 *n.* aircraft
~k'ung¹ hsüeh² ~空學 *n.* aeronautics
~k'ung¹ mu³ chien⁴ ~空母艦 *n.* aircraft carrier
~k'ung¹ tui⁴ ~空隊 *n.* air fleet
~yün⁴ ~運 *n.* air transportation
HANG² 行 *see* HSING²
HAO³ 好 *a.* good, fine, well, right; *adv.* well. ~⁴
v. be fond of
~³ ch'ih¹ ~吃 *a.* palatable. ~⁴ *a.* gluttonous
~hsiao⁴ ~笑 *a.* funny
~k'an⁴ ~看 *a.* beautiful, pretty, handsome
~yün⁴ ~運 *n.* good luck
~⁴ se⁴ ~色 *v.* be fond of beauty
HAO⁴ 號 *n.* sign, mark, title, bugle, signal, order,
name, firm; *v.* cry, call
~chao⁴ ~召 *v.* summon
~k'u¹ ~哭 *v.* cry
~ma³ ~碼 *n.* number
~ping¹ ~兵 *n.* bugler
~wai⁴ ~外 *n.* newspaper extra
HEI¹ 黑 *n.* & *a.* black, dark
~an⁴ ~暗 *a.* dark; *n.* darkness
~jen² ~人 *n.* negro
~mei² ~莓 *n.* blackberry
~ming² tan¹ ~名單 *n.* black list
~pan³ ~板 *n.* blackboard
~se⁴ ~色 *n.* black
~shih⁴ ~市 *n.* black market
HEN³ 很 *adv.* very, quite
~hao³ ~好 *a.* very good
HEN⁴ 恨 *v.* hate; *n.* hate, hatred
HENG² 橫 *a.* horizontal. ~⁴ *a.* perverse, wicked;
adv. crosswise
~² hsing² ~行 *n.* bad conduct
~⁴ huo⁴ ~禍 *n.* unexpected calamity
~pao⁴ ~暴 *a.* perverse
~ssu³ ~死 *n.* unnatural death
~ts'ai² ~財 *n.* windfall (unexpected profit)

67

HO¹ 喝 *v.* drink. ~⁴ *v.* shout
  ~¹ **chiu³** ~酒 *v.* drink wine
  ~**ch'a²** ~茶 *v.* drink tea
  ~⁴ **ts'ai³** ~采 *v.* applaud
HO² 何 *pron.* who, which, what; *adv.* how, why
  ~**i³** ~以 *adv.* why
  ~**jen²** ~人 *pron.* who
  ~**ku⁴** ~故 *adv.* why
  ~**shih²** ~時 *adv.* when
  ~**shih⁴** ~事 *pron.* what
  ~**ti⁴** ~地 *adv.* where
HO² 河 *n.* river
  ~**an⁴** ~岸 *n.* bank
  ~**ch'uan¹ chan⁴** ~川戰 *n.* river warfare
  ~**ch'uang²** ~床 *n.* river bed
  ~**liu²** ~流 *n.* stream
  ~**tao⁴** ~道 *n* river course
HO² 合 *v.* shut, close, enclose; *a.* suitable, accordant
  ~**chin¹** ~金 *n.* alloy
  ~**fa³** ~法 *a.* legal
  ~**ko²** ~格 *a.* qualified
  ~**li³** ~理 *a.* reasonable
  ~**suan⁴** ~算 *v.* add; *a.* profitable
  ~**t'ung²** ~同 *n.* contract, agreement
  ~**tso⁴** ~作 *v.* cooperate; *n.* cooperation
  ~**tso⁴ hua⁴** ~作化 *n.* co-operativisation**
  ~**tso⁴ nung² ch'ang³** ~作農場 *n.* Co-operative Farm**
HO² 和 *conj.* and; *a.* friendly
  ~**ai³** ~藹 *a.* genial
  ~**chieh³** ~解 *v.* compromise
  ~**ch'i⁴** ~氣 *a.* kind
  ~**feng¹** ~風 *n.* breeze
  ~**hao³** ~好 *v.* reconcile
  ~**hsieh²** ~諧 *a.* harmonious; *n.* harmony
  ~**nuan³** ~暖 *a.* warm
  ~**p'ing²** ~平 *a.* peaceful; *n.* peace
  ~**p'ing² hui⁴ i⁴** ~平會議 *n.* peace conference
  ~**p'ing² t'an² p'an⁴** ~平談判 *n.* peace negotiations

~shang⁴ ~尚 *n.* monk
~yüeh¹ ~約 *n.* peace treaty
HO⁴ 賀 *v.* congratulate
　~hsi³ ~喜 *v.* congratulate
　~hsin¹ nien² ~新年 *v.* offer New Year's greetings
HOU² 喉 *n.* throat
　~t'ung⁴ ~痛 *n.* sore throat
HOU⁴ 侯 *v.* wait
　~ch'e¹ shih⁴ ~車室 *n.* waiting room (station)
　~pu³ ~補 *n.* candidacy
　~pu³ che³ ~補者 *n.* candidate
　~shen³ ~審 *v.* wait trial
HOU⁴ 後 *prep.* after, behind; *a.* future, late; *adv.*
　afterwards
　~fang¹ ~方 *n.* zone of the interior, rear
　~fang¹ i¹ yüan⁴ ~方醫院 *n.* base hospital
　~fu⁴ ~父 *n.* stepfather
　~hui³ ~悔 *v.* regret
　~jen⁴ ~任 *n.* successor
　~lai² ~來 *adv.* afterwards
　~mu³ ~母 *n.* stepmother
　~pu⁴ ~部 *n.* back
　~tso⁴ li⁴ ~座力 n. force of recoil
　~wei⁴ ~衛 *n.* rear guard
　~yüan² ~緣 *n.* trailing edge
　~yüan² chün¹ ~援軍 *n.* re-enforcement
HOU⁴ 厚 *n.* thickness, density; *a.* thick
　~ch'ing² ~情 *a.* friendly
　~tai⁴ ~待 *v.* treat kindly
　~tao⁴ ~道 *a.* generous
　~yen² ~顏 *a.* shameless
HU¹ 呼 *v.* call, exclaim, cry
　~han³ ~喊 *n.* & *v.* shout
　~hao⁴ ~號 *v.* yell
　~hsi¹ ~吸 *v.* breathe
HU¹ 忽 *a.* careless; *v.* neglect
　~jan² ~然 *adv.* suddenly; *a.* sudden
　~lüeh⁴ ~略 *a.* careless, neglectful, negligent
HU² 湖 *n.* lake
HU² 胡 *a.* arbitrary; *adv.* recklessly; *n.* northern
　barbarians

69

~chiao¹ ~椒 *n.* pepper
~ch'in² ~琴 *n.* Chinese violin
~kua¹ ~瓜 *n.* cucumber
~luan⁴ ~亂 *a.* confused
~shuo¹ ~說 *n.* nonsense
~t'ao² ~桃 *n.* walnut
~t'ung² ~同 *n.* lane
HU² 壺 *n.* kettle, pot
HU³ 虎 *n.* tiger
~lieh⁴ la¹ ~列拉 *n.* cholera
HU⁴ 互 *adv.* mutually, each other
~ai⁴ ~愛 *v.* love each other
~chu⁴ ~助 *n.* mutual assistance
~chu⁴ hsiao³ tsu³ ~助小組 *n.* mutual aid team**
~hsiang¹ ~相 *adv.* mutually, each other
~hsiang¹ ho² tso⁴ ~相合作 *n.* cooperation**
~hsiang¹ i¹ lai⁴ ~相依賴 *n.* interdependence**
~hsiang¹ kuan⁴ t'ung¹ ~相貫通 *n.* interpenetration**
~hsiang¹ lien² lo⁴ ~相聯絡 *n.* interconnection**
~hsiang¹ shen⁴ t'ou⁴ ~相滲透 *n.* interpermeation**
HU⁴ 戶 *n.* door, family
~k'ou³ ~口 *n.* population
~k'ou³ chien³ ch'a² ~口檢查 *n.* census
~wai⁴ yün⁴ tung⁴ ~外運動 *n.* outdoor sports
HU⁴ 護 *v.* protect, guard; *n.* protection
~chao⁴ ~照 *n.* passport
~chiu⁴ ~救 *v.* rescue
~hang² tui⁴ ~航隊 *n.* convoy
~ping¹ ~兵 *n.* private bodyguard
~sung⁴ ~送 *v.* convoy
~wei⁴ ~衛 *v.* defend, protect
HUA¹ 花 *n.* flower
~ch'iu² ~球 *n.* bouquet
~ch'üan¹ ~圈 *n.* garland, wreath
~fang² ~房 *n.* greenhouse, hothouse
~fei⁴ ~費 *v.* spend, expend
~fen³ ~粉 *n.* pollen
~hung² ~紅 *n.* bonus
~jui³ ~蕊 *n.* bud

70

~kang¹ shih² ~岡石 *n.* granite
~kuan¹ ~冠 *n.* flower petals
~lan² ~籃 *n.* flower basket
~liu³ ping⁴ ~柳病 *n.* venereal disease
~ming² ts'e⁴ ~名册 *n.* roll (list of names)
~pan⁴ ~瓣 *n.* petal
~p'ing² ~瓶 *n.* vase
~yang⁴ ~樣 *n.* pattern
~yüan² ~園 *n.* garden
HUA² 華 *n.* China, flower, glory; *a.* stately, beautiful
~ch'iao² ~僑 *n.* overseas Chinese
~ch'iao² shih⁴ wu⁴ wei³ yüan² hui⁴ ~僑事務委員會 *n.* Commission of Overseas Chinese Affairs**
~li⁴ ~麗 *a.* pompous
~pei³ hsing² cheng⁴ wei³ yüan² hui⁴ ~北行政委員會 *n.* North China Administrative Committee**
~pei³ jen² min² ko² ming⁴ ta⁴ hsüeh² ~北人民革命大學 *n.* North China People's Revolutionary University**
~tan⁴ ~誕 *n.* birthday
HUA² 劃 *v.* divide, mark, cut
~² fen¹ ~分 *v.* divide
~p'o⁴ ~破 *v.* scratch
~⁴ i¹ ~一 *a.* uniform
HUA⁴ 話 *n.* word, speech, spoken language
HUA⁴ 化 *v.* change, alter, melt, convert, dissolve
~ho² wu⁴ ~合物 *n.* compound (*chem.*)
~hsüeh² ~學 *n.* chemistry
~hsüeh² chan⁴ ~學戰 *n.* chemical warfare
~shih² ~石 *n.* fossil
~yu² ch'i⁴ ~油器 *n.* carburetor
HUA⁴ 畫 *v.* draw, paint; *n.* picture, drawing
~chia¹ ~家 *n.* painter, artist
~chia⁴ ~架 *n.* picture easel
~fang³ ~舫 *n.* excursion barge
~pu⁴ ~布 *n.* painting canvas
HUAI² 懷 *n.* bosom; *v.* conceal, think of
~hen⁴ ~恨 *v.* hate

71

~i² ~疑 v. doubt, suspect; a. skeptical
~nien⁴ ~念 v. think of
~pao⁴ ~抱 n. bosom; v. cherish, nestle
~yün⁴ ~孕 a. pregnant; n. pregnancy
HUAI⁴ 壞 a. vicious, corrupt; v. destroy, ruin, spoil
~ch'u⁴ ~處 n. defect
~ch'uan² ~船 n. wreck
~jen² ~人 n. bad man
~yün⁴ ~運 n. bad luck
HUAN¹ 歡 v. rejoice, like; n. joy, delight; a. merry, jolly
~hsi³ ~喜 n. joy, delight, happiness
~ying² ~迎 v. welcome
~ying² hui⁴ ~迎會 n. reception (party)
HUAN² 還 v. return, repay, compensate. HAI² adv. still
HUAN² 環 n. ring, loop, coil, eye, eyelet, bracelet; v. surround
~chi¹ ~擊 v. return fire
~ching⁴ ~境 n. surroundings
~jao⁴ ~繞 v. surround, circle
~shih⁴ ~視 v. look around
HUAN⁴ 換 v. change, exchange, replace
~ch'i⁴ ~氣 v. ventilate
~ch'ien² ~錢 v. exchange money
~nao³ ~腦 n. brain-changing**
HUANG¹ 慌 a. nervous
~chang¹ ~張 a. nervous, excited
~luan⁴ ~亂 n. disorder
~mang² ~忙 a. hurried
HUANG¹ 荒 a. barren, wild; n. famine
~liang² ~涼 a. desert
~lin² ~林 n. wildwood
~miu⁴ ~謬 a. absurd
~nien² ~年 n. famine
~p'i⁴ ~僻 a. desolate
~tan⁴ ~誕 a. fabulous
~wu² ~蕪 a. weedy
~yin² ~淫 a. dissipated
HUANG² 黃 n. & a. yellow

72

~chin¹ ~金 *n.* gold; *a.* golden
~chin¹ shih² tai⁴ ~金時代 *n.* golden age
~chung³ ~種 *n.* yellow race
~feng¹ ~蜂 *n.* wasp
~ho² ~河 *n.* Yellow River
~hun¹ ~昏 *n.* dusk
~huo⁴ ~禍 *n.* yellow peril
~kua¹ ~瓜 *n.* cucumber
~la⁴ ~臘 *n.* wax
~se⁴ ~色 *n.* yellow
~se⁴ yao⁴ ~色藥 *n.* picric acid, trinitrophenol
~shu³ lang² ~鼠狼 *n.* weasel
~tan³ ping⁴ ~胆病 *n.* jaundice
~tou⁴ ~豆 *n.* soy bean
~t'ung² ~銅 *n.* brass
~ying¹ ~鶯 *n.* chaffinch
HUANG² 蝗 *n.* locust
HUI¹ 灰 *n.* ash, dust, lime, mortar; *a.* gray
~ch'en² ~塵 *a.* dusty
~se⁴ ~色 *n.* & *a.* gray
HUI¹ 揮 *v.* move, shake, rouse, wag
~huo⁴ ~霍 *v.* squander
~shou³ ~手 *v.* wave the hand
HUI² 回 *n.* turn, time; *v.* return
~chia¹ ~家 *v.* return home
~chiao⁴ ~教 *n.* Mohammedanism
~chiao⁴ kuo² ~教國 *n.* Moslem states
~chiao⁴ t'ang² ~教堂 *n.* Mosque
~chiao⁴ t'u² ~教徒 *n.* Mohammedan, Moslem
~ch'ü⁴ ~去 *v.* return
~i⁴ ~憶 *v.* recall, remember
~i⁴ lu⁴ ~憶錄 *n.* memoirs
~kuei¹ hsien⁴ ~歸線 *n.* Tropics
~kuei¹ je⁴ ~歸熱 *n.* relapsing fever
~sheng¹ ~聲 *n.* echo
~ta² ~答 *n.* & *v.* answer
~tsui³ ~嘴 *v.* retort
~yung⁴ ~佣 *n.* commission (money)
HUI³ 悔 *v.* repent; *n.* repentance
~kai³ ~改 *v.* repent
~kuo⁴ ~過 *v.* repent

73

~tsui⁴ ~罪 *v.* repent

HUI³ 毀 *v.* injure, break, spoil

~huai⁴ ~壞 *v.* destroy; *n.* destruction

~mieh⁴ ~滅 *v.* destroy

~pang⁴ ~謗 *v.* slander

~shang¹ ~傷 *v.* injure, hurt

HUI⁴ 會 *v.* meet together, assemble, know. K'UAI⁴ *v.* calculate; *n.* society, guild

~chan⁴ ~戰 *n.* war battle

~chien⁴ ~見 *n.* interview

~ch'ang³ ~場 *n.* place of meeting

~ho² ~合 *v.* meet together

~hua⁴ ~話 *n.* conversation

~i⁴ ~議 *n.* conference

~k'o⁴ shih⁴ ~客室 *n.* drawing room, parlor

~shang¹ ~商 *v.* consult, confer

~shih¹ ~師 *n.* join forces (*mil.*)

k'uai⁴ chi⁴ ~計 *n.* accountant

~chi⁴ hsüeh² ~計學 *n.* accounting

~chi⁴ yüan² ~計員 *n.* accountant

HUN¹ 婚 *v.* marry; *n.* marriage, wedding

~li³ ~禮 *n.* wedding

~yin¹ ~姻 *n.* marriage

~yin¹ fa³ ~姻法 *n.* Marriage Law**

~yin¹ tzu⁴ yu² ~姻自由 *n.* freedom of marriage

HUN⁴ 混 *a.* mingled, mixed, confused

~chan⁴ ~戰 *n.* dog fight

~ho² ~合 *v.* mix

~ho² wu⁴ ~合物 *n.* compound

~luan⁴ ~亂 *n.* chaos

HUNG¹ 轟 *n.* roar, boom

~cha⁴ ~炸 *v.* bomb; *n.* bombardment

~cha⁴ chi¹ ~炸機 *n.* bomber

~chi¹ ~擊 *v.* shell; *n.* bombardment

HUNG² 紅 *n.* red, scarlet

~chün¹ ~軍 *n.* Communist Army

~ch'a² ~茶 *n.* black tea

~hsüeh⁴ ch'iu² ~血球 *n.* red blood corpuscle

~li⁴ ~利 *n.* bouns

~pao³ shih² ~寶石 *n.* ruby

~se⁴ ~色 *n.* red

74

~shih² tzu⁴ hui⁴ ~十字會 *n.* Red Cross
~shih² tzu⁴ i¹ yüan⁴ ~十字醫院 *n.* Red Cross Hospital
HUO² 活 *n.* living, livelihood
~ch'i¹ ts'un² k'uan³ ~期存款 *n.* checking account
~p'o¹ ~潑 *a.* active, lively
~tung⁴ ~動 *n.* activity; *a.* active, movable
HUO³ 火 *n.* fire
~chi¹ ~雞 *n.* turkey
~chien⁴ ~箭 *n.* rocket
~chiu³ ~酒 *n.* alcohol
~ch'ai² ~柴 *n.* match
~ch'e¹ ~車 *n.* train
~ch'e¹ t'ou² ~車頭 *n.* locomotive
~fu¹ ~夫 *n.* fireman
~hsien³ ~險 *n.* fire insurance
~hsien⁴ ~線 *n.* firing line
~hsing¹ ~星 *n.* Mars (planet)
~lu² ~爐 *n.* stove
~pa³ ~把 *n.* torch
~shan¹ ~山 *n.* volcano
~shih² ~石 *n.* flint
~t'ui³ ~腿 *n.* ham
~tsai¹ ~災 *n.* conflagration
~tsang⁴ ~葬 *n.* cremation
~yao⁴ ~藥 *n.* gunpowder, powder
~yen⁴ ~燄 *n.* flame
~yen⁴ fang⁴ she⁴ ch'i⁴ ~燄放射器 *n.* flame thrower
HUO³ 伙 *n.* companion, furniture
~pan⁴ ~伴 *n.* companion, partner
~shih² ~食 *n.* food
HUO⁴ 貨 *v.* deal (business); *n.* goods, merchandise, cargo (for sale)
~chan⁴ ~棧 *n.* warehouse
~ch'e¹ ~車 *n.* wagon, truck
~pi⁴ ~幣 *n.* money
~tan¹ ~單 *n.* invoice
~wu⁴ ~物 *n.* merchandise, goods, cargo
~wu⁴ chiao¹ huan⁴ ~物交換 *n.* barter

75

~yang⁴ ~樣 *n.* samples of goods
HUO⁴ 禍 *n.* misfortune, calamity
~hai⁴ ~害 *n.* damage, injury
~huan⁴ ~患 *n.* misfortune
~luan⁴ ~亂 *n.* disturbance
HUO⁴ 或 *adv.* perhaps, maybe, possibly
~che³ ~者 *adv.* perhaps
HUO⁴ 獲 *v.* catch, obtain, get
~li⁴ ~利 *v.* make profit
~sheng⁴ ~勝 *v.* win
~te² ~得 *v.* obtain
~tsui⁴ ~罪 *v.* commit a crime

HS

HSI¹ 西 *n.* west; *a.* west, western
~fang¹ ~方 *a.* western
~jen² ~人 *n.* Westerner, foreigner
~kua¹ 瓜 *n.* watermelon
~nan² fang¹ ~南方 *a.* southwestern
~yu² chi⁴ ~遊記 *n.* Pilgrimage to the West (Chinese novel)
HSI¹ 希 *a.* rare, few, strange; *adv.* rarely, seldom
~ch'i² ~奇 *a.* wonderful, curious, strange
~han³ ~罕 *a.* rare; *adv.* seldom, rarely
~wang⁴ ~望 *n. & v.* hope
HSI¹ 稀 *a.* rare, few, seldom, scarce
~fan⁴ ~飯 *n.* rice gruel
~pao² ~薄 *a.* this
~shao³ ~少 *a.* rare; *adv.* seldom
~shu¹ ~疏 *a.* sparse
HSI¹ 吸 *v.* inhale, suck, attract
~li⁴ ~力 *n.* attraction
~mo⁴ chih³ ~墨紙 *n.* blotter, blotting paper
~shou¹ ~收 *n.* absorption
~t'ieh³ shih² ~鉄石 *n.* loadstone
~yin³ ~引 *n.* attraction
HSI² 習 *n.* custom, usage; *v.* practise, learn
~ch'ang² ~常 *a.* common, usual
~kuan⁴ ~慣 *n.* habit, custom

76

~su² ~俗 *n.* custom, usage
~t'i² ~題 *n.* problem
~tzu⁴ t'ieh³ ~字帖 *n.* copybook
HSI² 惜 *v.* pity, be sympathetic, spare, care for
HSI² 息 *v.* cease, stop, rest
HSI² 席 *n.* mat, seat, banquet
HSI² 錫 *n.* tin, gifts; *v.* give
  ~chiang⁴ ~匠 *n.* tinsmith
  ~ch'i⁴ ~器 *n.* tinware
  ~po² ~箔 *n.* tin foil
HSI³ 喜 *n.* joy, delight; *a.* glad, cheerful
  ~chiu³ ~酒 *n.* wedding feast
  ~chü⁴ ~劇 *n.* comedy
  ~ch'iao¹ ~鵲 *n.* magpie
  ~huan¹ ~歡 *v.* like; *a.* happy
  ~hsin⁴ ~信 *n.* happy news
  ~le⁴ ~樂 *a.* joy
  ~yüeh⁴ ~悅 *a.* pleasant
HSI³ 洗 *v.* wash, cleanse
  ~ch'ing ~清 *v.* make clean
  ~i¹ chi¹ ch'i⁴ ~衣機器 *n.* washing machine
  ~i¹ tso⁴ ~衣作 *n.* laundry
  ~li³ ~禮 *n.* baptism
  ~nao³ ~腦 *n.* brain-washing**
  ~shou³ ~手 *v.* wash hands
  ~shou³ chien¹ ~手間 *n.* washroom
  ~t'ou² ~頭 *v.* shampoo
  ~tsao³ ~澡 *v.* bathe; *n.* bath
  ~ts'a¹ ~擦 *v.* wash
HSI⁴ 細 *a.* fine, thin, slender, delicate; *adv.* carefully
  ~ch'ang² ~長 *a.* spindling, slender
  ~hsiao³ ~小 *a.* small
  ~hsin¹ ~心 *a.* careful
  ~pao¹ ~胞 *n.* cell (living matter)
  ~tse² ~則 *n.* regulation
  ~yü³ ~雨 *n.* drizzle
HSI⁴ 戲 *n.* drama, play; *v.* play, joke
  ~chü⁴ ~劇 *n.* drama
  ~chü⁴ chia¹ ~劇家 *n.* dramatist
  ~t'ai² ~臺 *n.* theater stage

77

~yen² ~言 *v.* joke
~yüan⁴ ~院 *n.* theater
HSI⁴ 系 *n.* connection, university department, system
~p'u³ ~譜 *n.* genealogy
~shu⁴ ~數 *n.* joint agent
~t'ung³ ~統 *n.* system, clique
HSI⁴ 係 *v.* belong to
HSIA¹ 瞎 *a.* blind, heedless; *adv.* blindly, heedlessly
~nao⁴ ~鬧 *n.* nonsense
~shuo¹ ~説 *n.* lie
~tzu¹ ~子 *n.* blinder
HSIA⁴ 下 *n.* bottom; *adv.* below, down, under; *a.* inferior, mean, low; *v.* descend, go down
~chi² ~級 *n.* inferior, junior, low grade
~chien⁴ ~賤 *a.* mean, base
~ch'e¹ ~車 *v.* get out of a car
~ch'i² ~棋 *v.* play chess
~ch'uan² ~船 *v.* disembark
~hsüeh² ~學 *n.* elementary study
~hsüeh³ ~雪 *v.* snow
~jen² ~人 *n.* servant, attendant
~k'ou³ ling⁴ ~口令 *v.* give commands (in drill)
~lou² ~樓 *v.* come downstairs
~mao² ~錨 *v.* anchor
~pan¹ ~班 *v.* go off duty
~pan⁴ ch'i² ~半旗 *v.* half-mast a flag
~shen¹ ~身 *n.* lower part of the body, privates
~shih⁴ ~士 *n.* sergeant (army)
~shu³ ~屬 *n.* subordinates
~teng³ ~等 *n.* inferior (quality)
~t'a⁴ ~榻 *v.* lodge
~ts'eng² she⁴ hui⁴ ~層社會 *n.* lower class
~tz'u⁴ ~次 *n.* next time
~wu³ ~午 *n.* afternoon
~wu⁴ ~霧 *a.* foggy
~yu² ~游 *adv. & a.* downstream
~yüeh⁴ ~月 *n.* next month
HSIA⁴ 夏 *n.* summer
~chi⁴ ~季 *n.* summer

78

~chih⁴ ~至 *n.* summer solstice
HSIANG¹ 香 *n.* incense; *a.* fragrant
~chiao¹ ~蕉 *n.* banana
~chün⁴ ~菌 *n.* mushroom
~ch'i⁴ ~氣 *n.* perfume, fragrance
~k'o⁴ ~客 *n.* pilgrim
~liao⁴ ~料 *n.* spice
~lu² ~炉 *n.* censer
~pin¹ chiu³ ~檳酒 *n.* champagne
~shui³ ~水 *n.* perfume
~yen¹ ~煙 *n.* cigarette
HSIANG¹ 箱 *n.* box, chest
~tzu¹ ~子 *n.* suitcase, trunk
HSIANG¹ 相 *a.* reciprocal
~cheng¹ 爭 *v.* quarrel
~chu⁴ ~助 *v.* help each other
~ch'ih² ~持 *n.* stalemate
~fan³ ~反 *a.* opposite
~fu² ~符 *v.* correspond
~hui⁴ ~會 *v.* meet
~hsin⁴ ~信 *v.* believe
~i¹ ~依 *a.* interdependent
~lien² ~連 *v.* connect
~pi³ ~比 *v.* compare
~shih⁴ ~識 *n.* acquaintance
~ssu⁴ ~似 *a.* alike, similar
~teng³ ~等 *a.* equal; *n.* equality
~tui⁴ lun⁴ ~對論 *n.* theory of relativity
~t'ung² ~同 *a.* same
~mao⁴ ~貌 *n.* appearance
~p'ien⁴ ~片 *n.* photograph
HSIANG¹ 郷 *n.* village, country
~ch'ih⁴ wei⁴ tui⁴ ~赤衛隊 *n.* township Communist guards**
~hsia⁴ ~下 *n.* country, rural district
~ts'un¹ ~村 *n.* village
~ts'un¹ chiao⁴ yü⁴ ~村教育 *n.* rural education
~ts'un¹ hao² shen¹ chieh¹ chi² ~村豪紳階級 *n.* landed gentry in the countryside**
HSIANG² 詳 *v.* report, examine; *adv.* minutely
HSIANG² 降 *see* CHIANG⁴

79

HSIANG³ 想 *v.* think about, reflect, consider
~chia¹ ~家 *a.* homesick
~hsiang⁴ ~像 *v.* imagine; *n.* fancy imagination
~hsiang⁴ li⁴ ~像力 *n.* imagination
~nien⁴ ~念 *v.* think
~tao⁴ ~到 *v.* remember
HSIANG³ 享 *v.* enjoy
~shou⁴ ~受 *v.* enjoy
~yu³ ~有 *v.* possess
HSIANG³ 響 *n.* sound, noise, echo; *a.* noisy
~wei³ she² ~尾蛇 *n.* rattlesnake
~ying⁴ ~應 *n.* echo (response); *v.* respond
HSIANG⁴ 向 *prep.* toward
~ch'ien² ~前 *adv.* forward, ahead, onward
~hou⁴ ~後 *adv.* backward, behind
~hsia⁴ ~下 *adv.* downward, down
~jih⁴ k'uei² ~日葵 *n.* sunflower
~lai² ~來 *adv.* hitherto, until now
~li⁴ ~例 *adv.* habitably
~nei⁴ ~內 *adv.* inward
~shang⁴ ~上 *adv.* upward, above
~wai⁴ ~外 *adv.* outward, beyond
HSIANG⁴ 像 *n.* image; *v.* resemble
~mao⁴ ~貌 *n.* appearance
~p'ien⁴ ~片 *n.* photograph, picture
HSIANG⁴ 象 *n.* elephant
~ch'i² ~棋 *n.* chess
~hsing² wen² tzu⁴ ~形文字 *n.* hieroglyphics
~pi² ~鼻 *n.* elephant's trunk
~ya² ~牙 *n.* ivory
~ya² shan⁴ ~牙扇 *n.* ivory fan
HSIANG⁴ 項 *n.* nape, neck, kind, sort
~ch'üan¹ ~圈 *n.* necklace
~mu⁴ ~目 *n.* item
HSIANG⁴ 巷 *n.* lane, alley
~chan⁴ ~戰 *n.* street fighting
HSIAO¹ 消 *v.* melt, disappear, diminish
~chi² ~極 *a.* passive, negative
~ch'ien³ ~遣 *n.* pastime, amusement, recreation
~ch'u² ~除 *v.* remove
~fang² tui⁴ ~防隊 *n.* fire station (place or per-

80

sonnel)

~fei⁴ ho² tso⁴ she⁴ ~費合作社 *n.* post exchange (army)

~hao⁴ ~耗 *v.* waste ; *n.* ammunition expenditure

~hao⁴ chan⁴ ~耗戰 *n.* war of attrition

~hao⁴ p'in³ ~耗品 *n.* expendable property

~hua⁴ ~化 *v.* digest; *n.* digestion

~hua⁴ pu⁴ liang² ~化不良 *n.* indigestion

~hsi² ~息 *n.* information, news

~mieh⁴ ~滅 *v.* annihilate

~shih¹ ~失 *v.* vanish, disappear

~shou⁴ ~瘦 *a.* lean

~tu² ~毒 *n.* decontamination, disinfection

HSIAO¹ 削 *v.* cut, sharpen ; *a.* steep

~jo⁴ ~弱 *v.* weaken

~pi⁴ ~壁 *n.* cliff, precipice

HSIAO³ 曉 *n.* dawn, light; *v.* know, understand

HSIAO³ 小 *a.* little, small, tiny, petty, slight, minute, young

~chieh³ ~姐 *n.* Miss, girl, unmarried woman

~ch'an³ ~産 *n.* abortion

~ch'i⁴ ~氣 *a.* narrow-minded ; *adv.* narrow-mindedly

~ch'ou³ ~丑 *n.* clown

~fan⁴ ~販 *n.* peddler

~fei⁴ ~費 *n.* tip (money)

~hsin¹ ~心 *a.* careful; *adv.* carefully

~hsüeh² hsiao⁴ ~學校 *n.* primary school

~kung¹ ~工 *n.* coolie

~lu⁴ ~路 *n.* small path

~mai⁴ ~麥 *n.* rye

~pien⁴ ~便 *v.* urinate; *n.* urine

~shu⁴ ~數 *a.* & *n.* decimal

~shuo¹ ~説 *n.* fiction, novel, story

~t'uan² t'i³ chu³ i⁴ ~団體主義 *n.* cliquism**

~tzu¹ ch'an³ chieh¹ chi² ~資産階級 *n.* petty bourgeoisie**

HSIAO⁴ 效 *v.* imitate ; *n.* result

~fa³ ~法 *v.* imitate

~lü⁴ ~率 *n.* efficiency, proficiency

~yung⁴ ~用 *n.* utility

HSIAO⁴ 笑 *v.* smile, laugh, ridicule
~hua⁴ ~話 *n.* joke
~ping³ ~柄 *n.* laughingstock
HSIAO⁴ 校 *see* CHIAO⁴
HSIEH¹ 些 *a.* little, few; *adv.* slightly
~wei¹ ~微 *adv.* slightly
HSIEH¹ 歇 *v.* rest, stop
HSIEH² 鞋 *n.* shoe
~chiang⁴ ~匠 *n.* shoemaker
~ken¹ ~跟 *n.* shoe heel
~pa² ~拔 *n.* shoehorn
~shua¹ ~刷 *n.* shoe brush
~tai⁴ ~帶 *n.* shoelace, shoestring
~ti³ ~底 *n.* shoe sole
HSIEH² 協 *n.* agreement, mutual help
~ho² ~和 *v.* harmonize; *n.* harmony
~hui⁴ ~會 *n.* association
~li⁴ ~力 *v.* cooperate
~shang¹ ~商 *v.* negotiate, discuss; *n.* negotiation
~ting⁴ ~定 *n.* agreement
~t'iao² ~調 *v.* coordinate
~t'ung² ~同 *v.* cooperate; *n.* cooperation
HSIEH² 斜 *a.* transverse, oblique, irregular
~chiao³ ~角 *n.* oblique angle
~mien⁴ ~面 *n.* slope
~p'o¹ ~坡 *n.* ramp, slope
~she⁴ ~射 *n.* oblique fire
HSIEH³ 寫 *v.* write
~hsin⁴ ~信 *v.* write a letter
~i⁴ ~意 *a.* comfortable
~sheng¹ ~生 *v.* draw a picture
~shih² chu³ i⁴ ~實主義 *n.* realism (art)
~shih² p'ai⁴ ~實派 *n.* realist (art)
~tso⁴ ~作 *v.* write (literature)
~tzu⁴ chien¹ ~字間 *n.* office
HSIEH⁴ 謝 *v.* thank
~chüeh² ~絕 *v.* refuse
~tsui⁴ ~罪 *v.* apologize; *n.* apology
~wei¹ ~萎 *v.* fade; *a.* faded
HSIEH⁴ 械 *n.* arm, weapon, tool

~tou⁴ ~鬥 v. fight with weapons
HSIEN¹ 仙 n. fairy, cent
~ching⁴ ~境 n. fairyland
~nü³ ~女 n. fairy
HSIEN¹ 先 prep. adv. & conj. before; a. previous
~chao⁴ ~兆 n. omen
~chien⁴ ~見 n. foresight
~chih¹ ~知 n. prophet
~ch'i¹ ~期 a. premature, advance (ahead of time)
~ch'ü¹ ~驅 n. forerunner, herald
~feng¹ ~鋒 n. pioneer, vanguard, spearhead
~hou⁴ ~後 adv. in succession, one after another
~li⁴ ~例 n. example, precedent
~sheng¹ ~生 n. teacher
~t'ou² pu⁴ tui⁴ ~頭部隊 n. leading elements of column
HSIEN¹ 鮮 a. fresh, new. ~³ a. rare, few
~hua¹ ~花 n. fresh flower
~kuo³ ~果 n. fresh fruit
~mei³ ~美 n. fresh and delicious
~yen⁴ ~艶 a. attractive
HSIEN² 嫌 v. dislike, loathe
~ch'i⁴ ~棄 v. reject
~i² ~疑 a. suspicious; n. suspicion
~i² fan⁴ ~疑犯 n. suspect
~wu⁴ ~惡 v. dislike
HSIEN² 閒 a. vacant, idle; n. leisure
~hsia² ~暇 n. leisure
~t'an² ~談 n. gossip
HSIEN³ 險 n. danger; a. dangerous
~cha⁴ ~詐 a. treacherous; n. treachery
~e⁴ ~惡 a. vicious
HSIEN³ 顯 v. display, show; a. apparent, clear, glorious
~ho⁴ ~赫 a. prominent
~ming² ~明 a. apparent
~shih⁴ ~示 v. show
~wei¹ ching⁴ ~微鏡 n. microscope
HSIEN⁴ 現 v. appear, display; adv. now; a. visible
~chin¹ ~金 n. cash

83

~chuang⁴ ~狀 *n.* status quo
~ch'u¹ ~出 *v.* appear
~hsiang⁴ ~象 *n.* phenomena
~i⁴ ~役 *n.* active service, active duty
~k'uan³ chiao¹ i⁴ ~款交易 *n.* cash sale
~shih² chu³ i⁴ ~實主義 *n.* realism
~tsai⁴ ~在 *adv.* now, present
HSIEN⁴ 限 *n.* & *v.* limit; *n.* limitation
~chih⁴ ~制 *v.* limit; *n.* limitation
~ch'i¹ ~期 *n.* deadline
HSIEN⁴ 縣 *n.* district, country
~ch'ih⁴ wei⁴ tsung³ tui⁴ ~赤衛總隊 *n.* County Communist Guards**
HSIEN⁴ 線 *n.* thread, yarn, cord, line
~chou² ~軸 *n.* spool
~so³ ~索 *n.* clue
HSIEN⁴ 獻 *v.* offer, give, present
~chi⁴ ~ 計 *v.* give advice
~chi⁴ ~祭 *v.* sacrifice
~chin¹ ~金 *n.* monetary contribution
~hua¹ ~花 *v.* present a bouquet
HSIN¹ 心 *n.* heart
~ai⁴ ~愛 *a.* beloved
~chiao¹ ~焦 *n.* worried
~fu⁴ ~腹 *a.* intimate
~hsüeh⁴ ~血 *n.* lifeblood
~li³ chan⁴ cheng¹ ~理戰爭 *n.* psychological warfare
~li³ hsüeh² ~理學 *n.* psychology; *a.* psychological
~ling² ~靈 *n.* soul
~luan⁴ ~亂 *a.* confused
~t'iao⁴ ~跳 *n.* pulse
~t'ung⁴ ~痛 *n.* heartache
~yüan⁴ ~願 *n.* hope, desire
HSIN¹ 新 *a.* new, fresh, modern, recent
~chin⁴ 近 *adv.* recently
~hsien¹ ~鮮 *a.* fresh
~lang² ~郎 *n.* bridegroom
~min² chu³ chu³ i⁴ ~民主主義 *n.* New Democracy**

~niang² ~娘 *n.* bride
~nien² ~年 *n.* New Year
~ping¹ ~兵 *n.* recruit
~sheng¹ huo² yün⁴ tung⁴ ~生活運動 *n.* New Life Movement*
~shih⁴ ~式 *n.* new style
~ssu⁴ chün¹ ~四軍 *n.* New Fourth Army**
~wen² ~聞 *n.* press, news
~wen² chi⁴ che³ ~聞記者 *n.* journalist, news-man
~wen² tsung³ shu³ ~聞總署 *n.* Press Administration**
~yüeh¹ ~約 *n.* New Testament
HSIN¹ 辛 *a.* pungent, toilsome, grievous
~ch'in² ~勤 *a.* toilsome, laborious
~la⁴ ~辣 *a.* peppery, hot
~lao² ~勞 *a.* industrious, diligent
HSIN⁴ 信 *v.* believe, trust; *n.* letter, information; *a.* faithful
~cha² ~札 *n.* letter
~chien¹ ~箋 *n.* letter-paper
~ch'ai¹ ~差 *n.* mailman, postman
~feng¹ ~封 *n.* envelope
~hao⁴ ~號 *n.* signal
~hao⁴ ch'iang¹ ~號鎗 *n.* pyrotechnics projector
~hao⁴ tan⁴ ~號彈 *n.* signal shells, pyrotechnics
~hsi² ~息 *n.* news, information
~hsiang¹ ~箱 *n.* mailbox
~jen⁴ ~任 *v.* trust, believe
~kuan³ ~管 *n.* fuze
~t'iao² ~條 *n.* creed
~t'u² ~徒 *n.* disciple, follower
~wu⁴ ~物 *n.* pledge, security
~yang³ ~仰 *n.* belief
~yung⁴ ~用 *n.* credit
HSING¹ 興 *n.* fashion; *v.* rise; *a.* flourishing. ~⁴ *n.* high spirits
~¹ fen⁴ ~奮 *a.* excited
~fen⁴ chi⁴ ~奮劑 *n.* stimulant
~lung² ~隆 *a.* flourishing; *n.* prosperity
~⁴ ch'ü⁴ ~趣 *n.* interest

85

HSING¹ 星 *n.* star
~**ch'i¹** ~期 *n.* week
~**ch'i¹ erh⁴** ~期二 *n.* Tuesday
~**ch'i¹ i¹** ~期一 *n.* Monday
~**ch'i¹ jih⁴** ~期日 *n.* Sunday
~**ch'i¹ liu⁴** ~期六 *n.* Saturday
~**ch'i¹ san¹** ~期三 *n.* Wednesday
~**ch'i¹ ssu⁴** ~期四 *n.* Thursday
~**ch'i¹ wu³** ~期五 *n.* Friday
~**hsiang⁴ chia¹** ~相家 *n.* fortuneteller
~**kuang¹** ~光 *n.* starlight
~**su⁴** ~宿 *n.* constellation
HSING² 行 walk, act; *n.* conduct, behavior.
 HANG² *n.* row, line, store
~**cheng⁴** ~政 *n.* administration
~**cheng⁴ yüan⁴** ~政院 *n.* Executive Yuan*
~**hui⁴** ~賄 *n.* bribery
~**hsing¹** ~星 *n.* planet
~**li³** ~李 *n.* baggage
~**li³** ~禮 *v.* salute
~**lieh⁴** ~列 *n.* array, procession
~**tz'u⁴** ~刺 *v.* assassinate, murder
~**wei²** ~爲 *n.* conduct, behavior
hang² chang³ ~長 *n.* managing director (bank)
HSING² 形 *n.* shape, form, figure
~**chuang⁴** ~狀 *n.* shape, form
~**erh² shang⁴ hsüeh²** ~而上学 *n.* metaphysics
~**jung²** ~容 *v.* modify, describe
~**jung² tz'u²** ~容詞 *n.* adjective
~**shih⁴** ~勢 *n.* situation, condition
~**shih⁴** ~式 *n.* form, shape
~**shih⁴ chu³ i⁴** ~式主義 *n.* formalism
HSING³ 醒 *v.* wake up, awake, make sober; *a.* awake, sober
~**mu⁴** ~目 *a.* clear, attractive
~**wu⁴** ~悟 *v.* become aware
HSING³ 省 *see* **SHENG³**
HSING⁴ 姓 *n.* surname
~**ming²** ~名 *n.* name
~**ming² chieh¹ chi²** ~名階級 *n.* personnel identity (*mil.*)

~p'u³ ~譜 *n.* genealogy
HSING⁴ 性 *n.* sex, nature, temper
~chi² ~急 *a.* hot-tempered
~chiao¹ ~交 *n.* sexual intercourse
~chih² ~質 *n.* quality
~ch'ing² ~情 n. temper
~kan³ ~感 *a.* sexy
~ming⁴ ~命 *n.* life
~pieh² ~別 *n.* sex
~ping⁴ ~病 *n.* venereal disease
~yü⁴ ~慾 *n.* sexuality
HSING⁴ 幸 *n.* luck; *a.* lucky, fortunate
~erh² ~而 *adv.* fortunately
~fu² ~福 *n.* fortune
~yün⁴ ~運 *n.* good luck, fortune
HSIU¹ 休 *v.* rest, resign, retire, divorce, cease
~chan⁴ ~戰 *n.* armistice, truce
~ch'i⁴ ~棄 *v.* divorce a wife
~hsi² ~息 *n.* rest (after work)
~yeh⁴ ~業 *n.* recess
HSIU¹ 修 *v.* repair, mend
~cheng⁴ ~正 *v.* amend
~kai³ ~改 *v.* correct, revise
~li³ ~理 *v.* repair
~shih⁴ ~飾 *v.* decorate
~tao⁴ yüan⁴ ~道院 *n.* monastery
~yang³ ~養 *n.* tolerance
~yeh⁴ cheng⁴ shu¹ ~業證書 *n.* certificate of attendance
HSIU¹ 羞 *v.* blush, feel ashamed; *n.* viand, delicacy
~ch'ih³ ~恥 *n.* shame
~ch'üeh⁴ ~怯 *a.* shy; *adv.* shyly
~ju³ ~辱 *v.* insult
~k'uei⁴ ~愧 *a.* ashamed
HSIU⁴ 秀 *a.* elegant, fair, pretty
~li⁴ ~麗 *a.* beautiful
~ya³ ~雅 *a.* graceful; grace
HSIU⁴ 袖 *n.* sleeve
~k'ou³ ~口 *n.* cuff
HSIUNG¹ 兄 *n.* older brother

87

~ti⁴ ~弟 *n.* brother
HSIUNG¹ 兇 *a.* fierce, savage, cruel, wild
~ch'i⁴ ~器 *n.* weapon
~e⁴ ~惡 *a.* malignant
~meng³ ~猛 *n.* violence
~shou³ ~手 *n.* murderer
HSIUNG¹ 胸 *n.* chest
~chin¹ ~襟 *n.* mind, feeling
~pi⁴ t'eng² ~壁疼 *n.* pleurodynia
~t'ang² ~膛 *n.* thorax
HSIUNG² 雄 *a.* brave, masculine; *n.* male, hero
~chuang⁴ ~壯 *a.* strong
~hsin¹ ~心 *n.* ambition
~pien⁴ ~辯 *n.* eloquence
~pien⁴ chia¹ ~辯家 *n.* debater
~te¹ ~的 *a.* male
HSÜ¹ 須 *a.* necessary; *v. aux.* must, ought
HSÜ¹ 虛 *a.* empty, vacant, vain, weak, useless
~hsin¹ ~心 *a.* humble (feeling)
~jo⁴ ~弱 *a.* weak
~wei⁴ ~僞 *a.* false loyalty
HSÜ¹ 需 *n. & v.* need, demand; *n.* necessity
~ch'iu² ~求 *n. & v.* demand
~yao⁴ ~要 *v.* need; *n.* necessity; *a.* necessary
HSÜ³ 許 *a.* a few; *v.* grant, permit, promise
~chiu³ ~久 *n.* a long time
~k'o³ ~可 *v.* promise
~no⁴ ~諾 *v.* grant, allow
~to¹ ~多 *a.* many, numerous
HSÜ⁴ 續 *v.* continue, succeed
~chia⁴ ~假 *v.* extend leave
~yin⁴ ~印 *v.* reprint
HSÜ⁴ 序 *n.* introduction, preface
~wen² ~文 *n.* preface
~yen² ~言 *n.* preface, introduction
HSÜAN¹ 宣 *v.* declare, announce, make known
~chan⁴ ~戰 *v.* declare war; *n.* declaration of war
~ch'uan² ~傳 *v.* propagandize, propagate by propaganda
~ch'uan² kung¹ tso⁴ ~傳工作 *n.* propaganda work

88

~pu⁴ ~布 *v.* announce; *n.* announcement
~shih⁴ ~誓 *v.* swear
~tu² ~讀 *v.* read
~yang² ~揚 *v.* make known
~yen² ~言 *v.* declare; *n.* declaration
HSÜAN³ 選 *v.* elect, select, choose
~chü³ ~舉 *v.* elect; *n.* election
~chü³ ch'üan² ~舉權 *n.* suffrage
~chü³ p'iao⁴ ~舉票 *n.* ballot
~k'o¹ ~科 *n.* selective course
~tse² ~擇 *v.* select; *n.* selection
HSÜEH² 學 *v.* learn, study
~che³ ~者 *n.* scholar
~chih⁴ ~制 *n.* system of education
~ch'ao² ~潮 *n.* student's strike
~ch'i¹ ~期 *n.* school term
~fei⁴ ~費 *n.* tuition
~hsi² ~習 *n.* & *v.* study; *v.* learn
~hsiao⁴ ~校 *n.* school, academy, college,
~k'o¹ ~科 *n.* course, curriculum (school)
~sheng¹ ~生 *n.* pupil, student
~shu⁴ ~術 *n.* learning
~shuo¹ ~說 *n.* tenet
~t'u² ~徒 *n.* apprentice
~wei⁴ ~位 *n.* college degree
~wen⁴ ~問 *n.* knowledge
~yeh⁴ ~業 *n.* studies
~yu³ ~友 *n.* schoolmate, classmate
~yüan² ~員 *n.* student-officer
~yüan⁴ ~院 *n.* college
HSÜEH³ 雪 *n.* snow
~ching³ ~景 *n.* snow scenery
~ch'e¹ ~車 *n.* sleigh
~ch'ieh² yen¹ ~茄煙 *n.* cigar
~ch'iu² ~球 *n.* snowball
~hua¹ ~花 *n.* snowflake
~hua¹ kao¹ ~花膏 *n.* vanishing cream
~hsieh² ~鞋 *n.* snowshoe
~jen² ~人 *n.* snowman
~li² ~犁 *n.* snowplow
~⁴ ch'ih³ ~恥 *v.* revenge

89

~pai² ~白 *a.* snow-white

HSÜEH⁴ 血 *n.* blood

~ch'ing¹ ~清 *n.* serum

~ch'iu² ~球 *n.* corpuscle

~hsing² ~型 *n.* blood type, blood group

~i⁴ ~液 *n.* blood

~kuan³ ~管 *n.* blood vessel

~k'u⁴ ~庫 *n.* blood bank

~mo⁴ ~脈 *n.* pulse

~t'ung³ ~統 *n.* blood relation

~ya¹ ~壓 *n.* blood pressure

HSÜN² 尋 *v.* find

~chao³ ~找 *v.* find

~ch'ang² ~常 *a.* common, usual, ordinary, deferred message

~ch'iu² ~求 *v.* search

~fang³ ~訪 *v.* visit

~ssu¹ ~思 *v.* consider

~ssu³ ~死 *v.* commit suicide

HSÜN⁴ 訓 *v.* teach, instruct, advise; *n.* precept, advice, training

~chieh⁴ ~戒 *v.* warn, admonish

~hua⁴ ~話 *v.* give a speech (*off.*)

~lien⁴ ~練 *n.* training; *v.* train

~ling⁴ ~令 *n.* letter of instruction

~shih⁴ ~示 *v.* instruct; *n.* instruction

HSÜN⁴ 訊 *n.* trial, message

~wen⁴ ~問 *v.* interrogate prisoners; *n.* interrogation

~wen⁴ ch'u⁴ ~問處 *n.* information office

I

I¹ 一 *a.* a, an, one; *n.* one

~chi⁴ ~季 *n.* one fourth of a year

~chih⁴ hsing⁴ ~致性 *n.* coincidence**

~ch'u¹ hsi⁴ ~齣戲 *n.* play (drama)

~hsin¹ ~心 *adv.* heartily

~kai⁴ ~概 *n.* all; *adv.* entirely, all

~lan³ piao³ ~覽表 *n.* list, table, schedule

~lü⁴ ~律 *a.* uniform; *adv.* uniformly
~pan⁴ ~半 *n.* one half
~pien¹ tao³ ~遍倒 *n.* leaning to one side**
~tao⁴ ts'ai⁴ ~道菜 *n.* course (meal)
~ting⁴ ~定 *adv.* certainly, surely, decidedly
~yang⁴ ~樣 *a.* same; *adv.* alike, similarly
I¹ 衣 *n.* clothing, clothes
~chia⁴ ~架 *n.* hanger
~ch'u² ~櫥 n. clothes closet
~fu² ~服 *n.* clothing, clothes, garment
I¹ 依 *v.* trust, rely; *prep.* according to
~chao⁴ ~照 *adv.* according to
~fu⁴ ~附 *v.* adhere
~jan² ~然 *adv.* as before
~lai⁴ ~賴 *v.* depend upon
~t'zu⁴ ~次 *adv.* by order
~ts'ung² ~從 *v.* follow
I¹ 醫 *n.* doctor; *v.* heal, cure
~chih⁴ ~治 *v.* cure
~hsüeh² ~學 *n.* medical science
~hsüeh² po² shih⁴ ~學博士 *n.* medical doctor
~hsüeh² sheng¹ ~學生 *n.* medical student
~hsüeh² yüan⁴ ~學院 *n.* medical college
~sheng¹ ~生 *n.* doctor, practitioner
~yao⁴ ~藥 *n.* medicine
~yüan⁴ ~院 *n.* hospital
I² 宜 *a.* suitable, fit
I² 疑 *n.* suspicion; *v.* doubt, suspect
~huo⁴ ~惑 *v.* suspect; *n.* suspicion; *a.* suspicious
~i⁴ ~義 *n.* ambiguity
~wen⁴ ~問 *n.* question (doubt)
I² 姨 *n.* aunt
~fu⁴ ~父 *n.* husband of mother's sister (uncle)
~mu³ ~母 *n.* mother's sister (aunt)
I² 移 *v.* remove, shift, influence
~chiao¹ ~交 *v.* turn over an office to
~chih² ~植 *v.* transplant
~chü¹ ~居 *v.* change residence
~min² ~民 *v.* emigrate
~min² cheng⁴ ts'e⁴ ~民政策 n. emigration policy

91

~tung⁴ ~動 *v.* move, remove

I³ 乙 *v.* mark; *a.* & *n.* second

~teng³ ~等 *a.* second-class, grade B

I³ 以 *v.* do, use; *prep.* because of, with, by

~chan⁴ chih³ chan⁴ ~戰止戰 *n.* " war to end war "

~ch'ien² ~前 *adv.* ago, before

~hou⁴ ~後 *adv.* afterward

~hsia⁴ ~下 *adv.* & *prep.* below

~lai² ~來 *prep.* since

~mien³ ~免 *v.* avoid

~nei⁴ ~內 *prep.* within

~shang⁴ ~上 *adv.* & *prep.* above

~t'ai⁴ ~太 *n.* ether

~wai⁴ ~外 *prep.* besides

~wei² ~爲 *v.* consider, think

I³ 已 *adv.* already, yet; *a.* finished, passed

~ching¹ ~經 *adv.* already

~wang³ ~往 *a.* & *n.* past

I⁴ 益 *n.* benefit. advantage

I⁴ 異 *a.* different, strange, heterodox

~chiao⁴ ~教 *n.* paganism

~ch'ang² ~常 *a.* abnormal

~tuan¹ ~端 *n.* heresy

~yü⁴ ~域 *n.* foreign country

I⁴ 芸 *n.* handicraft, art

~neng² ~能 *n.* handicraft

~shu⁴ ~術 *n.* art; *a.* artistic

~shu⁴ chia¹ ~術家 *n.* artist

~shu⁴ huo² tung⁴ ~術活動 *n.* artistic activity

~shu⁴ hsüeh² yüan⁴ ~術學院 *n.* art college

I⁴ 義 *n.* righteousness, justice, meaning

~ch'i⁴ ~氣 *n.* heroism, chivalry

~ho² t'uan² yün⁴ tung⁴ ~和團運動 *n.* Boxer Movement

~shih⁴ ~士 *n.* patriot

~wu⁴ ~務 *n.* obligation, duty

~wu⁴ chiao⁴ yü⁴ ~務教育 *n.* free education

I⁴ 議 *v.* consider, deliberate upon, discuss, negotiate

~an⁴ ~案 *n.* bill (proposed law)

92

~chang³ ~長 n. Speaker
~chüeh² ~決 v. resolve by vote
~chüeh² an⁴ ~決案 n. resolution (solution)
~ho² ~和 v. negotiate peace
~yüan² ~員 n. senator, congressman
~yüan⁴ ~院 n. Congress (*U.S.*), British Parliament

I⁴ 意 n. thought, idea, intention, wish
~chien⁴ ~見 n. opinion, idea
~chih⁴ ~志 n. will
~hsiang⁴ ~向 n. intention
~i⁴ ~義 n. meaning
~i⁴ ~譯 n. free translation
~liao⁴ ~料 v. guess
~shih⁴ ~識 n. consciousness
~wai⁴ ~外 n. accident; *a.* accidental
~wai⁴ te¹ ~外的 *a.* accidental

I⁴ 易 v. change; *a.* easy
~jan² ~燃 *a.* inflammable

I⁴ 疫 n. plague, epidemic

J

JAN² 然 *adv.* however, but, so, thus
JAN³ 染 v. dye, stain, infect
~fang¹ ~坊 n. dye works
~liao⁴ ~料 n. dyestuff
~ping⁴ ~病 v. be sick
~se⁴ ~色 v. dye
~wu¹ ~污 v. stain

JANG⁴ 讓 v. cede, yield, give way, let
~k'ai¹ ~開 v. clear for traffic
~lu⁴ ~路 v. make way
~pu⁴ ~步 v. give ground to
~tu⁴ ~度 n. transference of property
~wei⁴ ~位 v. abdicate
~yü³ ~與 v. cede, give up

JAO⁴ 繞 v. wind, surround, avoid
~tao⁴ ~道 v. go round about

JE⁴ 熱 *a.* hot, warm; *n.* heat; *v.* warm

93

~cheng⁴ ~症 *n.* fever (disease)
~ch'ing² ~情 *n.* passion
~hsin¹ ~心 *n.* zeal, enthusiasm
~li⁴ ~力 *n.* heat power
~tai⁴ ~帶 *n.* Tropics
~tu⁴ ~度 *n.* fever
JEN² 人 *n.* person, people, human beings
~chung³ ~種 *n.* race
~ch'üan² ~權 *n.* human rights
~ko² ~格 *n.* personality
~k'ou³ ~口 *n.* population
~lei⁴ ~類 *n.* mankind, human being, human race, humankind
~li⁴ ch'e¹ ~力車 *n.* jinricksha, rickshaw
~min² ~民 *n.* people, subject
~min² cheng⁴ fu³ ~民政府 *n.* People's Government**
~min² chieh³ fang⁴ chün¹ ~民解放軍 *n.* People's Liberation Army**
~min² chien¹ ch'a² wei³ yüan² hui⁴ ~民監察委員會 *n.* Committee of People's Control**
~min² fa³ t'ing² ~民法廷 *n.* People's Tribunals**
~min² ko² ming⁴ chün¹ shih⁴ wei³ yüan² hui⁴ ~民革命軍事委員會 *n.* People's Revolutionary Military Council**
~min² min² chu³ chuan¹ cheng⁴ ~民民主專政 *n.* People's Democratic Dictatorship**
~min² p'ei² shen³ chih⁴ ~民陪審制 *n.* people's jury system**
~min² pi⁴ ~民幣 *n.* people's currency**
~min² yin² hang² ~民銀行 *n.* People's Bank of China**
~sheng¹ kuan¹ ~生觀 *n.* philosophy of life, view of life
~shih⁴ pu⁴ ~事部 *n.* Ministry of Personnel**
~tao⁴ ~道 *n.* humanity (being humane)
JEN⁴ 認 *v.* recognize, know, confess
~k'o³ ~可 *v.* consent
~shih⁴ ~識 *v.* know, recognize; *n.* recognition
~tsui⁴ ~罪 *v.* apologize; *n.* apology
JEN⁴ 任 *v.* appoint, assign, undertake, employ;

n. office
~hsing⁴ ~性 *a.* obstinate, headstrong
~i⁴ ~意 *a.* arbitrary
~ming⁴ ~命 *n.* appointment, assignment
~wu⁴ ~務 *n.* mission, role
~yung⁴ ~用 *v.* employ
JENG² 仍 *adv.* still, as before
~chiu⁴ ~舊 *adv.* as before, as usual
JIH⁴ 日 *n.* sun, day, daytime; *adv.* daily
~chi⁴ ~記 *n.* diary
~ch'i² ~期 *n.* date
~kuang¹ ~光 *n.* sunlight, sunshine
~kuei¹ ~規 *n.* sundial
~li⁴ ~曆 *n.* calender
~pao⁴ ~報 n. daily newspaper
~tzu¹ ~子 *n.* day
~yung⁴ p'in³ ~用品 *n.* daily necessities
JO⁴ 弱 *a.* weak, tender
~tien³ ~點 *n.* weak point
JOU² 柔 *a.* soft, tender, gentle, flexible
~jo⁴ ~弱 *a.* tender
~juan³ ~軟 *a.* soft
~juan³ t'i³ ts'ao¹ ~軟体操 *n.* calisthenics
~tao⁴ ~道 *n.* judo
JOU⁴ 肉 *n.* meat, flesh
~t'i³ ~體 *n.* body
~yü⁴ ~慾 *n.* lust (sex)
JU² 如 *conj.* as if; *a.* like, similar
~chin¹ ~今 *adv.* now, at present
~ho² ~何 *adv.* how
~hsia⁴ ~下 *adv.* as follows
~t'zu³ ~此 *adv.* so, thus
JU⁴ 入 *v.* enter, come in, step in
~ch'ang³ ch'üan⁴ 場券 *n.* admission ticket
~hsüeh² ~學 *v.* enter a school
~hsüeh² k'ao³ shih⁴ ~學考試 *n.* entrance examination
~k'ou³ ~口 *n.* import, importation, entry
~k'ou³ huo⁴ ~口貨 *n.* imported goods
~tang³ ~黨 *v.* join a party, side
JUAN³ 軟 *a.* soft, pliable, yielding

95

~jo⁴ 弱 *a.* weak
JUNG² 容 *v.* contain; *n.* manner
~chi¹ ~積 *n.* volume, capacity
~i⁴ ~易 *a.* easy
~jen³ ~忍 *v.* tolerate
~mao⁴ ~貌 *n.* appearance, countenance
~na⁴ ~納 *v.* admit (have room for)
JUNG² 榮 *n.* honor, glory
~ju⁴ ~辱 *n.* honor and disgrace
~kuang¹ ~光 *n.* splendor
~yao⁴ ~耀 *n.* honor, glory

K

KAI¹ 該 *v. aux.* must, ought
~ch'ien⁴ ~欠 *v.* owe
KAI³ 改 *v.* change
~cheng⁴ ~正 *v.* correct
~chuang¹ ~裝 *v.* reconstruct, rebuild, make over
~hsüan³ ~選 *n.* re-election
~ko² ~革 *n.* reform
~kuo⁴ ~過 *v.* reform (conduct)
~liang² ~良 *v.* reform, improve
~pien¹ ~編 *v.* reorganize units
~pien⁴ ~變 *v.* alter, change
~tsao⁴ ~造 *v.* reconstruct, rebuild, make over
KAI⁴ 概 *v.* level, adjust; *adv.* generally
~k'uo⁴ ~括 *adv.* generally
~nien⁴ ~念 *n.* conception
KAI⁴ 蓋 *n.* roof, covering; *v.* cover, build; *prep.* for
~fang² ~房 *v.* build houses
~yin⁴ ~印 *v.* stamp
KAN¹ 乾 *a.* dry, clean
~ching⁴ ~淨 *a.* clean
~ch'uan² wu⁴ ~船塢 *n.* drydock
~je⁴ ~熱 *n.* dry heat
~lao⁴ ~酪 *n.* cheese
~liang² ~糧 *n.* travel ration, reserve ration,

emergency ration
~te¹ ~的 *a.* dry
~tien⁴ ~電 *n.* dry battery, dry cell
~tsao⁴ ~燥 *a.* parched
~ts'ao³ ~草 *n.* hay
KAN¹ 肝 *n.* liver
~cheng⁴ ~症 *n.* cirrhosis
KAN¹ 甘 *a.* sweet, delicious, pleasant, willing
~che⁴ ~蔗 *n.* sugar cane
~hsin¹ ~心 *a.* willing
~ts'ao³ ~草 *n.* licorice
~yen² ~言 *n.* sweet words
KAN¹ 干 *n.* a shield; *v.* offend against
~fan⁴ ~犯 *v.* violate, transgress
~ko¹ ~戈 *n.* weapon
~she⁴ ~涉 *v.* meddle, interfere
KAN³ 感 *v.* influence; *n.* feeling; *a.* affected
~chi¹ ~激 *n.* gratitude
~chüeh² ~覺 *n.* feeling, sensation
~ch'ing² ~情 *n.* emotion; *a.* sentimental
~en¹ ~恩 *n.* gratitude
~hua⁴ yüan⁴ ~化院 *n.* reformatory
~hsieh⁴ ~謝 *v.* thank
~hsing⁴ chieh¹ tuan⁴ ~性階段 *n.* perceptual stage**
~mao⁴ ~ 冒 *n.* head cold
~tung⁴ ~動 *a.* impressive
KAN³ 敢 *v.* dare, be bold; *a.* presumptuous
~ssu³ tui⁴ ~死隊 *n.* shock troops
KAN³ 趕 *v.* pursue, follow after, eject; *adv.* quickly
~chin³ ~緊 *adv.* quickly, speedily
~k'uai⁴ ~快 *v.* speed
~tsou³ ~走 *v.* expel
KAN³ 稈 *n.* hay, the stalk of millet
KAN⁴ 幹 *a.* capable, skillful; *n.* trunk, stem, body
~lien⁴ ~練 *a.* skillful
~pu⁴ ~部 *n.* cadre (*mil.*)
KANG¹ 剛 *a.* firm, solid, hard; *adv.* just
~chih² ~直 *a.* righteous, upright
~ch'iang² ~強 *a.* obstinate, stubborn
~i⁴ ~毅 *n.* fortitude

97

~ts'ai² ~才 *adv.* just
KANG¹ 鋼 *n.* steel; *a.* hard
~ch'in² ~琴 *n.* piano
~ku³ shui³ ni² ~骨水泥 *n.* reinforced concrete
~k'uei¹ ~盔 *n.* steel helmet
~pan³ ~板 *n.* armor plate
~pi³ ~筆 *n.* fountain pen
KANG¹ 缸 *n.* jar, cistern
KANG³ 港 *n.* harbor, port
~fang² ~防 *n.* harbor defense
~k'ou³ ~口 *n.* harbor
KAO¹ 高 *a.* high, tall
~ao⁴ ~傲 *a.* proud
~chi² chung¹ hsüeh² ~級中學 *n.* senior middle school
~hsing⁴ ~興 *a.* happy
~kuei⁴ ~貴 *n.* dignity; *a.* noble
~shang⁴ ~尚 *a.* high-minded
~she⁴ p'ao⁴ ~射礮 *n.* anti-aircraft gun
~sheng¹ ~聲 *a.* loud
~tu⁴ ~度 *n.* height
~ya¹ ~壓 *v.* press
~yüan² ~原 *n.* plateau
KAO¹ 糕 *n.* sweets, cake, pastry
~ping³ ~餅 *n.* cake, pastry
KAO³ 稿 *n.* straw, sketch, draft
~chien⁴ ~件 *n.* manuscript, draft
KAO³ 搞 *v.* handle, make, execute
~huai⁴ ~壞 *v.* spoil, get out of order; *n.* break down
~t'ung¹ ~通 *v.* have understood
~t'ung¹ ssu¹ hsiang³ ~通思想 *v.* thoroughly understand and accept Communist policy**
KAO⁴ ~告 *v.* tell, inform, accuse
~chia⁴ ~假 *adv.* on leave
~chuang⁴ ~狀 *n.* lawsuit
~fen⁴ yung³ ~奮勇 *v.* volunteer
~pieh² ~別 *v.* say good-bye
~su⁴ ~訴 *v.* tell, inform
~shih⁴ ~示 *n.* bulletin
~t'ui⁴ ~退 *v.* leave

KEI³ 給 *v.* give. **CHI³** *v.* pay
KEN¹ 跟 *v.* follow, *n.* heel; *prep.* with
  ~ts'ung² che³ ~從者 *n.* follower
KEN¹ 根 *n.* root
  ~chih⁴ fa³ ~治法 *n.* radical treatment
  ~chü⁴ ~據 *v.* base on
  ~chü⁴ ti⁴ ~據地 *n.* base (*mil.*)
  ~ch'u² ~除 *v.* eradicate
  ~pen³ ~本 *n.* foundation
  ~yüan² ~源 *n.* origin, source
KENG¹ 更 *v.* alter, change. ~⁴ *adv.* more, again
  ~cheng⁴ ~正 *v.* correct
  ~hsin¹ ~新 *v.* renew; *n.* renewal
  ~i¹ ~衣 *v.* change clothes
  ~kai³ ~改 *v.* change
  ~⁴ to¹ ~多 *adv.* more
KENG¹ 耕 *v.* plow, cultivate
  ~chung⁴ ~種 *v.* plow and sow
  ~t'ien² ~田 *v.* plow the field
  ~tso⁴ ~作 *n.* farm
KO¹ 哥 *n.* older brother
KO¹ 歌 *n.* song; *v.* sing
  ~chi⁴ ~劇 *n.* opera, operetta
  ~chi⁴ yüan⁴ ~劇院 *n.* opera house
  ~ch'ang⁴ ~唱 *v.* sing
  ~ch'ang⁴ chia¹ ~唱家 *n.* singer
  ~ch'ü³ ~曲 *n.* song
  ~nü³ ~女 *n.* female vocalist
  ~sung⁴ ~頌 *v.* praise with carols
  ~yao² ~謠 *n.* ballad
KO¹ 割 *v.* cut
  ~chü⁴ ~據 *v.* amputate
  ~jang⁴ ~讓 *n.* cession
KO² 隔 *n.* partition, shelf; *v.* interpose; *adv.* next to
  ~jih⁴ ~日 *adv.* every other day
  ~k'ai¹ ~開 *v.* separate, divide
  ~li² ~離 *n.* isolation, quarantine; *v.* separate
  ~mo⁴ ~膜 *n.* misunderstanding, diaphragm
  ~pi³ ~壁 *n.* next door, neighbor
KO² 革 *n.* leather; *v.* renew, dismiss

~chih² ~職 *v.* fire (dismiss)
~ch'u² ~除 *v.* dismiss
~hsin¹ ~新 *v.* reform
~ming⁴ ~命 *n.* revolution
~ming⁴ chün¹ ~命軍 *n.* revolutionary army
~ming⁴ tang³ ~命黨 *n.* revolutionary party
~ming⁴ tang³ yüan² ~命黨員 *n.* revolutionist
~ming⁴ yün⁴ tung⁴ ~命運動 *n.* revolutionary movement
KO² 格 *n.* grid, pattern
~shih⁴ ~式 *n.* style, form
~wai⁴ ~外 *a.* extraordinary
~yen² ~言 *n.* proverb
KO⁴ 個 *n.* unit, piece
~jen² ~人 *n.* individual
~jen² chu³ i⁴ ~人主義 *n.* individualism
~jen² chu³ i⁴ che³ ~人主義者 *n.* individualist
~pieh² ~別 *a.* individual
KO⁴ 各 *a.* each, every, all, various
~chung³ ~種 *n.* all kinds
~ch'u⁴ ~處 *adv.* everywhere
~jen² ~人 *pron.* everyone, everybody
~ti⁴ ~地 *adv.* everywhere
~yang⁴ te¹ ~樣的 *a.* various
KOU¹ 溝 *n.* drain, ditch, groove
~huo⁴ ~壑 *n.* gully
KOU³ 狗 *n.* dog
~fei⁴ ~吠 *n.* bark
KOU⁴ 够 *v.* suffice; *a.* enough, adequate
KU¹ 估 *v.* estimate, value
~chi⁴ ~計 *v.* guess
~chia⁴ ~價 *v.* appraise, estimate value
~liang² ~量 *v.* consider
KU¹ 姑 *n.* paternal aunt
~hsi²~息 *v.* spoil
~mu³ ~母 *n.* father's sister (aunt)
~niang² ~娘 *n.* miss
~yeh² ~爺 *n.* son-in-law
KU³ 古 *n.* antiquity, oldness; *a.* antique, ancient, old-fashioned, out-of-date
~chi⁴ ~蹟 *n.* relics, remains, ruins

100

~jen² ~人 *n.* the ancients
~tai⁴ ~代 *n.* antiquity
~tien³ ~典 *n.* classics; *a.* classical
~tung³ ~董 *n.* curio, antique
~wen² ~文 *n.* paleography, ancient writing
KU³ 股 *n.* thigh, share, stock. [suffix] section, branch
~fen⁴ ~份 *n.* share, stock (company)
~fen⁴ kung¹ ssu¹ ~份公司 *n.* stock company
~hsi² ~息 *n.* monetary dividend
~pen³ ~本 *n.* capital (money)
~p'iao⁴ ~票 *n.* stock share certificate ·
~p'iao⁴ chiao¹ i⁴ so³ ~票交易所 *n.* stock exchange
~p'iao⁴ shih⁴ ch'ang³ ~票市場 *n.* stock market
~tung¹ ~東 *n.* shareholder, stockholder
KU³ 骨 *n.* bone
~che² ~折 *n.* fracture
~chieh² ~節 *n.* bone joint
~kan⁴ ~幹 *n.* backbone (of an army, etc.)
~ko² ~骼 *n.* skeleton
~sui³ ~髓 *n.* marrow
KU³ 鼓 *n.* drum
~chang³ ~掌 *v.* applaud; *n.* applause
~ch'ui¹ ~吹 *v.* inspire
~li⁴ ~勵 *v.* encourage
~tung⁴ ~動 *v.* stimulate
~wu³ ~舞 *v.* inspire
KU³ 穀 *n.* grain, corn
KU⁴ 固 *a.* stable, steadfast, firm, secure
~chieh² ~結 *v.* consolidate
~chih² ~執 *a.* obstinate, stubborn
~shou³ ~守 *v.* persist
~ting⁴ ~定 *a.* fixed
~t'i³ ~體 *a.* & *n.* solid
KU⁴ 雇 *v.* employ, hire; *n.* employment
~chu³ ~主 *n.* employer
~yung⁴ ~用 *v.* employ
~yüan² ~員 *n.* employee
KU⁴ 顧 *v.* look after, regard, consider
~chi⁴ ~忌 *v.* fear

101

~k'o⁴ ~客 *n.* customer, patron, patroness
~nien⁴ ~念 *v.* regard
~wen⁴ ~問 *n.* adviser
KU⁴ 故 *n.* cause, reason; *a.* late, deceased; *conj.* therefore, so
~hsiang¹ ~鄉 *n.* native place
~i⁴ ~意 *adv.* purposely, intentionally
~shih⁴ ~事 *n.* story
KUA¹ 瓜 *n.* melon
~fen¹ ~分 *v.* divide
KUA⁴ 掛 *v.* hang up, suspend
~hao⁴ ~號 *v.* register; *n.* registration
~hao⁴ hsin⁴ chien⁴ ~號信件 *n.* registered letter
~kou¹ ~鉤 *n.* pintle (*mil.*)
~nien⁴ ~念 *v.* worry
KUAI⁴ 怪 *n.* monster; *v.* blame; *a.* strange
~i⁴ ~異 *n.* whim
~jen² ~人 *n.* strange fellow
~p'i³ ~癖 *a.* queer
~shih⁴ ~事 *n.* miracle
~wu⁴ ~物 *n.* monster
KUAN¹ 關 *n.* barrier, custom house; *v.* shut, close
~chieh² ~節 *n.* bone joint
~chieh² yen² ~節炎 *n.* arthritis
~hsi⁴ ~係 *n.* relation
~hsiang³ ~餉 *v.* pay
~hsin¹ ~心 *v.* concern
~k'ou³ ~口 *n.* mountain pass
~shui⁴ ~稅 *n.* tariff, customs
~yü² ~於 *prep.* concerning
KUAN¹ 官 *n.* officer, official
~chang³ ~長 *n.* officer
~chih² ~職 *n.* rank (position)
~fang¹ ~方 *a.* government official
~fang¹ chan⁴ pao⁴ ~方戰報 *n.* war communique
~liao² ~僚 *n.* bureaucracy
~liao² tzu¹ pen³ chieh¹ chi² ~僚資本階級 *n.* bureaucratic-capitalist class**
~neng² ~能 *n.* sense
~ssu¹ ~司 *n.* lawsuit
~yüan² ~員 *n.* official

102

KUAN¹ 觀 *v.* look, consider; *n.* view, sight
  ~chung⁴ ~衆 *n.* audience (confer)
  ~ch'a² ~察 *v.* observe
  ~nien⁴ ~念 *n.* idea
  ~ts'e⁴ ~測 *v.* observe
KUAN³ 館 *n.* restaurant, guest house, room
KUAN³ 管 *n.* tube, pipe; *v.* govern, rule
  ~chang⁴ ~帳 *n.* cashier
  ~chih⁴ ~制 *v.* control
  ~li³ ~理 *v.* manage; *n.* administration
  ~li³ ch'üan² ~理權 *n.* control
  ~li³ tan¹ wei⁴ ~理單位 *n.* administrative unit
  ~li³ yüan² ~理員 *n.* manager
  ~shih⁴ ~事 *n.* steward
KUAN⁴ 慣 *a.* habitual; *adv.* usually
  ~ch'ang² ~常 *adv.* usually, always
  ~hsing⁴ ~性 *n.* inertia
  ~li⁴ ~例 *n.* habit, custom
  ~yung⁴ ~用 *n.* usage
  ~yü² ~於 *v.* be used to
KUANG¹ 光 *n.* light, brightness, glory
  ~fu⁴ ~復 *v.* recover by conquest
  ~hua² ~滑 *a.* smooth
  ~hui¹ ~輝 *a.* brilliant
  ~hsien⁴ ~線 *n.* ray
  ~hsüeh² ~學 *n.* optics
  ~jung² ~榮 *n.* glory, honor
  ~lun² ~輪 *n.* halo
  ~ming² ~明 *a.* bright
  ~tse² ~澤 *n.* luster; *a.* lustrous
  ~ts'ai³ ~彩 *n.* splendor
  ~yin¹ ~陰 *n.* time
KUANG³ 広 *a.* wide, broad, large
  ~kao⁴ ~告 *v.* advertise; *n.* advertisement
  ~po⁴ ~播 *n. & v.* broadcast
  ~po⁴ tien⁴ t'ai² ~播電臺 *n.* broadcasting station
  ~po⁴ yüan² ~播員 *n.* announcer
  ~ta⁴ ~大 *a.* vast
KUEI¹ 規 *n.* compass, rule, custom
  ~chü⁴ ~矩 *n.* regulation
  ~ch'üan⁴ ~勸 *v.* advise

103

~fan⁴ ~範 *n.* model, standard

~ting⁴ ~定 *n.* regulation; *a.* authorized

~ting⁴ fu² chuang¹ ~定服裝 *n.* prescribed uniform

KUEI¹ 歸 *v.* return, restore, belong to

~hua⁴ ~化 *v.* naturalize; *n.* naturalization

~shun⁴ ~順 *v.* surrender

~t'ien¹ ~天 *v.* die; *n.* death

KUEI³ 鬼 *n.* ghost, devil

~hua⁴ ~話 *n.* lying

~huo³ ~火 *n.* will-o'-the-wisp, jack-o'-lantern

~kuai⁴ ~怪 *n.* devil, demon

KUEI⁴ 貴 *a.* honorable, noble, dignified, costly, precious

~chung⁴ ~重 *a.* precious

~tsu² ~族 *n.* aristocrat, noble

~tsu² chih⁴ tu⁴ ~族制度 *n*, aristocracy, nobility

KUEI⁴ 櫃 *n.* box, case, chest

~t'ai² ~枱 *v.* store counter

KUN³ 滾 *v.* boil, roll, move back

~ch'u¹ ch'ü⁴ ~出去 *v.* get out

~k'ai¹ ~開 *v.* get away

~shui³ ~水 *n.* boiling water

KUN⁴ 棍 *n.* stick, rowdy, club

~pang⁴ ~棒 *n.* club, stick

~t'u² ~徒 *n.* rascal

~tzu¹ ~子 *n.* stick

KUNG¹ 工 *n.* work, job, labor

~chiang⁴ ~匠 *n.* artisan, craftsman

~chü⁴ ~具 *n.* tool, instrument

~ch'ang³ ~場 *n.* workshop

~ch'ang³ ~廠 *n.* factory, plant, mill

~ch'eng² ~程 *n.* construction work

~ch'eng² shih¹ ~程師 *n.* engineer

~hui⁴ ~會 *n.* labor union

~jen² ~人 *n.* workman, laborer

~jen² chieh¹ chi² ~人階級 *n.* working class**

~jen² yeh⁴ yü² wen² hua⁴ hsüeh² hsiao⁴ ~人業餘文化學校 *n.* Workers' Spare Time Literacy School**

~nung² hung² chün¹ ~農紅軍 *n.* Workers' and

104

Peasants' Communist Army**

~ping¹ ~兵 *n.* engineer troops

~ping¹ hsüeh² hsiao⁴ ~兵學校 *n.* Engineering School*

~shang¹ yeh⁴ lien² ho² hui⁴ ~商業聯合會 *n.* Federation of Industry and Commerce**

~t'ou² ~頭 *n.* foreman

~tso⁴ ~作 *n.* work

~tzu¹ ~資 *n.* wages

~yeh⁴ ~業 *n.* industry; *a.* industrial

KUNG¹ 公 *a.* public, open

~an¹ pu⁴ ~安部 *n.* Ministry of Public Safety**

~chai⁴ ~債 *n.* public loan

~chai⁴ ch'üan⁴ ~債券 *n.* bond

~cheng⁴ jen² ~證人 *n.* notary public, notary

~chi¹ chin¹ ~積金 *n.* reserve fund

~chih² ~職 *n.* public duty

~chin¹ ~斤 *n.* kilogram

~chu³ ~主 *n.* princess

~chüeh² ~爵 *n.* Duke

~ch'an³ ~産 *n.* government property

~fei⁴ ~費 *n.* public expenditure

~fen¹ ~分 *n.* centimeter

~kuan³ ~館 *n.* residence, mansion

~kung¹ ~公 *n.* father-in-law (woman's)

~kung⁴ ~共 *a.* common, public

~kung⁴ ch'i⁴ ch'e¹ ~共汽車 *n.* bus

~kung⁴ t'u² shu¹ kuan³ ~共圖書館 *n.* public library

~kung⁴ wei⁴ sheng¹ ~共衛生 *n.* public health

~k'ai¹ pi⁴ mi⁴ ~開祕密 *n.* open secret

~li³ ~理 *n.* axiom

~li³ ~里 *n.* kilometer

~li⁴ ~例 *n.* regulation

~lu⁴ ~路 *n.* highroad, highway

~min² ~民 *n.* citizen

~pao⁴ ~報 *n.* bulletin

~pu⁴ ~布 *v.* proclaim, declare publicly

~p'ing² ~平 *a.* fair

~shih⁴ ~式 *n.* formula

~shih⁴ ~事 *n.* official business

105

~shih⁴ ~使 *n.* vice ambassador

~shih⁴ kuan³ ~使館 *n.* legation

~ssu¹ ~司 *n.* company

~te² ~德 *a.* public-spirited

~wen² ~文 *n.* official documents

~wu⁴ ~務 *n.* public affair, official business

~yung⁴ shih⁴ yeh⁴ ~用事業 *n.* public utility

~yü⁴ ~寓 *n.* apartment house

~yüan² ~園 *n.* park

KUNG¹ 功 *n.* merit, achievement, honor; *a.* meritorious

~k‘o⁴ ~課 *n.* lesson

~k‘o⁴ piao³ ~課表 *n.* curriculum table

~yung⁴ ~用 *n.* function, use

KUNG¹ 攻 *v.* attack

~chi¹ ~擊 *n.* & *v.* attack

~fan⁴ ~犯 *v.* invade, attack

~tu² ~讀 *v.* study

~wei² ~圍 besiege

KUNG¹ 供 *v.* supply, provide, confess. ~⁴ *v.* offer

~¹ chi³ ~給 *v.* supply

~chi³ chih⁴ ~給制 *n.* A system of providing free board and lodging for government officials and employees with a small amount of money for miscellaneous expenses**

~tz‘u² ~詞 *n.* confession

~⁴ feng⁴ ~奉 *v.* devote

~hsien⁴ ~献 *n.* devotion, dedication

~yang³ ~養 *v.* maintain (provide for)

KUNG⁴ 共 *v.* share; *adv.* altogether, wholly, entirely

~ch‘an³ chu³ i⁴ ~産主義 *n.* Communism

~ch‘an³ tang³ ~産黨 *n.* Communist Party

~ch‘an³ tang³ yüan² ~産黨員 *n.* Communist

~ho² kuo² ~和國 *n.* republic

~kan⁴ ~幹 *n.* Communist cadre

~ming² ~鳴 *n.* resonance

~t‘ung² ~同 *adv.* together

~t‘ung² kang¹ ling³ ~同綱領 *n.* Common Programme**

KUO¹ 鍋 *n.* pot, boiler, kettle

106

KUO² 國 *n.* nation, state, country

~chai⁴ ~債 *n.* national debts

~chi² ~籍 *n.* nationality

~chi⁴ ~際 *a.* international

~chi⁴ chu³ i⁴ ~際主義 *n.* internationalism

~chi⁴ fa³ t'ing² ~際法廷 *n.* International Court of Justice

~chi⁴ fu⁴ nü³ chieh² ~際婦女節 *n.* International Woman's Day

~chi⁴ hua⁴ ~際化 *v.* internationalize

~chi⁴ huo⁴ pi⁴ chi¹ chin¹ hui⁴ ~際貨幣基金會 *n.* international monetary fund

~chi⁴ ko¹ ~際歌 *n.* Internationale

~chi⁴ kuan¹ hsi⁴ ~際關係 *n.* international relations

~chi⁴ kung¹ fa³ ~際公法 *n.* international law

~chi⁴ lien² meng² ~際聯盟 *n.* League of Nations

~chi⁴ tsu³ chih¹ ~際組織 *n.* international organization

~chi⁴ yü³ ~際語 *n.* international language

~chia¹ chi⁴ hua⁴ wei³ yüan² hui⁴ ~家計劃委員會 *n.* State Planning Committee**

~chia¹ chu³ i⁴ ~家主義 *n.* nationalism

~chia¹ hua⁴~ ~家化 *v.* nationalize

~chia¹ she⁴ hui⁴ chu³ i⁴ ~家社會主義 *n.* state socialism

~chia¹ tzu¹ pen³ chu³ i⁴ ~家資本主義 *n.* state capitalism**

~chia¹ yin² hang² ~家銀行 *n.* national bank

~ch'i² ~旗 *n.* national flag

~fang² ~防 *n.* national defense

~fang² i¹ hsüeh² yüan⁴ ~防醫學院 *n.* National Defense Medical Hospital*

~fang² pu⁴ ~防部 *n.* Department of Defense (*U.S.*)

~fang² ta⁴ hsüeh² ~防大学 *n.* National Defense College*

~hui¹ ~徽 *n.* national emblem

~hui⁴ ~會 *n.* parliament

~ko¹ ~歌 *n.* national anthem

~k'u⁴ ~庫 *n.* treasury (nation)
~min² ~民 *n.* citizen, people
~min² cheng⁴ fu³ ~民政府 *n.* National Government
~min² ta⁴ hui⁴ ~民大會 *n.* National Assembly
~min² tang³ ~民黨 *n.* Kuomintang
~shih⁴ fan⁴ ~事犯 *n.* political criminal
~tu¹ ~都 *n.* national capital
~t'u³ ~土 *n.* territory
~wai⁴ mao⁴ i⁴ ~外貿易 *n.* foreign trade
~wang² ~王 *n.* king, ruler
~wu⁴ ch'ing¹ ~務卿 *n.* Secretary of State(*U.S.*)
~wu⁴ yüan⁴ ~務院 *n.* Department of State (*U.S.*)
~ying² nung² ch'ang³ ~營農場 *n.* State Farm**
~yü³ ~語 *n.* national language
KUO³ 果 *n.* fruit, result, effect; *a.* resolute
~chiang⁴ ~醬 *n.* jam, jelly
~jan² ~然 *adv.* surely, certainly
~shih² ~實 *n.* fruit
~tuan⁴ ~斷 *n.* decision
~yüan² ~園 *n.* orchard
KUO⁴ 過 *v.* pass, cross; *n.* fault, error; *adv.* too
~ch'ü⁴ ~去 *n.* & *a.* past
~hou⁴ ~後 *adv.* afterward, later
~shih¹ ~失 *n.* fault, offense
~tu⁴ ~度 *a.* excessive
~tu⁴ ch'i¹ ~度期 *n.* transition period
~yü² ~於 *prep.* over, above

K'

K'AI¹ 開 *v.* open, begin; *n.* boil
~chan⁴ ~戰 *n.* outbreak of war
~ch'iang¹ ~鎗 *v.* fire (gun)
~hua¹ ~花 *v.* bloom
~hua⁴ ~化 *a.* civilized
~hui⁴ ~會 *v.* hold a meeting
~hsiao³ ch'ai¹ ~小差 *v.* desert (*mil.*)
~kuan¹ ~關 *n.* switch (elec.)

108

~k'en³ ~墾 v. cultivate
~k'uang⁴ ~鑛 v. open mines
~k'uo⁴ ti⁴ ~濶地 n. open terrain
~she⁴ ~設 v. establish, open
~shih³ ~始 v. begin, start; n. beginning
~shih⁴ ~釋 v. release
~shui³ ~水 n. boiled water
~tao¹ ~刀 n. operation (med.)
~t'ing² ~庭 v. open the court
~yao⁴ fang¹ ~葯方 v. prescribe (med.)
K'AN⁴ 看 v. see, look at. ~¹ v. watch
~¹ hu⁴ ~護 v. look after
~hu⁴ fu⁴ ~護婦 n. nurse
~men² ~門 n. doorkeeper, doorman
~shou³ ~守 v. guard, watch
~⁴ wang⁴ ~望 v. visit
K'ANG¹ 康 n. peace, repose, prosperity
~chien⁴ ~健 a. healthy
~le⁴ 樂 a. happy
~ning² ~寧 n. peaceful happiness and abundance
K'ANG⁴ 抗 v. resist, oppose
~chü⁴ ~拒 v. resist
~i⁴ ~議 n. & v. protest; v. object
~jih⁴ min² tsu² t'ung³ i¹ chen⁴ hsien⁴ ~日民族統一陣線 n. Anti-Japanese National United Front**
~mei³ yüan² ch'ao² yün⁴ tung⁴ ~美援朝運動 n. Resist-America and Aid-Korea Movement**
~pien⁴ ~辯 n. defense (lawsuit)
K'AO³ 考 v. test, examine; n. test, examination
~cheng⁴ ~證 v. prove; n. verification
~ch'a² ~查 v. investigate
~lü⁴ ~慮 v. consider
~shih⁴ ~試 n. examination (test)
~shih⁴ yüan⁴ ~試院 n. Examination Yuan*
K'AO⁴ 靠 v. lean on, trust; a. near to
~chin⁴ ~近 a. near to
~pu² chu⁴ ~不住 a. unreliable
~te² chu⁴ ~得住 a. reliable, trustworthy
K'EN³ 肯 v. consent, agree, permit, allow
~hsü³ ~許 v. assent, agree

109

~ting⁴ ~定 *a.* certain, sure; *adv.* certainly, surely

K'O¹ 科 *n.* family department (biology), section, arm, branch (army)

~fa² ~罰 *v.* punish; *n.* punishment

~hsüeh² ~學 *n.* science

~hsüeh² chia¹ ~學家 *n.* scientist

~hsüeh² huo² tung⁴ ~學活動 *n.* scientific activity

~hsüeh² kuan³ li³ ~學管理 *n.* scientific management

~hsüeh² yüan⁴ ~學院 *n.* Academia Sinica**

~yüan² ~員 *n.* clerk

K'O¹ 刻 *v.* carve, sculpture, engrave; ~⁴ *n.* one fourth of an hour

~⁴ k'u³ ~苦 *v.* mortify (overcome bodily desires)

~po² ~薄 *a.* cruel

K'O¹ 顆 *n.* (numerative of small round things)

K'O³ 可 *v. aux.* may, can

~hsiao⁴ ~笑 *a.* absurd, foolish, ridiculous

~i³ ~以 *v. aux. & v.* may

~jen² ~人 *a.* charming

~k'ao⁴ ~靠 *a.* reliable; *n.* reliability

~lien² ~憐 *a.* piteous, pitiful

~neng² ~能 *n.* possibility; *a.* possible

~p'a⁴ ~怕 *a.* dreadful, terrible

~e⁴ ~惡 *a.* detestable

K'O³ 渴 *n.* thirst; *a.* thirsty

~mu⁴ ~慕 *v.* desire earnestly

~nien⁴ ~念 *v.* long for

~wang⁴ ~望 *v.* expect

K'O⁴ 客 *n.* guest, visitor

~chan⁴ ~棧 *n.* hotel, inn

~chi¹ ~機 *n.* passenger airplane

~ch'e¹ ~車 *n.* passenger train

~ch'i⁴ ~氣 *a.* polite, courteous

~jen² ~人 *n.* guest, visitor

~kuan¹ ~觀 *a.* objective (impersonal)

~kuan¹ chu³ i⁴ ~觀主義 *n.* objectivism

~t'ing¹ ~廳 *n.* parlor, sitting room

K'O⁴ 課 *n.* lesson, exercise, task

~ch'eng² ~程 *n.* curriculum
~ch'eng² piao³ ~程表 *n.* curriculum table
K'O⁴ 克 *v.* overcome, conquer
~fu² ~服 *v.* conquer
~fu⁴ ~復 *v.* recapture
~nan² ~難 *v.* conquer difficulties
K'OU³ 口 *n.* mouth, opening, gap, entrance
~an⁴ 岸 *n.* port
~chi¹ ~吃 *n. & v.* stammer
~chiao³ ~角 *n. & v.* quarrel
~ch'in² ~琴 *n.* harmonica
~hao⁴ ~號 *n.* slogan
~ling⁴ 令 *n.* command, password (*mil.*)
~shih⁴ ~試 *n.* oral examination
~ts'ai² ~才 *n.* eloquence
~wei⁴ ~味 *n.* taste
K'OU⁴ 扣 *n.* button; *v.* knock, rap
~chu⁴ ~住 *n.* fasten with buttons
~liu² ~留 *v.* detain; *n.* detention
~wen⁴ ~問 *v.* ask, inquire
K'U¹ 哭 *v.* weep, cry
~ch'i⁴ ~泣 *v.* weep
K'U³ 苦 *a.* painful; *n.* pain
~ch'u³ ~楚 *n.* torture, distress
~kung¹ ~工 *n.* hard work
~li⁴ ~力 *n.* coolie
~t'ung⁴ ~痛 *n.* pain
K'U⁴ 褲 *n.* trousers, pantaloons
K'UA³ 垮 *v.* fail, collapse, defeat
K'UAI⁴ 塊 *n.* clod, lump
K'UAI⁴ 快 *a.* fast, quick, rapid, swift
~chieh² ~捷 *adv.* promptly
~ch'e¹ ~車 *n.* express train
~hsin⁴ ~信 *n.* express mail
~le⁴~樂 *n.* happiness; *a.* happy
~p'ao³ ~跑 *v.* run quickly
K'UAI⁴ 會 *see* HUI⁴
K'UAN¹ 寬 *a.* broad, large, indulgent
~hou⁴ ~厚 *a.* kind
~jung² ~容 *v.* tolerate; *n.* toleration
~shu⁴ ~恕 *v.* excuse

111

~ta⁴ ~大 *a.* wide, broad, spacious

~wei⁴ ~慰 *v.* console

~yü² ~餘 *a.* abundant

K'UAN³ 款 *n.* article, amount of money; *v.* entertain

~liu² ~留 *v.* detain

~shih⁴ ~式 *n.* style, pattern

~tai⁴ ~待 *v.* treat well

K'UANG¹ 筐 *n.* basket

K'UANG² 狂 *a.* crazy, violent, mad

~feng¹ ~風 *n.* gust, hurricane

~huan¹ chieh² ~歡節 *n.* carnival (festival)

~hsi³ ~喜 *v.* make extremely joyful

~hsiang³ ~想 *n.* extravagent thoughts

~hsiang³ ch'ü³ ~想曲 *n.* fantasia

~hsiao⁴ ~笑 *v.* laugh foolishly

~nu⁴ ~怒 *n.* fury, frenzy

~pao⁴ ~暴 *a.* violent; *n.* violence

~t'u² ~徒 *n.* profligate

~yen² ~言 *n.* nonsense

~yin³ ~飲 *v.* guzzle

K'UANG⁴ 礦 *n.* mine, ore; *a.* mineral

~hsüeh² chia¹ ~學家 *n.* mineralogist

~kung¹ ~工 *n.* miner

~k'eng¹ ~坑 *n.* mine shaft

~miao² ~苗 *n.* ore

~wu⁴ ~物 *n.* mineral

~wu⁴ hsüeh² ~物學 *n.* mineralogy

~yu² ~油 *n.* mineral oil

K'UANG⁴ 況 *adv.* moreover, also, besides, in addition

~ch'ieh³ ~且 *adv.* moreover, besides

K'UEI¹ 虧 *n.* wanting, defect; *v.* injure, harm

~ch'ien⁴ ~欠 *v.* be in debt

~hsin¹ ~心 *a.* discreditable

~k'ung¹ ~空 *n.* deficit, shortage

K'UN⁴ 困 *n.* poverty, confinement; *v.* confine; *a.* confined, fatigued

~k'u³ ~苦 *n.* poverty

~nan² ~難 *n.* difficulty

~tou⁴ ~鬥 *v.* resist desperately

112

K'UNG¹ 空 *a.* empty, vacant

~**chan⁴** ~戰 *n.* aerial combat

~**chien¹** ~間 *n.* space

~**chung¹ chao⁴ hsiang⁴** ~中照相 *n.* aerial photography

~**chung¹ chen¹ ch'a²** ~中偵察 *n.* air reconnaissance

~**chung¹ fang² yü⁴** ~中防禦 *n.* air defense (planes)

~**chung¹ kuan¹ ts'e⁴** ~中觀測 *n.* aerial observation

~**chung¹ kung¹ chi¹** ~中攻擊 *n.* air attack

~**chün¹ chi¹ hsieh⁴ hsüeh² hsiao⁴** ~軍機械學校 *n.* Air Force Mechanics School*

~**chün¹ chi¹ ti⁴** ~軍基地 *n.* air base

~**chün¹ chih³ hui¹ ts'an¹ mou² hsüeh² hsiao⁴** ~軍指揮參謀學校 *n.* Air Force Command and Staff College*

~**chün¹ chün¹ kuan¹ hsüeh² hsiao⁴** ~軍軍官學校 *n.* Air Force Academy*

~**chün¹ hsüeh² sheng¹** ~軍學生 *n.* aviation cadet

~**chün¹ t'ung¹ hsin⁴ hsüeh² hsiao⁴** ~軍通信學校 *n.* Air Force Signal School*

~**chün¹ tsung³ ssu¹ ling⁴ pu⁴** ~軍總司令部 *n.* Air Force Headquarters*

~**chün¹ wu³ kuan¹** ~軍武官 *n.* air attache

~**chün¹ yü⁴ pei⁴ hsüeh² hsiao⁴** ~軍豫備學校 *n.* Air Force Preparatory School*

~**ch'i⁴** ~氣 *n.* air

~**hsi** ~襲 *n.* air raid

~**hsi² ching³ pao⁴** ~襲警報 *n.* air raid alarm

~**pao¹** ~包 *n.* blank ammunition

~**yün⁴** ~運 *n.* airborne

~**yün⁴ pu⁴ tui⁴** ~運部隊 *n.* airborne troops

K'UNG³ 恐 *conj.* lest

~**ho⁴** ~嚇 *v.* intimidate; *n.* intimidation

~**huang¹** ~慌 *n.* panic

~**pu⁴** ~怖 *a.* terrible, dreadful; *n.* terror

K'UNG³ 孔 *n.* hole, opening

~**chiao⁴** ~教 *n.* Confucianism

~**ch'iao³** ~雀 *n.* peacock

113

~fu¹ tzu³ ~夫子 *n.* Confucius
~tzu³ te¹ ~子的 *n.* Confucian
K'UO⁴ 擴 *v.* stretch, expand
~chang¹ ~張 *v.* expand
~ch'ung¹ ~充 *v.* expand, extend
~ta⁴ ~大 *v.* magnify
~ta⁴ ch'i⁴ ~大器 *n.* loudspeaker

L

LA¹ 拉 *v.* drag, pull, draw
~ch'e³ ~扯 *v.* pull and drag
~fa¹ ~發 *n.* detonation by pulling
LA¹ 啦 [a final particle]
LA⁴ 辣 *a.* acrid, pungent, biting
~chiao¹ ~椒 *n.* pepper
~shou³ ~手 *a.* cruel, difficult
~wei⁴ ~味 *a.* pungent
LAI² 來 *v.* come, arrive
~fu⁴ ch'iang¹ ~復鎗 *n.* rifle
~fu⁴ hsien⁴ ~復線 *n.* rifling
~hui² p'iao⁴ ~回票 *n.* round trip ticket
~jen² ~人 *n.* comer
~yüan² ~源 *n.* source, origin
LAN² 籃 *n.* basket
~ch'iu²~球 *n.* basketball
LAN² 藍 *n.* blue, indigo
~se⁴ ~色 *n.* & *a.* blue
~t'ien¹ ~天 *n.* blue sky
LAN³ 懶 *n.* idleness; *a.* lazy, remiss
~fu⁴ ~婦 *n.* slut
~jen² ~人 *n.* idler
~to⁴ ~惰 *a.* lazy
LAN⁴ 爛 *a.* rotten, ruined, overcooked
~chih³ ~紙 *n.* waste paper
~man⁴ ~縵 *a.* splendid, brilliant
~pu⁴ ~布 *n.* rag
LANG⁴ 浪 *n.* wave, billow
~fei⁴ ~費 *v.* squander, waste
~hua¹ ~花 *n.* spray

114

~man⁴ ~漫 *a.* romantic; *n.* romance
~man⁴ chu³ i⁴ ~漫主義 *n.* romanticism
~tang⁴ ~蕩 *a.* dissipated
~tzu³ ~子 *n.* spendthrift
LAO² 勞 *n.* labor; *v.* toil. ~4 *v.* reward
~hsin¹ ~心 *n.* labor
~kung¹ pu⁴ ~工部 *n.* Department of Labor (*U.S.*)
~kung¹ tui⁴ ~工隊 *n.* labor troops
~k'u³ ~苦 *a.* toilsome, laborious; *n.* hardship
~li⁴ ~力 *n.* labor
~mo² ~模 *n.* Labor Model**
~tung⁴ ~動 *n.* labor
~tung⁴ chieh¹ chi² ~動階級 *n.* labor class
~tung⁴ chieh² ~動節 *n.* Labor Day
~tung⁴ mo² fan⁴ ~動模範 *n.* Labor Model**
~tung⁴ pao³ hsien³ t'iao² li⁴ ~動保險條例 *n.* Labor Insurance Regulations**
~tung⁴ ying¹ hsiung² ~動英雄 *n.* Labor Hero**
~⁴ chün¹ yün⁴ tung⁴ ~軍運動 *n.* A Comfort-the-Soldiers Movement
LAO³ 老 *a.* old, aged
~chu³ ku⁴ ~主顧 *n.* patron, regular customer
~hu³ ~虎 *n.* tiger
~jo⁴ ~弱 *a.* old and weak
~nien² ~年 *n.* old age
~pao³ ~鴇 *n.* procuress
~p'o² ~婆 *n.* wife
~shu³ ~鼠 *n.* mouse, rat
~ta⁴ ko¹ ~大哥 *n.* Big Brother (Russia)**
~tzu³ ~子 *n.* Lao-tse (Chinese philosopher)
~yu³ ~友 *n.* old friend
LAO⁴ 落 *v.* fall, drop
~ch'eng² ~成 *n.* completion (building)
~hsüan³ ~選 *v.* fail in election
~lei⁴ ~淚 *v.* weep
~wu³ ~伍 *a.* retrogressive
~yeh⁴ ~葉 *n.* fall of the leaf
~yü³ ~雨 *v.* rain
~tui⁴ ~隊 *n.* band, orchestra, ensemble
LE¹ 樂 *a.* happy, joyful, pleasant; *n.* pleasure, joy.

115

YÜEH⁴ *n.* music. **YAO⁴** *v.* rejoice
~i⁴ ~意 *adv.* willingly
~kuan¹ ~觀 *a.* optimistic; *n.* optimism
~t'ien¹ p'ai⁴ ~天派 *n.* optimist
yüeh⁴ ch'i⁴ ~器 *n.* musical instruments
~p'u³ ~譜 *n.* score (music)
LEI² 雷 *n.* thunder
~ming² ~鳴 *n.* thunderclap
~tien⁴ ~電 *n.* thunderbolt
~yü³ ~雨 *n.* thunderstorm
~yün² ~雲 *n.* thundercloud
LEI³ 累 *adv.* often, repeatedly. ~⁴ *v.* involve, tire
~chi¹ ~積 *v.* accumulate
LEI⁴ 淚 *n.* tear
LEI⁴ 類 *n.* species, kind, class
~pieh² ~別 *v.* classify; *n.* classification
~ssu⁴ ~似 *a.* similar
LENG³ 冷 *a.* cold, chilly
~chan⁴ ~戰 *n.* cold war
~ching⁴ ~靜 *a.* quiet
~hsiao⁴ ~笑 *v.* sneer
~hsüeh⁴ ~血 *a.* cold-blooded
~shui³ yü⁴ ~水浴 *n.* cold bath
~tan⁴ ~淡 *a.* indifferent, cold
LI² 離 *n.* distance; *v.* leave, separate
~ch'i² ~奇 *a.* eccentric
~ch'i⁴ ~棄 *v.* desert
~ho² ~合 *n.* parting or meeting
~hun¹ ~婚 *n.* & *v.* divorce
~pieh² ~別 *v.* depart, leave; *n.* departure
LI² 犁 *n.* plow
~tao¹ ~刀 *n.* scythe
~t'ien² ~田 *v.* plow
LI³ 理 *n.* reason, law; *v.* arrange, manage
~chieh³ ~解 *n.* understanding
~fa³ ~髮 *n.* haircut
~fa³ chiang⁴ ~髮匠 *n.* barber
~fa³ tien⁴ ~髮店 *n.* barbershop
~hua⁴ ~化 *n.* physics and chemistry
~hui⁴ ~會 *v.* apprehend
~hsiang³ ~想 *n.* idea; *a.* ideal

~hsiang³ chia¹ ~想家 *n.* idealist

~hsing⁴ ~性 *n.* reason

~hsüeh² yüan⁴ ~學院 *n.* college of science

~k'o¹ ~科 *n.* natural science

~lun⁴ ~論 *n.* theory; *a.* theoretical, theoretic

~yu² ~由 *n.* reason

LI³ 裡 *n.* inside, lining; *a.* inner

LI³ 李 *n.* plum

LI³ 禮 *n.* etiquette, ceremony, gift, worship, present

~chieh² ~節 *n.* formality

~fu² ~服 *n.* full dress

~mao⁴ ~貌 *n.* manners

~pai⁴ ~拜 *n.* & *v.* worship

~pai⁴ erh⁴ ~拜二 *n.* Tuesday

~pai⁴ i¹ ~拜一 *n.* Monday

~pai⁴ jih⁴ ~拜日 *n.* Sunday

~pai⁴ liu⁴ ~拜六 *n.* Saturday

~pai⁴ san¹ ~拜三 *n.* Wednesday

~pai⁴ ssu⁴ ~拜四 *n.* Thursday

~pai⁴ t'ang² ~拜堂 *n.* church

~pai⁴ wu³ ~拜五 *n.* Friday

~wu⁴ ~物 *n.* present, gift

LI³ 里 *n.* Chinese measure for old standard of length, about one third mile

LI⁴ 力 *n.* strength, power, force, energy, vigor

~ch'i⁴ ~氣 *n.* vigor, strength

~ch'iang² ~強 *a.* strong

~liang⁴ ~量 *n.* power, force, strength

~ta⁴ ~大 *a.* powerful

LI⁴ 利 *v.* benefit; *n.* profit

~chi³ ~己 *a.* selfish

~chi³ chu³ i⁴ ~己主義 *n.* egoism, selfishness

~hai⁴ ~害 *a.* severe, strict

~hsi² ~息 *a.* interest (money)

~i⁴ ~益 *n.* advantage, benefit, profit

~t'o¹ chu³ i⁴ ~他主義 *n.* altruism

~yung⁴ ~用 *v.* utilize

LI⁴ 立 *v.* stand, erect, set up, establish; *a.* erect, upright

~an⁴ ~案 *v.* register

117

~fa³ ~法 *a.* lawmaking, legislative; *n.* legislation

~fa³ yüan⁴ ~法院 *n.* Legislative Yuan*

~fang¹ ken¹ ~方根 *n.* cubic root

~hsien⁴ ~憲 *v.* establish a constitution

~k'o⁴ ~刻 *a.* immediate; *adv.* immediately

~t'i³ ~體 *n.* cubic, solid

LI⁴ 例 *n.* precedent, example, regulation

~hsing² kung¹ shih⁴ ~行公事 *n.* routine matters (*off.*)

~ju² ~如 *adv.* for instance, for example

~wai⁴ ~外 *n.* exception

LI⁴ 粒 *n.* grain, kernel

LI⁴ 歷 *a.* successive; *v.* experience

~ch'ao² ~朝 *n.* successive dynasties

~shih³ ~史 *n.* history, chronicle

~shih³ chia¹ ~史家 *n.* historian

~tai⁴ ~代 *n.* successive generations

LI⁴ 麗 *a.* elegant, graceful, beautiful

~jen² ~人 *n.* feminine beauty

LI⁴ 隸 *n.* underling, subordinate; *v.* be attached to

~shu³ ~屬 *v.* be attached to (*mil.*)

LIANG² 糧 *n.* food, ration, grain, provisions, fodder, forage

~shih² ~食 *n.* food, provisions

~shih² pu⁴ ~食部 *n.* Ministry of Food**

~ts'ao³ ~草 *n.* fodder, forage

LIANG² 量 *v.* measure, consider. ~⁴ *n.* quantity

LIANG² 良 *a.* good, virtuous

~chih¹ ~知 *n.* intuition

~hsin¹ ~心 *n.* conscience

~jen² ~人 *n.* good man, husband

~shan⁴ ~善 *a.* good, fine, nice

~yao⁴ ~藥 *n.* good medicine

~yen² ~言 *n.* good advice

~yu³ ~友 *n.* good friend

LIANG² 涼 *a.* cool

~shuang³ ~爽 *a.* cool

LIANG² 梁 *n.* sorghum, bridge, beam

LIANG³ 兩 *a.* two, both; *n.* tael (Chinese weight for 37.8 grams)

~chiao³ kuei¹ ~脚規 *n.* compass

~tz'u⁴ ~次 *adv.* twice

LIANG⁴ 亮 *a.* bright, clear, brilliant

~kuang¹ ~光 *n.* light

LIAO³ 了 *a.* finished, ended, completed, done

~chieh² ~結 *a.* finished, ended, concluded; *v.* settle, conclude

~chieh³ ~解 *n.* understanding; *v.* understand

~pu⁴ ch'i³ ~不起 *a.* extraordinary; *adv.* extraordinarily

LIAO⁴ 料 *n.* material; *v.* imagine

~hsiang³ ~想 *v.* guess, imagine

~li³ ~理 *v.* arrange

LIEH⁴ 列 *v.* arrange, put in the proper order; *n.* row, file

~c'he¹ ~車 *n.* train

~ch'iang² ~強 *n.* world powers

~hsi² ~席 *v.* attend

~ping¹ ~兵 *n.* private (army)

LIEH⁴ 烈 *a.* fierce, violent

~hsing⁴ ~性 *a.* vicious horse

~shih⁴ ~士 *n.* patriot, hero

LIEH⁴ 劣 *a.* vile, bad, low, mean, poor, inferior; *n.* inferiority

~huo⁴ ~貨 *n.* low-grade goods

~hsing² ~行 *n.* bad behavior, misconduct

~shen¹ ~紳 *n.* deprived gentry

LIEN² 聯 *v.* connect, assemble, unite, combine

~chün¹ ~軍 *n.* allied armies

~ho² ~合 *v.* join, unite; *a.* joint

~ho² cheng⁴ fu³ ~合政府 *n.* coalition government

~ho² ch'in² wu⁴ tsung³ ssu¹ ling⁴ pu⁴ ~合勤務總司令部 *n.* Combined Service Forces Headquarters

~ho² kuo² ~合國 *n.* United Nations

~lei⁴ ~累 *v.* implicate, involve (in difficulty)

~lo⁴ ~絡 *n.* liaison, contact; *v.* maintain contact

~lo⁴ kuan¹ ~絡官 *n.* liaison officer

LIEN² 連 *n.* company (army); *v.* connect, continue

119

~chang³ ~長 *n.* company commander, battery commander

~chieh¹ ~接 *v.* connect; *n.* coupling, join

~ho² ~合 *v.* combine; *a.* joint

~hsi⁴ ~繫 *v.* contact

~hsü⁴ ~續 *v.* continue

~ho² tso⁴ chan⁴ ~合作戰 *n.* combined operations, joint operations

~hsiang³ ~想 *v.* associate (in thought)

~lo⁴ ~絡 *v.* affiliate

~meng² ~盟 *n.* alliance

~pang¹ ~邦 *n.* federation

~pang¹ cheng⁴ fu³ ~邦政府 *n.* federal government

~pang¹ chu³ i⁴ ~邦主義 *n.* federalism

LIEN² 憐 *v.* pity

~ai⁴ ~愛 *v.* love, regard

~hsi² ~惜 *v.* sympathize

~min³ ~憫 *v.* pity

LIEN² 鐮 *n.* sickle

~tao¹ ~刀 *n.* scythe, sickle

LIEN³ 臉 *n.* face, honor

~hou⁴ ~厚 *a.* shameless

~mien⁴ ~面 *n.* reputation

~p'en² ~盆 *n.* washbowl, washbasin

LIEN⁴ 練 *v.* practise, train, drill

~hsi² ~習 *v.* practice, train; *n.* exercise

~hsi² pu⁴ ~習簿 *n.* exercise book

~ping¹ ~兵 *v.* train troops

LIEN⁴ 煉 *v.* refine, purify, smelt

~chih⁴ ch'ang³ ~製廠 *n.* refinery

~ju³ ~乳 *n.* condensed milk

~tan¹ shu⁴ ~丹術 *n.* alchemy

~t'ang² ~糖 *n.* refined sugar

LIN² 林 *n.* forest, wood

~hsüeh² ~學 *n.* foresty

~yeh⁴ pu⁴ ~業部 *n.* Ministry of Foresty**

LIN² 臨 *v.* attend

~pieh² ~別 *a.* farewell

~p'en² ~盆 *n.* confinement (birth)

~shih² ~時 *a.* temporary; *adv.* temporarily

120

~shih² hui⁴ i⁴ ~時會議 *n.* temporary meeting
LIN² 鄰 *a.* neighboring
~chin⁴ ~近 *a.* neighboring
~chü¹ ~居 *n.* neighbor
~kuo² ~國 *n.* neighboring countries
LING² 鈴 *n.* bell
LING² 靈 *n.* soul, spiritual
~ch'iao³ ~巧 *a.* ingenious
~hun² ~魂 *n.* soul
~yen⁴ ~驗 *a.* efficacious
LING² 零 *n.* zero, naught
~chien⁴ ~件 *n.* accessories, spare part ·
~lo⁴ ~落 *a.* scattered
~shou⁴ ~售 *n.* & *v.* retail
~shou⁴ shang⁴ ~售商 *n.* retailer
~tu⁴ ~度 *n.* zero degree
~t'ou² ~頭 *n.* change (money)
~yung⁴ ch'ien² ~用錢 *n.* pocket money
LING³ 領 *n.* collar; *v.* receive, accept, lead
~chang¹ ~章 *n.* collar insignia
~ch'ing² ~情 *v.* receive kindness
~hai³ ~海 *n.* marginal sea
~hua¹ ~花 *n.* collar pin (ornament)
~hsiu⁴ ~袖 *n.* leader, chief, head
~kang³ ~港 *n.* ship pilot
~shih⁴ ~事 *n.* consul
~shih⁴ kuan³ ~事館 *n.* consulate
~shih⁴ ts'ai² p'an⁴ ch'üan² ~事裁判權 *n.* consular jurisdiction
~shou⁴ ~受 *v.* accept, receive
~tai⁴ ~帶 *n.* necktie
~tao³ ~導 *v.* direct, lead
~t'u³ ~土 *n.* territory, dominion
~t'u³ wan² cheng³ ~土完整 *n.* territorial integrity
~tzu¹ ~子 *n.* collar
LING⁴ 令 *n.* order, command. *v.* direct, make
~ming² ~名 *n.* reputation
LING⁴ 另 *a.* another, extra, more
~chia¹ ~加 *a.* additional
~wai⁴ ~外 *n.* extra

LIU² 留 *v.* remain, stay
  ~hsin¹ ~心 *v.* pay attention
  ~sheng¹ chi¹ ~聲機 *n.* phonograph
LIU² 流 *v.* flow, pass
  ~chih² ~質 *n.* liquid, fluid
  ~ch'ang⁴ ~暢 *a.* fluent
  ~han⁴ ~汗 *v.* perspire
  ~hsien⁴ hsing² ~線型 *n.* streamline
  ~hsing¹ ~星 *n.* meteor, shooting star
  ~hsing² ~行 *v.* prevail, circulate; *a.* popular, prevalent
  ~hsing² kan³ mao⁴ ~行感冒 *n.* influenza
  ~hsüeh⁴ ~血 *n.* bloodshed
  ~lei⁴ ~淚 *v.* shed tears
  ~lo⁴ ~落 *v.* wander
  ~mang² ~氓 *n.* rascal
  ~pi⁴ ~弊 *n.* evil practice
  ~shui³ ~水 *n.* running water
  ~shui³ chang⁴ ~水帳 *n.* cashbook
  ~tan⁴ ~彈 *n.* stray bullet
  ~t'ung¹ ~通 *v.* circulate; *n.* circulation
  ~wang² ~亡 *a.* fugitive
  ~yen² ~言 *n.* rumor
  ~yü⁴ ~域 *n.* river basin
LIU⁴ 六 *n.* & *a.* six
  ~chiao³ hsing² ~角形 *n.* hexagon
  ~yüeh⁴ ~月 *n.* June
LOU² 樓 *n.* upper-story, tower
  ~hsia⁴ ~下 *adv.* downstairs
  ~shang⁴ ~上 *adv.* upstairs
  ~t'i¹ ~梯 *n.* staircase, stairway, stairs
LU² 爐 *n.* stove
LU⁴ 陸 *n.* dry land, continent
  ~chün¹ ~軍 *n.* army
  ~chün¹ chih³ hui¹ ts'an¹ mou² hsüeh² hsiao⁴ ~軍指揮參謀學校 *n.* Army Command and Staff College*
  ~chün¹ chuang¹ chia³ ping¹ hsüeh² hsiao⁴ ~軍裝甲兵學校 *n.* Armored Force School*
  ~chün¹ chün¹ kuan¹ hsüeh² hsiao⁴ ~軍軍官學校 *n.* Army Academy*

~chün¹ li³ chieh² ~軍禮節 *n.* military courtesy

~chün¹ pu⁴ ~軍部 *n.* War Department (*U.S.*)

~chün¹ pu⁴ chang³ ~軍部長 *n.* Secretary of the Army

~chün¹ pu⁴ ping¹ hsüeh² hsiao⁴ ~軍步兵學校 *n.* Infantry School*

~chün¹ p'ao⁴ ping¹ hsüeh² hsiao⁴ ~軍砲兵學校 *n.* Artillery School*

~chün¹ tsung³ ssu¹ ling⁴ ~軍總司令 *n.* Commander in Chief (*mil.*)

~chün¹ tsung³ ssu¹ ling⁴ pu⁴ ~軍總司令部 *n.* Ground Forces Headquarters*

~chün¹ wu³ kuan¹ ~軍武官 *n.* military attache

~hsü⁴ ~續 *a.* continuous; *adv.* continuously

~k'ung¹ t'ung¹ hsin⁴ ~空通信 *n.* air-ground communication

~ti⁴ ~地 *n.* land

~yün⁴ ~運 *n.* land transportation

LU⁴ 露 *n.* dew

~shui³ ~水 *n.* dewdrop

~t'ai² ~臺 *n.* balcony

~t'ien¹ ~天 *n.* open air

~yen² ~岩 *n.* exposed rock

~ying² ~營 *n. & v.* bivouac

~ying² ti⁴ ~營地 *n.* bivouac area

LU⁴ 路 *n.* road, path

~ch'eng² ~程 *n.* journey

LUAN⁴ 亂 *n.* trouble, disorder, rebellion

~chiao⁴ ~叫 *v.* shout

~lun² ~倫 *n.* incest

~min² ~民 *n.* lawless mob, rebel

~shih⁴ ~世 *n.* chaotic period

LUN² 輪 *n.* wheel, circle, turn, disk; *v.* turn, revolve

~ch'uan² ~船 *n.* steamer, steamboat, steamship

~liu² ~流 *v.* reverse, rotate; *n.* rotation

~tu⁴ ~渡 *n.* steam ferry

~t'ai¹ ~胎 *n.* tire

LUN⁴ 論 *v.* discuss, debate, criticize

~li³ hsüeh² ~理學 *n.* logic

~li³ hsüeh² chia¹ ~理學家 *n.* logician

123

~**wen²** ~文 *n.* essay, thesis
LÜ² 驢 *n.* ass, donkey
LÜ³ 旅 *n.* troop, brigade
~**fei⁴** ~費 *n.* traveling expenses
~**hsing²** ~行 *n.* & *v.* travel
~**kuan³** ~館 *n.* hotel, inn
~**k'o⁴** ~客 *n.* traveler, passenger
LÜ⁴ 律 *n.* law, rule, regulation, code
~**chieh⁴** ~誡 *n.* commandment
~**li⁴** ~例 *n.* law
~**shih¹** ~師 *n.* lawyer, attorney
~**tien³** ~典 *n.* code
LÜ⁴ 綠 *a.* & *n.* green
~**ch'a²** ~茶 *n.* green tea
~**lin²** ~林 *n.* greenwood
~**se⁴** ~色 *a.* green
~**teng¹** ~燈 *n.* green traffic light
~**tou⁴** ~豆 *n.* green beans
~**yü⁴** ~玉 *n.* emerald
LÜ⁴ 率 *see* SHUAI⁴
LÜEH⁴ 略 *a.* simple; *adv.* briefly, simply; *v.* abbreviate
~**t'ung²** ~同 *a.* alike, similar

M

MA¹ 麼 [an interrogative particle]
MA¹ 嗎 [an interrogative form]
MA¹ 媽 *n.* mother, mamma
MA² 麻 *n.* hemp
~**ch'üeh⁴** ~雀 *n.* sparrow. ~**chiang⁴** 雀＝將 *n.* mahjong
~**mu⁴** ~木 *a.* torpid
~**pi⁴** ~痺 *n.* palsy
~**pu⁴** ~布 *n.* linen
~**sheng²** ~繩 *n.* marline
~**tzu³** ~子 *n.* pockmark
~**yao⁴** ~藥 *n.* narcotics
MA³ 馬 *n.* horse
~**an¹** ~鞍 *n.* saddle

~chang³ ~掌 *n.* horseshoe
~chiu⁴ ~廐 *n.* stable
~ch'e¹ ~車 *n.* carriage
~ch'e¹ fu¹ ~車夫 *n.* coachman
~fu¹ ~夫 *n.* groom
~hsi⁴ ~戲 *n.* circus
~hsüeh¹ ~靴 *n.* field boots, riding boots
~kan¹ ~乾 *n.* forage, fodder
~k'o⁴ ssu¹ 克斯 *n.* Marx
~li⁴ ~力 *n.* horsepower
~lieh⁴ chu³ i⁴ ~列主義 *n.* Marxism-Leninism**
~lu⁴ ~路 *n.* road
~pei⁴ ~背 *n.* horseback
~pien¹ ~鞭 *n.* horse whip
~shu⁴ ~術 *n.* horsemanship
~teng⁴ ~蹬 *n.* stirrup
~tui⁴ ~隊 *n.* cavalry
~t'ung³ ~桶 *n.* toilet stool
~ts'ao² ~槽 *n.* manger
~tz'u⁴ ~刺 *n.* spurs
~ying² ~蠅 *n.* horsefly
MA⁴ 罵 *v.* curse, scold
MAI² 埋 *v.* bury
~fu² ~伏 *n.* ambush
~tsang⁴ ~葬 *v.* bury
MAI³ 買 *v.* buy, purchase
~chia⁴ ~價 *n.* cost price
~huo⁴ ~貨 *v.* purchase goods
~mai⁴ ~賣 *n.* trade, business
~pan⁴ ~辦 *n.* compradore
MAI⁴ 賣 *v.* sell; *n.* sale
~chia⁴ ~價 *n.* selling price
~chu³ ~主 *n.* seller
~kuo² ~國 *n.* treason
~kuo² tsei² ~國賊 *n.* traitor
~nung⁴ ~弄 *v.* show off
~p'iao⁴ ch'u⁴ ~票處 *n.* booking office
~yin² ~淫 *n.* prostitution
MAI⁴ 麥 *n.* wheat, barley
~chiu³ ~酒 *n.* ale
~fen³ ~粉 *n.* flour

125

~p'ien⁴ ~片 *n.* white oats

MAN³ 滿 *a.* full, complete; *n.* Manchu

~chou¹ ~洲 *n.* Manchuria

~chou¹ jen² ~洲人 *n.* Manchu, Manchurian

~chou¹ kuo² ~洲國 *n.* Manchukuo

~ch'i¹ ~期 *n.* expiration

~fen¹ ~分 *n.* full mark

~tsu² ~足 *v.* satisfy

~yüeh⁴ ~月 *n.* full moon

MAN⁴ 慢 *a.* slow, remiss, neglectful

~kun³ ~滾 *n.* slow roll (aviation)

~pu⁴ ~步 *v.* walk slowly

~tai⁴ ~待 *v.* treat impolitely

MANG² 忙 *v.* keep busy; *a.* busy

~luan⁴ ~亂 *a.* excited, anxious

~su² ~速 *adv.* quickly, hurriedly

MAO¹ 貓 *n.* cat, kitten, puss

~t'ou² ying¹ ~頭鷹 *n.* owl

MAO² 毛 *n.* feather, hair, dime; *a.* coarse, rough

~chin¹ ~巾 *n.* towel

~pi³ ~筆 *n.* brush-pen

~ping⁴ ~病 *n.* disease, defect, fault, shortcoming

MAO⁴ 冒 *v.* risk, pretend, counterfeit

~ch'ung¹ ~充 *v.* pretend

~fan⁴ ~犯 *v.* offend

~hsien³ ~險 *v.* risk, adventure

~hsien³ chia¹ ~險家 *n.* adventurer

~hsien³ hsing⁴ ~險性 *n.* adventurism**

~shih¹ ~失 *a.* rude

~shih¹ kuei³ ~失鬼 *n.* blunderer

MAO⁴ 帽 *n.* cap, hat, headgear

~chang¹ ~章 *n.* hat insignia

~tien⁴ ~店 *n.* haberdasher

~yen² ~簷 *n.* visor

MEI² 没 *adv.* not. **MO⁴** *v.* die, varnish, sink; *a.* dead, gone

~yung⁴ ~用 *a.* useless

mo⁴ shou¹ ~收 *v.* confiscate; *n.* confiscation

MEI² 煤 *n.* coal

~ch'i⁴ ~氣 *n.* carbon monoxide

~k'uang⁴ ~礦 *n.* coal mine

~k'uang⁴ kung¹ ssu¹ ~礦公司 *n.* coal mining company

~yu² ~油 *n.* kerosene

MEI² 眉 *n.* eyebrow

~mao² ~毛 *n.* eyebrow

MEI³ 每 *a.* every, each; *prep.* per

~chi⁴ ~季 *a.* quarterly, one fourth of a year

~chou¹ ~週 *a.* & *adv.* weekly

~hsiao³ shih² ~小時 *prep.* per hour

~jih⁴ ~日 *a.* & *adv.* daily

~ko⁴ ~個 *a.* each

~mei³ ~每 *adv.* often, always

~nien² ~年 *a.* & *adv.* yearly

~yüeh⁴ ~月 *a.* & *adv.* monthly

MEI³ 美 *a.* beautiful, pretty, lovely; *n.* beauty

~ching³ ~景 *a.* beautiful scenery

~chiu³ ~酒 *n.* good wine

~hsüeh² ~學 *n.* aesthetics

~jen² ~人 *n.* a feminine beauty

~kuo² hai³ chün¹ ~國海軍 *n.* Navy (*U.S.*)

~kuo² k'ung¹ chün¹ ~國空軍 *n.* Air Force(*U.S.*)

~kuo² lu⁴ chün¹ ~國陸軍 *n.* Army (*U.S.*)

~kuo² lu⁴ chün¹ chün¹ kuan¹ hsüeh² hsiao⁴ ~國陸軍軍官學校 *n.* Military Academy (*U.S.*)

~li⁴ ~麗 *a.* beautiful, pretty; *n.* beauty

~miao⁴ ~妙 *a.* excellent

~shu⁴ ~術 *n.* fine arts

~shu⁴ chia¹ ~術家 *n.* artist

~shu⁴ kuan³ ~術館 *n.* art museum

~shu⁴ p'in³ ~術品 *n.* work of art

~te² ~德 *n.* virtue

~wei⁴ ~味 *n.* delicious

~yü⁴ ~譽 *n.* good reputation, good name

MEI⁴ 妹 *n.* younger sister

~fu¹ ~夫 *n.* younger sister's husband (brother-in-law)

MEN² 門 *n.* door, gate

~hu⁴ ~戶 *n.* door

~k'ou³ ~口 *n.* doorway, entrance

~p'ai² ~牌 *n.* door number

~shuan¹ ~閂 *n.* gate bar

127

~t‘u² ~徒 *n.* disciple, follower

MEN² 們 [word used to signify plural number of the pronoun I, you, he, she, and it]

MEN⁴ 悶 *a.* depressed

~ssu³ ~死 *v.* suffocate

MENG³ 猛 *a.* violent, fierce, brave, savage

~kung¹ 攻 *v.* make a heavy attack

~lieh⁴ ~烈 *a.* fierce attack, intense fire

~shou⁴ ~獸 *n.* wild beast

MENG⁴ 夢 *n. & v.* dream

~hsiang³ ~想 *v.* dream of, fancy

~i² ~遺 *n.* seminal emission

~mo² ~魔 *n.* nightmare

~yu² ~遊 *n.* sleepwalking

MI² 迷 *a.* intoxicated

~huo⁴ ~惑 *a.* puzzled

~hsin⁴~信 *n.* superstition

~lu⁴ ~路 *a. & adv.* astray; *v.* lose one's way

~luan⁴ ~亂 *n.* perplexity

~t‘u² ~途 *v.* stray

MI³ 米 *n.* rice

~fan⁴ ~飯 *n.* cooked rice

~t‘ang¹ ~湯 *n.* rice water

~t‘u⁴ ~突 *n.* meter

MI⁴ 密 *a.* dense, thick, confidential, secret, private, close, intimate

~ch‘ieh⁴ ~切 *a.* close association

~ma³ ~碼 *n.* secret cipher, secret code

~shih³ ~使 *n.* emissary

~wei⁴ ~位 *n.* mil

MIAO² 苗 *n.* sprout, descendant, Southwestern Chinese tribe

~t‘iao² ~條 *a.* graceful

MIAO⁴ 廟 *n.* temple, fair

MIEH⁴ 滅 *v.* extinguish, destroy, exterminate

~huo³ ch‘i⁴ ~火器 *n.* fire extinguisher

~shih¹ ~虱 *v.* delouse

~ting³ ~頂 *v.* be drowned

~wang² ~亡 *v.* destroy

MIEN² 棉 *n.* cotton

~hua¹ ~花 *n.* raw cotton

~hsü⁴ ~絮 *n.* cotton rags
~pu⁴ ~布 *n.* calico, cotton cloth
~sha¹ ~紗 *n.* cotton yarn
~yao⁴ ~藥 *n.* nitrocellulose
MIEN³ 免 *v.* take off, avoid, dismiss
~chih² ~職 *v.* dismiss from service
~ch'u² ~除 *v.* relieve from duty, avoid
~shui⁴ ~税 *a.* tax-exempt
~tsui⁴ ~罪 *v.* acquit; *n.* acquittal
MIEN⁴ 面 *n.* face, surface
~chi¹ ~積 *n.* area
~chin¹ ~巾 *n.* towel
~ch'ih⁴ ~赤 *v.* flush
~mao⁴ ~貌 *n.* appearance
~se⁴ ~色 *n.* complexion
~shih⁴ ~試 *n.* oral examination
MIEN⁴ 麵 *n.* noodle
~fen³ ~粉 *n.* flour
MIN² 民 *n.* people, citizen
~cheng¹ ~政 *n.* civil administration
~chu³ ~主 *n.* democracy
~chu³ chien⁴ kuo² hui⁴ ~主建國會 *n.* China Democratic National Construction Association**
~chu³ tang³ ~主黨 *n.* Democratic Party
~chung⁴ yün⁴ tung⁴ ~衆運動 *n.* popular movement
~ch'üan² ~權 *n.* people's rights
~ch'üan² chu³ i⁴ ~權主義 *n.* principle of democracy*
~fa³ ~法 *n.* civil law
~i⁴ ~意 *n.* public opinion
~sheng¹ ~生 *n.* livelihood
~sheng¹ chu³ i⁴ ~生主義 *n.* principle of people's livelihood*
~tsu² ~族 *n.* nation, race; *a.* national
~tsu² chu³ i⁴ ~族主義 *n.* nationalism*
~tsu² shih⁴ wu⁴ wei³ yüan² hui⁴ ~族事務委員會 Commission of Nationalities Affairs**
~tsu² tzu¹ ch'an³ chieh¹ chi² ~族資産階級 *n.* national bourgeoisie**

129

MING² 名 *n.* name, title; *a.* famous, noted
~ch'eng¹ ~稱 *n.* title
~jen² ~人 *n.* celebrity
~kuei⁴ ~貴 *a.* valuable
~p'ien⁴ ~片 *n.* calling card
~tzu⁴ ~字 *n.* name
~tz'u² ~詞 *n.* noun
~wang⁴ ~望 *n.* reputation, fame
~yü⁴ ~譽 *n.* fame, reputation
MING² 明 *a.* bright, apparent, plain
~ch'üeh⁴ ~確 *a.* evident
~hsin⁴ p'ien⁴ ~信片 *n.* post card
~hsing¹ ~星 *n.* movie star
~jih⁴ ~日 *n.* & *adv.* tomorrow
~liang⁴ ~亮 *a.* bright, brilliant
~pai² ~白 *v.* understand; *a.* clear
MING⁴ 命 *n.* fate, lot, destiny, life, decree, order; *v.* order, command
~an⁴ ~案 *n.* murder
~chung⁴ kung¹ suan⁴ ~中公算 *n.* vulnerability factor
~chung⁴ shu⁴ ~中數 *n.* number of hits
~chung⁴ tan⁴ ~中彈 *n.* sensing a direct hit
~ling⁴ ~令 *n.* & *v.* command; *v.* order
~ling⁴ chu³ i⁴ ~令主義 *n.* frequent issue of orders**
~yün⁴ ~運 *n.* fate, destiny
MO¹ 摸 *v.* touch, feel
~so³ ~索 *v.* seek for, feel out
MO² 磨 ~⁴ *n.* mill; *v.* rub, polish, grind
~² li⁴ ~礪 *n.* discipline
~nan⁴ ~難 *n.* misfortune
~sun³ ~損 *v.* wear (deteriorate)
~tao¹ shih² ~刀石 *n.* grindstone
~tien⁴ chi¹ ~電機 *n.* generator, dynamo
~ts'a¹ ~擦 *n.* friction (physical or personal)
~fang¹ ~坊 *n.* mill
MO² 模 *see* MU²
MO⁴ 末 *a.* final, last
~chan⁴ ~站 *n.* railroad terminal, terminus
~liao³ ~了 *n.* end

~tuan¹ ~端 *a.* terminal; *n.* extremity

~tso⁴ ~座 *n.* lowest seat

MO⁴ 莫 *v. aux.* don't; *adv.* not; *a.* great

MO⁴ 墨 *n.* Chinese ink

~shui³ ~水 *n.* ink

~shui³ chia⁴ ~水架 *n.* inkstand

MO⁴ 没 *see* MEI²

MOU² 謀 *n.* strategy; *v.* plot, scheme

~p'an⁴ ~叛 *v.* rebel; *n.* rebellion

~sha¹ ~殺 *v.* assassinate, murder

~sheng¹ ~生 *v.* earn a living

~shih⁴ ~事 *v.* look for a job

~shih⁴ ~士 *n.* adviser

MOU³ 某 *n.* certain person, someone

MU² 模 *n.* pattern, fashion, mold. MO² *n.* model (after someone)

~yang⁴ ~樣 *n.* pattern, model, fashion

mo² fan⁴ ~範 *n.* model

~fan⁴ kung¹ jen² ~範工人 *n.* model workers**

~fang³ ~倣 *v.* imitate; *n.* imitation

~hu² ~糊 *a.* vague

~hsing² ~型 *n.* mold

~t'e⁴ erh¹ ~特兒 *n.* artists model

MU³ 母 *n.* mother, mamma

~chiu⁴ ~舅 *n.* mother's brother (uncle)

~ch'in¹ ~親 *n.* mother

~hsiao⁴ ~校 *n.* mother school

~i² ~姨 *n.* mother's sister (aunt)

~nü³ ~女 *n.* mother and daughter

~tzu³ ~子 *n.* mother and son

~yin¹ ~音 *n.* vowel

MU³ 畝 *n.* Chinese measure for 0.1636 acre

MU⁴ 木 *n.* wood, timber; *a.* wooden

~chiang⁴ ~匠 *n.* carpenter

~hsing¹ ~星 *n.* Jupiter

~liao⁴ ~料 *n.* lumber, timber

~mien² ~棉 *n.* cotton

~nai³ i¹ ~乃伊 *n.* mummy

~ou³ ~偶 *n.* idol

~pan³ ~板 *n.* board, plank

~t'an⁴ ~炭 *n.* charcoal

MU⁴ 目 *n.* eye

~**hsia⁴** ~下 *adv.* at present, for the time being

~**li⁴** ~力 *n.* eyesight

~**lu⁴** ~錄 *n.* catalog, contents

~**piao¹** ~標 *n.* goal

~**ti⁴** ~的 *n.* aim, purpose, objective

N

NA² 拿 *v.* take, seize, arrest

~**huo⁴** ~獲 *v.* arrest, seize

~**lai²** ~來 *v.* bring here

~**tsou³** ~走 *v.* take away

NA⁴ 那 *pron.* that; *adv.* there. Also read **NAI³** and **NEI⁴**. [All read 3rd tond when interrogatives]

NAI³ 奶 *n.* milk, nipple

~**chao⁴** ~罩 *n.* bra, brassiere

~**mu³**~母 *n.* baby nurse

~**t'ou²** ~頭 *n.* nipple

~**t'ou² tun⁴** ~頭盾 *n.* nipple shield

~**yu²** ~油 *n.* butter

NAI⁴ 耐 *v.* suffer, endure

~**chiu³ te¹** ~久的 *a.* durable

~**hsing⁴** ~性 *n.* patience; *a.* patient

NAI⁴ 那 *see* **NA⁴**

NAN² 難 *a.* difficult, hard; *n.* difficulty. ~⁴ *n.* calamity

~⁴ **min²** ~民 *n.* refugee

NAN² 南 *a. & n.* south; *a.* southern

~**chi²** ~極 *n.* South Pole

~**fang¹** ~方 *n.* south; *a.* southern

~**kua¹** ~瓜 *n.* pumpkin

NAN² 男 *n.* man

~**chüeh²** ~爵 *n.* baron

~**hsing⁴** ~性 *n.* male; *a.* masculine

~**nü³ t'ung² hsüeh²** ~女同學 *n.* co-education

~**tzu¹** ~子 *n.* man

NAO³ 腦 *n.* brain

~**ch'ung¹ hsüeh⁴** ~充血 *n.* brain congestion

~**li⁴** ~力 *n.* brains

~mo⁴ yen² ~膜炎 *n.* meningitis
NAO⁴ 鬧 *a.* noisy
~chung¹ ~鐘 *n.* alarm clock
~shih⁴ ~市 *n.* busy street
~shih⁴ ~事 *v.* make disturbance
NEI⁴ 內 *a.* inner, inside; *prep.* within
~chan⁴ ~戰 *n.* civil war
~cheng⁴ pu⁴ ~政部 *n.* Ministry of the Interior*,
Department of the Interior (*U.S.*)
~chu⁴ ~助 *n.* wife
~jung² ~容 *n.* contents
~k'o¹ ~科 *n.* medical science
~luan⁴ ~亂 *n.* civil war
~meng³ ku³ tzu⁴ chih⁴ ch'ü¹ ~蒙古自治區 *n.*
Inner Mongolian Autonomous Region**
~pu⁴ ~部 *n.* interior, inside, inner part
~wu⁴ ~務 *n.* home affairs
~wu⁴ pu⁴ ~務部 *n.* Ministry of the Interior**
NEI⁴ 那 *see* NA⁴
NENG² 能 *v. aux.* can; *n.* capacity, ability; *a.*
capable, able
~kan⁴ ~幹 *a.* able
~li⁴ ~力 *n.* ability, capacity
NI² 呢 *n.* wool. [Also a final particle]
~jung² ~絨 *n.* woolens
NI² 泥 *n.* mud, clay
~shui³ chiang⁴ ~水匠 *n.* mason
~t'an¹ ~灘 *n.* muddy beach
~t'u³ ~土 *n.* mud, clay, soil, earth
NI³ 你 *pron.* you
~men² ~們 *pron.* you
~men² te¹ ~們的 *pron.* your, yours
~men² tzu⁴ chi³ ~們自己 *pron.* yourselves
~te¹ ~的 *pron.* your, yours
~tzu⁴ chi³ ~自己 *pron.* yourself
NIANG² 娘 *n.* miss, woman, mother, wife
NIAO³ 鳥 *n.* bird
~ch'ao² ~巢 *n.* nest
~lei⁴ hsüeh² ~類學 *n.* ornithology
NIAO⁴ 尿 *n.* urine; *v.* urinate; *a.* urinary
NIEN² 年 *n.* year; *a.* annual, yearly

133

~chi⁴ ~紀 *n.* age
~chia⁴ ~假 *n.* vacation, annual leave
~chien⁴ ~鑑 *n.* yearbook
~chin¹ ~金 *n.* annuity
~ch'ing¹ ~青 *a.* young
~lao³ ~老 *a.* old
~sui⁴ ~歲 *n.* age
~tai⁴ ~代 *n.* generation, dynasty, period, age
NIEN² 粘 *see* CHAN¹
NIEN⁴ 念 *v.* think, remember
~ching¹ ~經 *v.* chant psalms or prayers
~fo² chu¹ ~佛珠 *n.* rosary
~shu¹ ~書 *v.* read, study
NING² 寧 *n.* peace, repose, rest; *v.* prefer
~ching⁴ ~静 *a.* quiet, peaceful
~k'o³ ~可 *adv.* rather
NIU² 牛 *n.* cattle, cow, bull, ox
~jou⁴ ~肉 *n.* beef
~nai³ ~奶 *n.* milk
~p'ai³ ~排 *n.* beefsteak
~tou⁴ ~痘 *n.* cowpox
~yu² ~油 *n.* butter
NU² 奴 *n.* slave, servant
~i⁴ ~役 *n.* slavery
~li⁴ ~隸 *n.* slave
NU³ 努 *v.* endeavor
~li⁴ ~力 *v.* endeavor
NU⁴ 怒 *a.* angry; *n.* anger
~ch'i⁴ ~氣 *n.* anger
NUAN³ 暖 *a.* mild, warm
~ch'i⁴ ~氣 *n.* steam
~ho² ~和 *a.* warm climate
~hua¹ fang² ~花房 *n.* greenhouse, hothouse
NUNG² 農 *n.* agriculture, farmer; *v.* cultivate
~fu¹ ~夫 *n.* farmer, peasant
~min² chieh¹ chi² ~民階級 *n.* peasant class**
~ts'un¹ ~村 *a.* rural
~yeh⁴ ~業 *n.* agriculture
~yeh⁴ chia¹ ~業家 *n.* agriculturalist
~yeh⁴ pu⁴ ~業部 *n.* Department of Agriculture
(*U.S.*)

NUNG⁴ 弄 *v.* play, handle
NU³ ~女 *n.* female, girl, woman, maid, maiden
~ch'üan² ~權 *n.* woman's rights
~erh² ~兒 *n.* daughter
~hai² tzu¹ ~孩子 *n.* girl
~hsing⁴ ~性 *n.* female, womanhood
~hsü⁴ ~婿 *n.* son-in-law
~hsüeh² hsiao⁴ ~學校 *n.* girl's school
~hsüeh² sheng¹ ~學生 *n.* schoolgirl
~jen² ~人 *n.* woman
~ling² ~伶 *n.* actress
~p'eng² yu³ ~朋友 *n.* girl friend
~p'u² ~僕 *n.* maidservant
~shen² ~神 *n.* goddess
~shih⁴ ~士 *n.* Miss, lady
~wang² ~王 *n.* Queen
~wu¹ ~巫 *n.* witch, sorceress

O

OU³ 偶 *n.* idol, image; *v.* mate; *adv.* unexpectedly
~hsiang⁴ ~像 *n.* idol
~jan² ~然 *adv.* accidentally

P

PA¹ 八 *n. & a.* eight
~che² ~折 *n.* twenty percent discount
~ku³ tiao⁴ ~股調 *n.* ancient Chinese examination system (" eight-legged essay ")
~yüeh⁴ ~月 *n.* August
PA¹ 巴 *n.* an ancient State
~chieh² ~結 *v.* flatter
PA¹ 吧 *a.* dumb. [Also a final particle]
PA² 拔 *v.* uproot
~ch'u² ~除 *v.* uproot, extirpate
~ho² ~河 *n.* tug-of-war
~ken¹ ~根 *v.* uproot

135

~ts'ao³ ~草 v. pull up weeds

~ya² ~牙 v. extract teeth

~ya² ch'ien² ~牙鉗 n. forceps (med.)

PA³ 把 v. hold. ~⁴ n. handle

~ping³ ~柄 n. handle, evidence

~wo⁴ ~握 n. security

PA⁴ 爸 n. papa, daddy, pop, father

PA⁴ 罷 v. stop, cease

~kung¹ ~工 n. work strike; v. strike

~k'o⁴ ~課 n. student's strike

~mien³ ch'üan² ~免權 n. power of recall

PA⁴ 霸 n. tyrant; v. govern, encroach

~chan⁴ ~佔 v. occupy by force

PAI² 白 n. & a. white

~chin¹ ~金 n. platinum, white gold

~cho² ~濁 n. gonorrhea

~chou⁴ ~晝 n. daytime

~chung³ ~種 n. white race

~ch'i² ~旗 n. white flag

~e⁴ ~俄 n. White Russian

~fan² ~攀 n. alum

~hou² ~喉 n. diphtheria

~je⁴ ~熱 n. white heat

~kung¹ ~宮 n. White House (U.S.)

~lan² ti⁴ chiu³ ~蘭地酒 n. brandy

~se⁴ ~色 n. white

~tai⁴ ~帶 n. leucorrhea

~t'ien¹ ~天 n. daytime

~ts'ai⁴ ~菜 n. cabbage

PAI³ 百 n. & a. hundred

~ho² ~合 n. lily flower

~huo⁴ shang¹ tien⁴ ~貨商店 n. department store

~hsing⁴ ~姓 n. people, population

~k'o¹ ch'üan² shu¹ ~科全書 n. encyclopedia

~ling² niao³ ~靈鳥 n. lark

~wan⁴ ~萬 n. million

~yeh⁴ ch'uang¹ ~葉窗 n. venetian blind

PAI³ 擺 n. pendulum, ferry; v. unfold, expand, expose

~pu⁴ ~佈 v. arrange

136

~tu⁴ ~渡 *v.* ferry
~t'o¹ ~脱 *v.* get rid of
PAI⁴ 拜 *v.* worship
~chin¹ chu³ i⁴ ~金主義 *n.* mammonism
~fang⁸ ~訪 *v.* visit
~ling³ ~領 *v.* accept
~nien² ~年 *v.* make a New Year's call
~t'o¹ ~託 *v.* request
PAI⁴ 敗 *n.* defeat; *v.* defeat, ruin, destroy
~chang⁴ ~仗 *n.* defeat
~huai⁴ ~壞 *v.* ruin, destroy
~ping¹ ~兵 *n.* defeated troops
PAN¹ 搬 *v.* remove
~chia¹ ~家 *n.* change living quarters
~ch'ü⁴ ~去 *v.* move away
~nung⁴ ~弄 *v.* carry tales
~yün⁴ ~運 *n.* transportation
PAN¹ 般 *n.* sort, kind, class
PAN¹ 班 *n.* class, squad
~chang³ ~長 *n.* squad leader, class leader
PAN³ 板 *n.* plank, board, block, metal plate
~teng⁴ ~凳 *n.* bench
PAN⁴ 半 *n.* half; *v.* halve
~ching⁴ ~徑 *n.* radius
~jih⁴ ~日 *n.* half-day
~kuan¹ fang¹ ~官方 *a.* semi-official
~nien² ~年 *n.* half-year
~tao³ ~島 *n.* peninsula
~tien³ chung¹ ~點鐘 *n.* half-hour
~yeh⁴ ~夜 *n.* midnight
~yüan² ~圓 *n.* semicircle, half dollar
~yüeh⁴ ~月 *n.* half-month
PAN⁴ 辦 *v.* manage, act, execute
~fa³ ~法 *n.* method, plan
~kung¹ ch'u⁴ ~公處 *n.* office
~kung¹ shih⁴ ~公室 *n.* office
~kung¹ t'ing¹ ~公廳 *n.* office
~li³ ~理 *v.* manage, do
PANG¹ 幫 *n.* clique; *v.* help
~chu⁴ ~助 *v.* help, assist
~hsiung¹ ~兇 *n.* accomplice

137

~**shou³** ~手 *n.* helper, assistant
PAO¹ 包 *v.* wrap; *n.* pack, bundle
~**feng¹** ~封 *n.* enclosure
~**han²** ~含 *v.* contain
~**hsiang¹** ~箱 *n.* theater box
~**hsiang¹ hsi²** ~箱席 *n.* box seat
~**kuan³** ~管 *v.* guarantee
~**kung¹** ~工 *n.* contract work
~**kuo³** ~裹 *n.* parcel, package
~**k'uo⁴** ~括 *v.* include
~**lan³** ~攬 *v.* monopolize
~**pan⁴** ~辦 *n.* contract
~**wei²** ~圍 *v.* encircle, surround
PAO³ 飽 *v.* eat enough, satiate; *n.* satiety
~**ho²** ~和 *v.* saturate
~**ho² tien³** ~和點 *n.* saturation point
PAO³ 寶 *n.* jewel, gem; *a.* precious, valuable
~**chien⁴** ~劍 *n.* sacred sword
~**ching⁴** ~鏡 *n.* sacred mirror
~**hsi³** ~璽 *n.* privy seal
~**kuei⁴** ~貴 *a.* precious
~**k'u⁴** ~庫 *n.* treasury
~**shih²** ~石 *n.* precious stone, gem
~**tien⁴** ~殿 *n.* shrine
~**t'a³** ~塔 *n.* pagoda
~**tso⁴** ~座 *n.* jeweled seat, throne
~**wu⁴** ~物 *n.* treasure
PAO³ 保 *n.* guardian, protector, guarantee; *v.* recommend, protect, guarantee
~**chang⁴** ~障 *v.* guarantee
~**cheng⁴** ~證 *n.* & *v.* guarantee
~**cheng⁴ chin¹** ~證金 *n.* monetary security
~**cheng⁴ jen²** ~證人 *n.* guarantor
~**cheng⁴ shu¹** ~證書 *n.* letter of guarantee
~**chü³** ~舉 *v.* recommend
~**ch'ih² chung¹ li⁴** ~持中立 *v.* be neutral
~**ch'üan²** ~全 *v.* keep safe, preserve
~**hu⁴** ~護 *v.* protect; *n.* protection
~**hu⁴ jen²** ~護人 *n.* guardian
~**hsien³** ~險 *v.* insure; *n.* insurance
~**hsien³ fei⁴** ~險費 *n.* insurance premium

138

~hsien³ hsiang¹ ~險箱 *n.* safe

~hsien³ kung¹ ssu¹ ~險公司 *n.* insurance company

~hsien³ ssu¹ ~險絲 *n.* fuse (*elec.*)

~hsien³ tai⁴ ~險帶 *n.* safety belt

~hsien³ tan¹ ~險單 insurance policy

~kuan³ jen² ~管人 *n.* custodian

~liu² ~留 *v.* reserve

~mu³ ~姆 *n.* baby nurse

~piao¹ ~標 *v.* escort

~shou³ ~守 *v.* keep; *a.* conservative

~shou³ tang³ ~守党 *n.* conservative party

~ts‘un² ~存 *v.* keep, conserve

~wei⁴ ~衛 *v.* defend

~yang³ ~養 *v.* nourish; *n.* maintenance

PAO⁴ 報 *n.* journal, newspaper; *v.* report, recompense

~chih³ ~紙 *n.* newspaper

~ch‘ou² ~仇 *v.* revenge

~ch‘ou² ~酬 *n.* remuneration

~kao⁴ ~告 *v.* report

~ming² ~名 *v.* register

~ta² ~答 *v.* recompense

~ying⁴ ~應 *n.* retribution

PAO⁴ 抱 *v.* embrace, hold

~ch‘ien⁴ ~歉 *v.* feel sorry, apologize

~fu⁴ ~負 *n.* aspiration

~k‘uei⁴ ~愧 *v*, feel shame

~ping⁴ ~病 *v.* get sick

~pu⁴ p‘ing² ~不平 *v.* bear a grudge

~yüan⁴ ~怨 *v.* grudge

PAO⁴ 暴 *a.* violent; *v.* ill-treat, abuse. P‘U⁴ *v.* expose

~chün¹ ~君 *n.* tyrant

~feng¹ ~風 *n.* gale

~feng¹ yü³ ~風雨 *n.* storm

~p‘o⁴ ~破 *v.* demolish

~tung⁴ ~動 *n.* riot, uprising, revolt

~t‘u² ~徒 *n.* rebel

~tsao⁴ ~躁 *a.* hot-tempered

p‘u⁴ lou⁴ ~露 *v.* expose

139

PEI¹ 悲 *n.* grief, sadness
~**ai¹** ~哀 *a.* melancholy
~**chü⁴** ~劇 *a.* tragic; *n.* tragedy
~**ko¹** ~歌 *n.* monody
~**kuan¹** ~観 *a.* pessimistic
~**kuan¹ che³** ~観者 *n.* pessimist
~**kuan¹ chu³ i⁴** ~観主義 *n.* pessimism
~**shang¹** ~傷 *a.* sad
~**t'ung⁴** ~痛 *a.* grievous
PEI³ 北 *a.* & *n.* north; *a.* northern
~**chi²** ~極 *n.* North Pole
~**chi² hsing¹** ~極星 *n.* North Star
~**fang¹** ~方 *a.* & *n.* north; *a.* northern
~**wei⁴ san¹ shih² pa¹ tu⁴** ~緯三十八度 *n.* 38th Parallel
~**yang² chün¹ fa²** ~洋軍閥 *n.* northern warlords
PEI⁴ 被 *v.* cover; *n.* bedcover, quilt; *prep.* by (action)
~**ju⁴** ~褥 *n.* bedclothes, bedding
~**kao⁴** ~告 *n.* defendant
~**p'ien⁴** ~騙 *v.* be deceived
~**sha¹** ~殺 *n.* be killed
~**tan¹** ~單 *n.* sheet, bedspread
~**tan⁴ mien⁴** ~單面 *n.* beaten zone
~**tung⁴** ~動 *a.* passive
PEI⁴ 背 *n.* back, opposite
~**chi³** ~脊 *n.* backbone
~**ching³** ~景 *n.* background
~**mien⁴** ~面 *n.* opposite
~**p'an⁴** ~叛 *v.* rebel
~**sung⁴** ~誦 *v.* recite
~**t'ung⁴** ~痛 *n.* backache
~**yüeh¹** ~約 *v.* break the contract
PEI⁴ 倍 *a.* double
~**shu⁴** ~數 *n.* multiple
PEI⁴ 備 *v.* prepare
~**chien⁴** ~件 *n.* spare parts
~**wang⁴ lu⁴** ~忘錄 *n.* memorandum
PEI⁴ 輩 *n.* generation
PEN³ 本 *n.* capital, copy, volume, root, origin, beginning; *a.* original, natural

140

~chou¹ ~週 *n.* this week
~ch'ien² ~錢 *n.* monetary capital, principal
~jen² ~人 *adv.* in person
~jih⁴ ~日 *n.* today, this day
~kuo² ~國 *n.* native country
~kuo² yü³ ~國語 *n.* mother tongue
~li⁴ ~利 *n.* monetary principal and interest
~neng² ~能 *n.* instinct
~nien² ~年 *n.* this year
~p'iao⁴ ~票 *n.* bank note
~ti⁴ ~地 *n.* native
~wei⁴ ~位 *n.* standard
~wei⁴ chu³ i⁴ ~位主義 *n.* group egoism**
~yüeh⁴ ~月 *n.* this month
PI¹ 逼 *v.* press, compel
~p'o⁴ ~迫 *v.* force
PI² 鼻 *n.* nose
~ch'u¹ hsüeh⁴ ~出血 *n.* nosebleed
~k'ung³ ~孔 *n.* nostrils
~liang² ~梁 *n.* bridge of nose
~t'i⁴ ~涕 *n.* snivel
~tsu³ ~祖 *n.* founder, first ancestor
~yen¹ ~煙 *n.* snuff
PI³ 筆 *n.* pen, pencil, brush
~chi⁴ ~記 *n.* note
~chi⁴ ~跡 *n.* handwriting
~chi⁴ pu⁴ ~記簿 *n.* notebook
~hua⁴ ~畫 *n.* stroke (writing)
~ming² ~名 *n.* pen name
PI³ 比 *n.* comparison; *v.* compare
~chiao⁴ ~較 *v.* compare
~fang¹ ~方 *n.* & *prep.* for instance
~li⁴ ~例 *n.* proportion
~lü⁴ ~率 *n.* rate
~sai⁴ ~賽 *n.* contest, competition, match
~yü⁴ ~喻 *n.* metaphor, simile, analogy
PI⁴ 閉 *v.* close, shut
~hui⁴ ~會 *v.* adjourn a meeting
~mu⁴ ~幕 *v.* drop the curtain
PI⁴ 避 *v.* flee from, avoid, retire
~chen⁴ ch'i⁴ ~震器 *n.* absorber

~hsien² ~嫌 *v.* avoid suspicion

~lei² chen¹ ~雷針 *n.* lightning rod

~mien³ ~免 *v.* avoid, prevent

~nan⁴ ~難 *v.* flee for refuge

~shu³ ~暑 *v.* pass the summer

~tsui⁴ ~罪 *v.* avoid punishment

PI⁴ 必 *v. aux.* must, will, ought; *adv.* certainly, surely, necessarily

~hsü¹ ~需 *v.* require

~ting⁴ ~定 *adv.* certainly

PI⁴ 壁 *n.* wall

~hu³ ~虎 *n.* small lizard

PI⁴ 幣 *n.* money, coin, wealth, presents

~chih⁴ ~制 *n.* currency

PI⁴ 畢 *v.* finish

~ching⁴ ~竟 *adv.* after all, at last

~yeh⁴ ~業 *v.* graduate; *n.* graduation

~yeh⁴ k'ao³ shih⁴ ~業考試 *n.* graduation examination

~yeh⁴ sheng¹ ~業生 *n.* graduate

~yeh⁴ tien³ li³ ~業典禮 *n.* commencement ceremonies

~yeh⁴ wen² p'ing² ~業文憑 *n.* diploma

PIAO¹ 標 *n.* signal, flag, warrant

~chi⁴ ~記 *n.* mark, sign

~chun³ ~準 *n.* standard

~ch'iang¹ ~鎗 *n.* javelin

~pen³ ~本 *n.* specimen, sample

PIAO³ 表 *v.* display, show; *n.* time table, list, manifest, instrument gage

~chüeh² ~決 *v.* vote

~ch'ih³ ~尺 *n.* rear gun sight

~hsien⁴ ~現 *n.* demonstration, performance -

~ko² ~格 *n.* blank form

~mien⁴ ~面 *n.* surface

~shuai⁴ ~率 *n.* leadership examples

~ts'e⁴ ~冊 *n.* reference book

PIEH² 別 *v.* separate, part

~chen¹ ~針 *n.* pin

~ch'u⁴ ~處 *adv.* elsewhere

~hao⁴ ~號 *n.* nickname

142

~jen² ~人 *pron.* other
~ko⁴ ~個 *a.* else, other
~li² ~離 *v.* depart; *n.* departure
~shu⁴ ~墅 *n.* villa
PIEN¹ 邊 *n.* edge, side, margin, bank, frontier, boundary
~chiang¹ ~疆 *n.* frontier region
~ch'ü¹ ~區 *n.* frontier
~fang² ~防 *n.* frontier defense
~hsien⁴ ~線 *n.* boundary line
PIEH¹ 編 *v.* arrange, compose
~chi² ~輯 *v.* edit; *n.* editor
~chih¹ ~織 *v.* knit
~i⁴ ~譯 *v.* edit and translate
~p'ai² ~排 *v.* arrange
~ting⁴ ~訂 *v.* revise
PIEN⁴ 辨 *v.* distinguish, separate
~jen⁴ ~認 *v.* recognize, identify
~pieh² ~別 *v.* distinguish; *n.* distinction
PIEN⁴ 變 *v.* transform, change, reform; *n.* change, alternation; *a.* changeable
~ch'ien¹ ~遷 *n.* vicissitude
~hua⁴ ~化 *n.* change; *v.* transform
~hsi⁴ fa³ ~戲法 *n.* juggle
~hsing² ~形 *n.* metamorphosis
~hsing² ch'ung² ~形蟲 *n.* amoeba
~keng⁴ ~更 *v.* change, alter
~ku⁴ ~故 *n.* misfortune
~luan⁴ ~亂 *n.* rebellion
~t'ai⁴ ~態 *a.* abnormal
PIEN⁴ 遍 *n.* time, frequency. P'IEN⁴ *adv.* everywhere
PIEN⁴ 便 *n.* convenience
~cho² ~酌 *n.* informal dinner
~i¹ ~衣 *n.* ordinary dress
~i¹ tui⁴ ~衣隊 *n.* plainclothes men
~li⁴ ~利 *a.* convenient; *n.* convenience; *v.* facilitate
~pi⁴ ~祕 *n.* constipation
p'ien² i² ~宜 *a.* cheap
PING¹ 兵 *n.* soldier, enlisted men

143

~**chien⁴** ~艦 *n.* battleship, warship

~**ch'i⁴** ~器 *n.* arms, weapons

~**fa³** ~法 *n.* strategy

~**hsiang³** ~餉 *n.* soldiers' pay

~**kung¹** ~工 *n.* Ordnance (*mil.*)

~**kung¹ ch'ang³** ~工廠 *n.* arsenal

~**k'o¹** ~科 *n.* arm, branch (*mil.*)

~**li⁴** ~力 *n.* unit strength (*mil.*)

~**li⁴ p'ei⁴ pei⁴** ~力配備 *n.* distribution of troops

~**pien⁴** ~變 *n.* mutiny

~**ying²** ~營 *n.* barracks

PING¹ 冰 *n.* ice

~**chu⁴** ~柱 *n.* icicle

~**ch'i² lin²** ~淇淋 *n.* ice cream

~**ch'uan¹** ~川 *n.* glacier

~**hsiang¹** ~箱 *n.* icebox, refrigerator

~**hsieh²** ~鞋 *n.* iceskates

~**pao²** ~雹 *n.* hail (frozen rain)

~**shan¹** ~山 *n.* iceberg

~**tao³** ~島 *n.* iceberg

~**tung⁴** ~凍 *a.* frozen

PING³ 餅 *n.* cake, pastry

~**kan¹** ~乾 *n.* biscuit

PING⁴ 並 *adv.* also, equally; *conj.* and

~**chien¹** ~肩 *adv.* & *a.* abreast

~**ch'ieh³** ~且 *adv.* also, moreover

~**fei¹** ~非 *adv.* not

~**hsing²** ~行 *a.* parallel

PING⁴ 併 *v.* annex, unite

~**lieh⁴** ~列 *adv.* & *a.* abreast

~**t'un¹** ~吞 *v.* annex

PING⁴ 病 *n.* disease, illness, sickness

~**cheng¹** ~徵 *n.* sign of disease

~**chuang⁴** ~狀 *n.* symptom

~**chung⁴** ~重 *a.* very sick

~**jen²** ~人 *n.* patient

~**yü⁴** ~愈 *n.* health recovery

~**yüan⁴** ~院 *n.* hospital

PO¹ 波 *n.* wave, ripple

~**chi²** ~及 *v.* get involved

~**ch'ang²** ~長 *n.* wave length

~lang⁴ ~浪 *n.* wave, ripple
~lo² mi⁴ ~羅蜜 *n.* pineapple
~wen² ~紋 *n.* wave, ripple (shape)
PO¹ 剝 *v.* flay, peel
~hsüeh¹ chieh¹ chi² ~削階級 *n.* exploiting
class**
~to² ~奪 *v.* deprive
PO² 伯 *n.* uncle
~chüeh² ~儕 *n.* Earl, Count
~fu⁴ ~父 *n.* father's older brother (uncle)
~mu³ ~母 *n.* wife of father's older brother (aunt)
PO² 薄 ~⁴ *n.* peppermint; *a.* thin, shabby, slight
~² ch'ing² ~情 *a.* cold (feeling)
~jo⁴ ~弱 *n.* week, feeble
~ming⁴ ~命 *n.* unfortunate life
~mu⁴ ~暮 *n.* evening
~⁴ ho² ~荷 *n.* peppermint
PO⁴ 播 *v.* sow, spread abroad. ~³ *v.* winnow
~³ ku⁸ ~穀 *v.* winnow grain
~⁴ chung⁸ ~種 *v.* sow seeds
~nung⁴ ~弄 *v.* instigate
~sung⁴ ~送 *v.* broadcast
PU³ 捕 *v.* seize, arrest
~huo⁴ ~獲 *n. & v.* capture
PU³ 補 *v.* patch, mend
~chi³ ~給 *n.* supplies
~chiu⁴ ~救 *v.* rectify
~chu⁴ ~助 *a.* auxiliary
~ch'ung¹ ~充 *v.* refill, replenish
~ch'ung¹ tui⁴ ~充隊 *n.* troop replacement
PU⁴ 步 *n.* step, pace, infantry
~ch'iang¹ ~槍 *n.* rifle
~ch'iang¹ pa³ ch'ang³ ~槍靶場 *n.* rifle range
~ch'iang¹ pan¹ ~槍班 *n.* rifle squad
~hsing² ~行 *v.* go on foot
~ping¹ ~兵 *n.* infantry
~ping¹ p'ao⁴ ~兵砲 *n.* rifle
~shao⁴ ~哨 *n.* outguard
PU⁴ 部 *n.* bureau, department, ministry, headquarters, section, class, genus, category
~chang³ ~長 *n.* minister, head of a department

145

~**fen¹** ~分 *n.* part

~**hsia⁴** ~下 *n.* subordinate

~**lao⁴** ~落 *n.* tribe

PU⁴ 不 *adv.* no, not, never

~**an¹** ~安 *a.* uneasy

~**cheng⁴ ch'ang²** ~正常 *a.* abnormal, unusual

~**chi²** ~吉 *a.* unlucky

~**chi² ko²** ~及格 *a.* unqualified

~**chiu³** ~久 *adv.* before long

~**chung⁴ yao⁴** ~重要 *a.* unimportant

~**chüan⁴** ~倦 *a.* untiring

~**ch'in¹ fan⁴ t'iao² yüeh¹** ~侵犯條約 *n.* non aggression treaty

~**ch'ü¹** ~屈 *a.* persistent

~**fa³** ~法 *a.* unlawful, illegal

~**ho² tso⁴** ~合作 *n.* noncooperation

~**hsing⁴** ~幸 *a.* unlucky

~**i⁴** ~意 *a.* unexpected, accidental

~**kou⁴** ~够 *a.* insufficient

~**kuan¹ hsin¹** ~關心 *a.* unconcerned, indifferent

~**kuan⁴** ~慣 *a.* unaccustomed

~**nai⁴ fan²** ~耐煩 *n.* impatience; *a.* impatient

~**pi⁴** ~必 *a.* unnecessary, needless

~**pien⁴** ~變 *a.* unchangeable

~**p'ing² teng³** ~平等 *a.* unequal

~**p'ing² teng³ t'iao² yüeh¹** ~平等條約 *n.* unequal treaty

~**tang¹** ~當 *a.* improper, unsuitable, unfit

~**tung⁴ ch'an³** ~動産 *n.* real estate, real property

~**t'o³** ~妥 *a.* unsafe

~**wen³** ~穩 *a.* unsafe, unstable

~**yao⁴ chin³** ~要緊 *a.* unimportant, insignificant, trifling

PU⁴ 布 *n.* cloth; *v.* display, announce

~**chih⁴** ~置 *v.* arrange; *n.* arrangement

~**kao⁴** ~告 *v.* announce; *n.* announcement

~**shih¹** ~施 *n.* charity; *v.* relieve

PU⁴ 佈 *v.* declare, spread

~**chih⁴** ~置 *v.* arrange; *n.* arrangement

~**ching³** ~景 *n.* scenery

~**kao⁴** ~告 *v.* announce

P'

P'A² 爬 *v.* creep, crawl, climb
　~kao¹ ~高 *v.* climb (aviation)
　~shang⁴ ~上 *v.* climb up
P'A⁴ 怕 *v.* feel fear; *n.* fear, dread; *a.* fearful, dreadful
P'AI² 排 *v.* arrange, dispose, expel; *n.* row (line), platoon
　~chang³ ~長 *n.* platoon commander
　~chieh³ ~解 *v.* mediate, compromise
　~ch'ih⁴ ~斥 *v.* exclude, reject
　~ch'iu² ~球 *n.* volleyball
　~hsieh⁴ ~泄 *v.* excrete; *n.* excretion
　~hsieh⁴ wu⁴ ~泄物 *n.* excrement, excretion
　~ku³ ~骨 *n.* sparerib
　~lieh⁴ ~列 *v.* arrange
　~shui³ kou¹ ~水溝 *n.* drain
　~tzu⁴ chi¹ ~字機 *n.* linotype
　~wai⁴ ~外 *n.* exclusion
P'AI² 牌 *n.* card, medal, shield
P'AI⁴ 派 *v.* sent, assign; *n.* party
　~ch'ien³ ~遣 *v.* dispatch
　~pieh² ~別 *n.* branch, sect
　~ssu¹ ~司 *n.* pass
P'AN² 盤 *n.* dish, plate, expense; *v.* examine
　~ch'uan¹ ~川 *n.* traveling expense
　~suan⁴ ~算 *v.* calculate
　~tieh² ~碟 n. dish
P'AN⁴ 判 *v.* judge
　~chüeh² ~決 *n.* sentence, decision (law)
　~kuan¹ ~官 *n.* judge
　~tuan⁴ 斷 *v.* judge; *n.* judgement
　~tz'u² ~詞 *n.* law sentence
P'ANG² 旁 *prep.* by, near, beside; *n.* side
　~jen² ~人 *pron.* others
　~kuan¹ che³ ~觀者 *n.* bystander
　~pien¹ ~邊 *n.* side
P'AO³ 跑 *v.* run

147

~ma³ ~馬 *n.* races

~ma³ ch'ang³ ~馬場 *n.* horse racing co'urse

~pu⁴ ~步 *v.* run, exercise

~tao⁴ ~道 *n.* airdrome runway

P'AO⁴ 砲 *n.* gun, cannon, artillery piece

~chi¹ ~擊 *v.* bombard (artillery)

~chien⁴ ~艦 *n.* gunboat

~hui¹ ~灰 *n.* cannon fodder

~huo³ ~火 *n.* artillery fire, gunfire

~ping¹ ~兵 *n.* artillery units

~tan⁴ ~彈 *n.* shell

~t'ai² ~臺 *n.* fort

P'EI⁴ 配 *v.* match

~chi³ ~給 *v.* ration

~chien⁴ ~件 *n.* spare parts

~ou° ~偶 *n.* match (husband or wife)

P'EN² 盆 *n.* basin, tub

~ching³ ~景 *n.* flowerpot

P'ENG² 朋 *n.* friend, party, group

~tang³ ~黨 *n.* party, clique

~yu³ ~友 *n.* friend

P'ENG⁴ 碰 *v.* bump, crash

~chien⁴ ~見 *v.* meet

~p'o⁴ ~破 *v.* damage by collision

P'I¹ 匹 *n.* pair, mate

~³ fu¹ ~夫 *n.* common people

~ti² ~敵 *v.* get a match for

P'I¹ 批 *v.* criticize, comment

~fa¹ ~發 *n.* wholesale

~p'ing² ~評 *n.* criticism

P'I² 皮 *n.* skin, bark, fur

~huo⁴ ~貨 *n.* fur

~ko² ~革 *n.* leather

~pao¹ ~包 *n.* woman's handbag

~p'ao² ~袍 *n.* fur gown

~tai⁴ ~帶 *n.* waistband

~t'iao² ~條 *n.* strap

P'I² 疲 *a.* tired, exhausted, fatigued

~chüan⁴ ~倦 *a.* tired, fatigued; *n.* fatigue

P'IAO⁴ 票 *n.* ticket, banknote, warrant, bill

~fang² ~房 *n.* ticket office

148

~hui⁴ ~匯 *v.* remit by draft

~mien⁴ e² ~面額 *n.* face value

P'IEN¹ 偏 *a.* inclined, partial; *n.* leaning

~chien⁴ ~見 *n.* prejudice

~ch'a¹ ~差 *n.* deviation, bias

P'IEN¹ 篇 *n.* leaf, essay, chapter, page

~fu² ~幅 *n.* pages

P'IEN⁴ 片 *n.* piece, slice, strip, visiting card

~k'o⁴ ~刻 *n.* moment, instant

~mien⁴ ~面 *a.* one-sided; *n.* prejudice

~mien⁴ hsing⁴ ~面性 *n.* one-sidedness**

~yen² ~言 *n.* a few words

P'IEN⁴ 騙 *v.* cheat, deceive, dupe, swindle, defraud

~jen² ~人 *v.* defraud

~tzu¹ ~子 *n.* swindler

P'IEN⁴ 遍 *see* PIEN⁴

P'IN² 貧 *a.* poor

~hsüeh⁴ cheng⁴ ~血症 *n.* anemia

~jen² ~人 *n.* poor people

~k'u³ ~苦 *a.* poor

P'IN³ 品 *n.* behavior, conduct, goods, class

~chi² ~級 *n.* class, grade

~chih² ~質 *n.* brand, quality

~hsing² ~行 *n.* behavior, conduct

~ko² ~格 *n.* character

~mao⁴ ~貌 *n.* conduct and appearance

~p'ing² ~評 *v.* criticize

P'ING² ~平 *n.* flat, level; *a.* smooth, flat, level, plain

~ching⁴ ~静 *a.* quiet

~chün¹ ~均 *n.* average

~ch'ang² ~常 *a.* ordinary, common, usual

~fang¹ ~方 *n.* square (*math.*)

~hsing² ~行 *a.* parallel

~mien⁴ ~面 *n.* plane

~min² ~民 *n.* commons, commoner

~teng³ ~等 *n.* equality; *a.* equal

~yüan² ~原 *n.* plain

P'ING² 評 *v.* discuss, settle, criticize

~lun⁴ ~論 *v.* criticize

149

~p'an⁴ ~判 v. judge
~p'an⁴ yüan² ~判員 n. umpire, referee
P'ING² 瓶 n. bottle
P'ING² 憑 n. proof, evidence; v. lean upon, trust
to; adv. according to
~chü⁴ ~據 n. evidence, proof
~hsin⁴ ~信 v. believe
~tan¹ ~單 n. certificate
P'O¹ 坡 n. slope
~tu⁴ ~度 n. slope, gradient
P'O² 婆 n. grandmother, grandma, dame, husband's mother (mother-in-law)
~chia¹ ~家 n. husband's family
P'O⁴ 迫 v. compel, urge, force, press
~chin⁴ ~近 a. imminent
~ch'ieh⁴ ~切 a. urgent
~hsieh² ~脅 v. coerce
P'O⁴ 破 v. break, destroy
~ch'an³ ~産 n. bankruptcy
~fei⁴ ~費 v. spend
~huai⁴ ~壞 v. destroy
~lieh⁴ ~裂 v. crack
~sui⁴ ~碎 v. smash
~sun³ ~損 n. damage
P'U¹ 鋪 ~⁴ n. [same as 舖] shop, bed; v. spread
out
~¹ chang¹ ~張 v. overdo
~kai⁴ ~蓋 n. quilt
~⁴ tzu¹ ~子 n. shop
P'U¹ 撲 v. strike, quench, whip
~k'o⁴ p'ai² ~克牌 n. poker (card game)
~mieh⁴ ~滅 v. quench
P'U³ 普 a. all, general, universal; adv. everywhere
~chi² te¹ ~及的 a. universal
~pien⁴ ~遍 a. universal
~t'ung¹ ~通 a. common, general
P'U⁴ 暴 see PAO⁴

150

S

SA³ 灑 *v.* sprinkle
~**shui³** ~水 *v.* sprinkle with water
SAI¹ 塞 *v.* stop up, obstruct; *n.* cork, plug, stopper. ~⁴ *n.* frontier
~ **k'ou³** ~口 *n.* line jack
~**tse²** ~責 *v.* avoid responsibility
~**tzu¹** ~子 *n.* stopper, cork, plug
~⁴ **wai⁴** ~外 *n.* beyond the frontier
SAI⁴ 賽 *v.* contest, compete; *n.* rivalry, match
~**ch'uan²** ~船 *n.* boat race
~**kuo⁴** ~過 *v.* surpass
~**ma³** ~馬 *n.* horse race
~**ma³ ch'ang³** ~馬場 *n.* race course
~**p'ao³** ~跑 *n.* & *v.* race
SAN¹ 三 *n.* & *a.* three
~**chiao³** ~角 *n.* trigonometry
~**chiao³ chia⁴** ~脚架 *n.* tripod
~**chiao³ hsing²** ~角形 *n.* triangle
~**chiao³ lien⁴ ai⁴** ~角戀愛 *n.* triangular love
~**chiao³ pan³** ~角板 *n.* set square
~**ch'i¹ wu³ chien³ tsu¹** ~七五減租 *n.* 37.5% rent reduction*
~**fan³ yün⁴ tung⁴** ~反運動 *n.* three anti-movements**
~**ho² t'u³** ~合土 *n.* concrete
~**kuo² yen³ i⁴** ~國演義 *n.* Romance of the Three Kingdoms*
~**meng³ chan⁴ shu⁴** ~猛戰術 *n.* " three fierce movements " tactics**
~**min² chu³ i⁴** ~民主義 *n.* Three Principles of the People*
~**min² chu³ i⁴ ch'ing¹ nien² t'uan²** ~民主義青年團 *n.* Three Principles Youth Corps*
~**ming² chih⁴** ~明治 *n.* sandwich
~**pa¹ hsien⁴** ~八線 *n.* 38th Parallel
~**ta⁴ chi⁴ lü⁴ pa¹ hsiang⁴ chu⁴ i⁴** ~大紀律八項注意 *n.* Three Rules and Eight Remarks**

151

~tang⁴ ~檔 *n.* high gear
~tien³ lao⁴ ti⁴ ~點落地 *n.* three-point landing
~tzu⁴ ching¹ ~字經 *n.* Trimetrical Classic
~yüeh⁴ ~月 n. March
SAN⁴ 散 *v.* scatter, disperse. ~³ *v.* break up; *n.* powder
  ~³ chi⁴ ~劑 *n.* powder (*med.*)
  ~fei¹ ~飛 *n.* gunnery dispersion
  ~po⁴ ~播 *v.* spread
  ~pu⁴ ~步 *n.* walk
  ~wen² ~文 *n.* prose
  ~⁴ hui⁴ ~會 *a.* adjourned
  ~ping¹ tung⁴ ~兵洞 *n.* foxhole
  ~pu⁴ ~布 *v.* scatter
SANG¹ 桑 *n.* mulberry
  ~shu⁴ ~樹 *n.* mulberry tree
  ~tzu³ ~子 *n.* mulberry seed
  ~tzu³ ~梓 *n.* one's native place
SANG¹ 喪 *n.* funeral; *v.* die, mourn. ~⁴ *v.* lose, ruin, destroy.
  ~¹ li³ ~禮 *n.* funeral rites
  ~shih⁴ ~事 *n.* funeral
  ~⁴ shih¹ ~失 *v.* lose
  ~tan³ ~膽 *a.* discouraged
SAO³ 掃 *v.* sweep, brush
  ~ch'u² ~除 *v.* sweep
  ~ch'u² wen² mang² kung¹ tso⁴ wei³ yüan² hui⁴ ~除文盲工作委員會 *n.* Commission for Eliminating Illiteracy**
  ~ch'u⁴ ~帚 *n.* broom
  ~ch'u⁴ hsing¹ ~帚星 *n.* comet
  ~mu⁴ ~墓 *v.* visit the grave
  ~tang⁴ ~蕩 *v.* mop up
  ~ti⁴ ~地 *v.* clean a floor
SAO³ 嫂 *n.* wife of one's older brother (sister-in-law)
SE⁴ 色 *n.* color, tint
  ~ch'ing² ~情 *a.* obscene, erotic
  ~yü⁴ ~慾 *n.* lust (sex)
SEN¹ 森 *n.* forest, abundance; *a.* somber, thick
  ~lin² ~林 *n.* forest

~lin² hsüeh² ~林學 *n.* forestry
SO¹ 縮 *v.* shorten, abbreviate, draw back
~hsiao³ ~小 *v.* reduce (lose weight)
~hsieh³ ~寫 *n.* abbreviation
~shao³ ~少 *v.* decrease, reduce
~tuan³ ~短 *v.* shorten
SO³ 所 *n.* place. [suffix] station, department
~i³ ~以 *adv.* therefore, so
~te² shui⁴ ~得稅 *n.* income tax
~yu³ ~有 *n.* possession
~yu³ ch'üan² ~有權 *n.* ownership
SO³ 索 *n.* rope, cord ; *v.* demand, search
~cha⁴ ~詐 *v.* blackmail
~ch'iao² ~橋 *n.* cable bridge
~ch'ü³ ~取 *v.* demand
~p'ei² ~賠 *v.* claim damages
~yin³ ~引 *n.* index
SO³ 鎖 *n.* lock, chain ; *v.* lock
~lien⁴ ~鏈 *n.* shackles, bonds, chains
SU¹ 蘇 *v.* revive
~hsing³ ~醒 *v.* awake
SU² 俗 *a.* common ; *n.* custom
~hsi² ~習 *n.* custom
~t'ao⁴ te¹ ~套的 *a.* customary, conventional
~yü³ ~語 *n.* proverb
SU⁴ 速 *v.* invite, urge on ; *a.* quick, speedy, swift ;
 adv. speedily, quickly
~chan⁴ su⁴ chüeh² ~戰速決 *n.* a quick war and
 a quick decision
~chi⁴ ~記 *n.* shorthand
~she⁴ ~射 *n.* rapid fire
~she⁴ p'ao⁴ ~射砲 *n.* rapid-fire gun
~tu⁴ ~度 *n.* speed
~tu⁴ piao³ ~度表 *n.* speedometer
SU⁴ 素 *a.* plain, pure, simple
~chiao¹ ~交 *n.* old acquaintance
~hsing⁴ ~性 *n.* habit
~lai² ~來 *adv.* usually
~ts'ai⁴ ~菜 *n.* vegetable
~yüan⁴ ~願 *n.* original desire
SU⁴ 宿 *v.* lodge

153

~she⁴ ~舍 *n.* dormitory

~ying² ~營 *v.* encamp

~ying² ti⁴ ~營地 *n.* encampment

~yüan⁴ ~怨 *n.* grudge

SU⁴ 訴 *v.* tell, complain

~k'u³ ~苦 *v.* complain

~sung⁴ ~訟 *v.* accuse, charge

SUAN¹ 酸 *n.* acid; *a.* sour

~su⁴ ~素 *n.* acid

~t'ung⁴ ~痛 *a.* sore

SUAN⁴ 算 *v.* count, calculate, plan; *n* calculation

~hsüeh² ~學 *n.* mathematics

~ming⁴ che³ ~命者 *n.* fortune teller

~p'an² ~盤 *n.* abacus

~shu⁴ ~術 *n.* arithmetic

SUI¹ 雖 *conj.* although, but

~jan² ~然 *adv.* however

SUI² 隨 *v.* follow, accompany, imitate

~hou⁴ ~後 *adv.* afterward

~i⁴ ~意 *adv.* optionally, freely

~shih² ~時 *adv.* whenever

~ti⁴ ~地 *adv.* anywhere

~yüan² ~員 *n.* attache, aid-de-camp

SUI⁴ 歲 *n.* year, age; *a.* yearly, annual

~ch'u¹ ~出 *n.* year expenditure

~ch'u¹ ~初 *n.* beginning of the year

~mu⁴ ~暮 *n.* end of the year

~shou¹ ~收 *n.* annual income

~shu⁴ ~數 *n.* age

SUI⁴ 碎 *a.* broken; *n.* fragment

~p'ien⁴ ~片 *n.* fragment

~te¹ ~的 *a.* broken

SUN¹ 孫 *n.* grandson

~erh² nü³ ~兒女 *n.* child of one's son (grand-child)

SUN³ 損 *a.* injurious, damaged; *v.* injure

~hai⁴ ~害 *v.* injure, damage; *n.* harm

~shang¹ ~傷 *n.* injury

~shih¹ ~失 *n.* loss

SUNG¹ 鬆 *v.* untie, loosen, unfasten; *a.* loose, lax

SUNG⁴ 送 *v.* give, send

154

~li³ ~禮 *v.* present
~pieh² ~別 *v.* see off

SH

SHA¹ 沙 *n.* sand
~mo⁴ ~漠 *n.* desert
~ting¹ yü² ~丁魚 *n.* sardine
~t'an¹ ~灘 *n.* beach
SHA¹ 紗 *n.* yarn, gauze
~ch'uang¹ ~窗 *n.* window screen
~pu⁴ ~布 *n.* gauze
SHA¹ 殺 *v.* kill, slay; *n.* slaughter
SHAI⁴ 曬 *v.* dry
~kan¹ ~乾 *v.* make dry
SHAN¹ 山 *n.* mountain, hill
~feng¹ ~峰 *n.* peak
~hai³ ching¹ ~海經 *n.* Books of Mountains and Seas
~ku³ ~谷 *n.* valley, glen
~mo⁴ ~脈 *n.* mountain range
~shui³ ~水 *n.* landscape
~ting³ ~頂 *n.* hilltop
~tung⁴ ~洞 *n.* cave
~yang² ~羊 *n.* goat
SHAN³ 閃 *v.* shun, avoid; *n.* flash
~kuang¹ ~光 *n.* glare
~shuo⁴ ~爍 *v.* twinkle
~tien⁴ ~電 *n.* lightning
~tien⁴ chan⁴ ~電站 *n.* blitzkrieg
SHAN⁴ 善 *a.* good, honest, virtuous; *v.* approve
SHAN⁴ 扇 *n.* fan. ~¹ *v.* fan
SHANG¹ 商 *n.* trade, merchant; *v.* deliberate, consult
~chieh⁴ ~界 *n.* business circle
~ch'uan² ~船 *n.* merchantman
~fu⁴ ~埠 *n.* commercial port
~hao⁴ ~號 *n.* firm
~hui⁴ ~會 *n.* Chamber of Commerce
~hsüeh² yuan⁴ ~學院 *n.* college commerce

155

~i⁴ ~議 *v.* consult, discuss; *n.* consultation
~jen² ~人 *n.* merchant
~piao¹ ~標 *n.* trademark
~p'in³ ~品 *n.* commodity
~tien⁴ ~店 *n.* shop, store, firm
~wu⁴ ~務 *n.* commerce; *a.* commercial
~yeh⁴ ching⁴ cheng¹ ~業競争 *n.* commercial competition
~yeh⁴ hua⁴ ~業化 *v.* commercialize
~yeh⁴ hsün² huan² ~業循環 *n.* business cycle
~yeh⁴ pu⁴ ~業部 *n.* Ministry of Commerce**
SHANG¹ 傷 *n.* & *v.* wound; *n.* injury, harm; *v.* injure
~feng¹ ~風 *v.* catch cold
~hai⁴ ~害 *v.* injure, hurt
~han² cheng⁴ ~寒症 *n.* typhoid fever
~hen² ~痕 *n.* scar
~hsin¹ ~心 *n.* heartbreak
~wang² ~亡 *n.* casualties, dead and wounded
SHANG³ 賞 *v.* bestow, reward
~shih⁴ ~識 *v.* appreciate
~tz'u⁴ ~賜 *v.* bestow
SHANG⁴ 上 *adv.* above, up; *prep.* above, on; *a.* high, superior, excellent
~an⁴ ~岸 *v.* land, disembark
~chi² ~級 *n.* superior, superior grades, superior classes
~chiang⁴ ~将 *n.* general, admiral (*mil.*)
~chieh¹ ~街 *v.* go on the street
~ch'ien² ~前 *adv.* forward
~ch'uan² ~船 *v.* embark; *adv.* aboard
~hsia⁴ ~下 *adv.* up and down
~hsiao⁴ ~校 *n.* colonel, captain (*mil.*)
~hsüeh² ~學 *v.* go to school
~k'o⁴ ~課 *v.* attend a class
~lou² ~樓 *v.* go upstairs
~pan¹ ~班 *v.* go on duty
~su⁴ ~訴 *v.* appeal (law)
~suan⁴ ~算 *a.* profitable
~shen¹ ~身 *n.* upper part of the body
~shih⁴ ~士 *n.* master sergeant (army)

156

~ssu¹ ~司 *n.* superior
~tang⁴ ~當 *a.* cheated
~teng³ ~等 *a.* &. *adv.* first-class
~teng³ ping¹ ~等兵 *n.* coporal (army)
~ti⁴ ~帝 *n.* God
~ts'eng² she⁴ hui⁴ ~層社會 *n.* upper-class
~tz'u⁴ ~次 *n.* last time
~wei⁴ ~尉 *n.* captain, lieutenant (*mil.*)
~wu³ ~午 *n.* forenoon
~yu² ~游 *adv.* & *a.* upstream
~yüeh⁴ ~月 *n.* last month
SHANG⁴ 尚 *adv.* yet, notwithstanding
~wei⁴ ~未 *adv.* not yet
~wu³ ching¹ shen² ~武精神 *n.* militarism
SHAO¹ 稍 *a.* little; *adv.* gradually
SHAO¹ 燒 *a.* feverish; *v.* burn, roast
SHAO³ 少 *a.* few, little, rare, scarce; *adv.* rarely, seldom
~³ shu⁴ ~數 *n.* minority
~⁴ fu⁴ ~婦 *n.* young lady
~nien² ~年 *n.* youngster, youth
~nien² erh² t'ung² tui⁴ ~年兒童隊 *n.* Young Pioneers**
~nien² hsien¹ feng¹ tui¹ ~年先鋒隊 *n.* Young Vanguard**
~nü³ ~女 *n.* lass, girl
SHAO⁴ 紹 *v.* connect, continue
SHE² 舌 *n.* tongue
~chan⁴ ~戰 *v.* argue; *n.* argument
SHE² 蛇 *n.* snake, serpent
~hsing² ~行 *v.* crawl
SHE⁴ 設 *v.* establish, set up
~chi⁴ ~計 *n.* design
~hsiang³ ~想 *v.* imagine
~li⁴ ~立 *v.* establish, found
~pei⁴ ~備 *n.* equipment
SHE⁴ 射 *v.* shoot, fire
~chi¹ ~擊 *v.* fire, firearms
~chi¹ chih³ hui¹ ~擊指揮 *n.* fire control
~chi¹ shu⁴ ~擊術 *n.* gunnery
~chiao³ ~角 *n.* quadrant angle of elevation

157

~chieh⁴ ~界 *n.* field of fire
~chien⁴ ~箭 *v.* shoot arrows
~ching¹ kuan³ ~精管 *n.* body ejaculation
~chung⁴ ~中 *v.* shoot and hit
~ch'eng² ~程 *n.* range of target
~hsiang⁴ ~向 *n.* line of fire
~hsien⁴ ~線 *n.* line of elevation
~k'ou³ ~口 *n.* jet
~lieh⁴ ~獵 *n.* shooting and hunting
~mien⁴ ~面 *n.* plane of fire
SHE⁴ 社 *n.* society, association
~chiao¹ ~交 *n.* social
~hui⁴ ~會 *n.* society
~hui⁴ hsüeh² ~會學 *n.* sociology
~hui⁴ ko² ming⁴ ~會革命 *n.* social revolution
~hui⁴ k'o¹ hsüeh² ~會科學 *n.* social science
~hui⁴ tang³ ~會黨 *n.* Socialist Party
~hui⁴ te¹ ~會的 *n.* social
~lun⁴ ~論 *n.* editorial
SHE⁴ 涉 *v.* interfere
SHEN¹ 身 *n.* body, tree trunk, ship hull; *pron.* I, me, myself
~fen⁴ ~份 *n.* social or professional status
~hsien¹ shih⁴ tsu² ~先士卒 *v.* be at the head of one's men
~t'i³ ~體 *n.* body
~ts'ai² ~材 *n.* human figure
SHEN¹ 深 *a.* deep, profound
~ao⁴ ~奧 *a.* profound
~chiao¹ ~交 *a.* intimate
~ch'ieh⁴ ~切 *adv.* intensely
~ch'ing² ~情 *n.* deep affection
~hai³ ~海 *n.* deep sea
~hu¹ hsi¹ ~呼吸 *n.* deep breath
~hsin⁴ ~信 *v.* believe firmly
~ju⁴ ~入 *v.* penetrate
~miao⁴ ~妙 *a.* profound
~shui⁴ ~睡 *n.* sound sleep
~ssu¹ ~思 *n.* deep thinking
~yüan¹ ~淵 *n.* abyss
SHEN¹ 伸 *v.* stretch, draw out, extend, express

~chih² ~直 v. straighten
~hsieh⁴ ~謝 v. thank
~yüan¹ ~寃 v. redress an imagined wrong
SHEN² 神 n. god, goddess, deity
  ~ching¹ ~經 n. nerve
  ~ching¹ kuo⁴ min³ ~經過敏 n. nervousness
  ~ching¹ shuai¹ jo⁴ ~經衰弱 n. neurasthenia
  ~hua⁴ ~話 n. myth, mythology; a. mythical
  ~hsien¹ ~仙 n. fairy
SHEN² 什 see SHIH²
SHEN⁴ 甚 a. excessive, too much; adv. very
  ~hao³ 好 a. very well
  ~to¹ ~多 a. very much
SHENG¹ 生 n. student, pupil life, livelihood; v. produce, give birth to; a. raw, unfamiliar
  ~chang³ ~長 v. grow up; n. growth
  ~chi⁴ ~計 n. livelihood
  ~chiang¹ ~薑 n. ginger
  ~chih² ~殖 n. reproduction (biology)
  ~ch'i⁴ ~氣 v. become angry
  ~huo² ~活 n. livelihood, living
  ~huo² ch'eng² tu⁴ ~活程度 n. standard of living
  ~jih⁴ ~日 n. birthday
  ~k'o⁴ ~客 n. stranger
  ~li³ hsüeh² ~理學 n. psysiology
  ~ming⁴ ~命 n. life
  ~ping⁴ ~病 v. fall sick
  ~shou³ ~手 n. green-hand
  ~tung⁴ ~動 a. lively, spirited
  ~ts'ai⁴ ~菜 n. lettuce
  ~ts'un² ~存 n. living
  ~wu⁴ hsüeh² ~物學 n. biology
  ~yü⁴ ~育 v. give birth to; n. birth
SHENG¹ 聲 n. voice, sound, noise
  ~ch'eng¹ ~稱 v. declare
  ~lang⁴ ~浪 n. sound wave
  ~ming² ~明 v. declare
  ~shih⁴ ~勢 n. power, influence
  ~tai⁴ ~帶 n. vocal cords
  ~tiao⁴ ~調 n. tone
  ~tung¹ chi¹ hsi¹ ~東擊西 v. feint and strike

159

~ts'e⁴ ~測 *n.* sound ranging

~wang⁴ ~望 *n.* reputation

~yin¹ ~音 *n.* voice, sound

~yü⁴ ~譽 *n.* reputation

~yüeh⁴ ~樂 *n.* vocal music

~yüeh⁴ chia¹ ~樂家 *n.* vocalist

SHENG¹ 牲 *n.* livestock, cattle

~k'ou³ ~口 *n.* livestock

SHENG¹ 勝 *v.* sustain. ~⁴ *v.* conquer

~¹ jen⁴ ~任 *a.* competent

~⁴ chang⁴ ~仗 *n.* victory

~kuo⁴ ~過 *v.* outdo

~li⁴ ~利 *n.* victory

~li⁴ kung¹ chai⁴ yün⁴ tung⁴ ~利公債運動 *n.*
Victory Bond Campaign**

SHENG¹ 升 *n.* Chinese measure for 1.09 liquid
quarts or 1.035 liters; *v.* ascend, promote

~chiang⁴ chi¹ ~降機 *n.* elevator

~cho² ~擢 *n.* promotion

~shang⁴ ~上 *v.* rise

SHENG² 繩 *n.* cord, string, rope; *v.* tie, restrain,
correct

~so³ ~索 *n.* rope

~tzu³ ~子 *n.* rope, cord, string

SHENG³ 省 *a.* frugal; *n.* province; *v.* save.
HSING³ *v.* visit, perceive

~cheng⁴ fu³ ~政府 *n.* provincial government

~chien³ ~儉 *a.* frugal

~chien³ ~減 *v.* reduce

~chu³ hsi² ~主席 *n.* provincial governor

~ch'üeh⁴ ~却 *v.* spare

~fen¹ ~分 *n.* province

~lüeh⁴ ~略 *n.* abbreviate

~shih² ~時 *v.* save time

SHENG⁴ 盛 *a.* abundant, prosperous; *n.* abundance. CH'ENG² *v.* contain, hold

~hsing² ~行 *n.* prevalence

~ming² ~名 *a.* well-known, noted

SHENG⁴ 剩 *n.* surplus, leavings

~yü² ~餘 *n.* surplus, remainder

~yü² chia⁴ chih² ~餘價值 *n.* surplus profit**

SHIH¹ 失 *n.* loss, fault, mistake; *v.* lose, miss
~ch'ang² ~常 *a.* abnormal
~huo³ ~火 *v.* catch fire
~li³ ~禮 *n.* disrespect; *a.* disrespectful
~pai⁴ ~敗 *v.* defeat, fail; *n.* failure
~shen² ~神 *a.* abstracted, absent-minded
~tang⁴ ~當 *n.* improper
~wang⁴ ~望 *v.* disappoint; *n.* disappointment
~yeh⁴ ~業 *a.* unemployed; *n.* unemployment
~yüeh¹ ~約 *v.* break one's promise .
SHIH¹ 師 *n.* teacher, army division
~chang³ ~長 *n.* division commander, teacher ·
~fan⁴ hsüeh² hsiao⁴ ~範學校 *n.* normal school
SHIH¹ 濕 *a.* wet, moist, damp
~ch'i⁴ ~氣 *n.* moisture
~ti⁴ ~地 *n.* marsh
~tu⁴ ~度 *n.* humidity
SHIH¹ 詩 *n.* poem, poetry
~i⁴ ~意 *a.* poetic
~jen² ~人 *n.* poet
~yün⁴ ~韻 *n.* rhyme
SHIH² 十 *n. & a.* ten
~tzu⁴ chia⁴ ~字架 *n.* religious cross
~tzu⁴ chieh¹ ~字街 *n.* crossroad
~tzu⁴ chün¹ ~字軍 *n.* religious crusade
~yüeh⁴ ~月 *n.* October
SHIH² 拾 *v.* pick up; *a.* ten
~ch'ü³ ~取 *v.* pick up
SHIH² 什 *a.* miscellaneous
SHEN² mo¹ ~麼 *pron.* what
SHIH² 石 *n.* stone, rock
~hui¹ ~灰 *n.* lime
~kao¹ ~膏 *n.* gypsum
~kung¹ ~工 *n.* stonemason
~liu² ~榴 *n.* pomegranate
~mien² ~綿 *n.* asbestos
~pan³ ~版 *n.* slate
~t'ou² ~頭 *n.* stone, rock
~yin⁴ ~印 *n. & v.* lithograph
~ying¹ ~英 *n.* quartz
~yu² ~油 *n.* petroleum

161

SHIH² 實 *a.* real, actual; *n.* fact
~chi⁴ ~際 *a.* actual
~chien⁴ ~踐 *v.* practice
~chien⁴ lun⁴ ~踐論 *n.* " On Practice " **
~hsien⁴ ~現 *v.* realize; *n.* realization
~hsing² ~行 *v.* carry out
~li⁴ ~力 *n.* strength
~shih¹ ~施 *v.* carry out
~tan⁴ she⁴ chi¹ ~彈射擊 *n.* firing live ammunition
~tsai⁴ ~在 *a.* real, true
~yeh⁴ ~業 *n.* industry
~yen⁴ ~驗 *n.* experiment
~yen⁴ shih⁴ ~驗室 *n.* laboratory
~yung⁴ ~用 *a.* practical
SHIH² 時 *n.* time, season, hour
~cheng⁴ ~症 *n.* epidemic
~chi¹ ~機 *n.* opportunity
~chien¹ ~間 *n.* time, period, duration
~chien¹ piao³ ~間表 *n.* timetable
~chung¹ ~鐘 *n.* clock
~chü² ~局 *n.* situation (condition)
~ch'ang² ~常 *adv.* often
~k'o⁴ ~刻 *n.* time (hour)
~mao² ~髦 *a.* modern, fashionable, stylish
~tai⁴ ~代 *n.* age (period)
SHIH² 食 *v.* eat
~chih³ ~指 *n.* forefinger
~liang⁴ ~量 *n.* appetite
~liao⁴ ~料 *n.* foodstuff
~p'in³ ~品 *n.* food
~wu⁴ ~物 *n.* food, provisions
~yen² ~鹽 *n.* salt
~yü⁴ ~慾 *n.* appetite
SHIH³ 使 ~⁴ *n.* messenger, envoy; *v.* cause, use
~che³ ~者 *n.* messenger
~kuan³ ~館 *n.* legation, embassy
~ming⁴ ~命 *n.* mission
~nü³ ~女 *n.* maid, maidservant
~t'u² ~徒 *n.* apostle
~yung⁴ ~用 *v.* use, employ, spend

162

SHIH³ 始 *n.* beginning; *v.* begin; *a.* first
~chung¹ ~終 *adv.* from beginning to end, from first to last
SHIH³ 史 *n.* history
~ch'ien² ~前 *a.* prehistoric, prehistorical
SHIH⁴ 是 *v.* be; *adv.* yes
SHIH⁴ 市 *n.* municipality, city, town
~chang³ ~長 *n.* mayor
~cheng⁴ ~政 *n.* municipal administration
~chia⁴ ~價 *n.* market price, value
~min² ~民 *n.* citizen
SHIH⁴ 式 *n.* form, style, fashion, model
~yang⁴ ~樣 *n.* style, fashion, model
SHIH⁴ 世 *n.* generation, age, world
~chi⁴ ~紀 *n.* century
~chieh⁴ ~界 *n.* world, earth
~chieh⁴ yü³ ~界語 *n.* Esperanto
~su² ~俗 *a.* secular, worldly
~tai⁴ ~代 *n.* generation
SHIH⁴ 勢 *n.* power, authority, influence
~li⁴ ~力 *n.* influence (personal or political)
SHIH⁴ 試 *v.* try, examine; *n.* test
~fei¹ ~飛 *n.* test flight
~yen⁴ ~驗 *n.* test
~yen⁴ ch'ang³ ~驗場 *n.* proving ground
~yen⁴ shih⁴ ~驗室 *n.* laboratory
~yung⁴ ~用 *n.* probation
SHIH⁴ 士 *n.* scholar
~ch'i⁴ ~氣 *n.* morale
~ping¹ ~兵 *n.* soldier
SHIH⁴ 室 *n.* room, chamber, apartment
~nei⁴ ~內 *a.* indoor; *adv.* indoors
~wai⁴ ~外 *a.* outdoor; *adv.* outdoors
SHIH⁴ 示 *v.* proclaim, show
~wei¹ yün⁴ tung⁴ ~威運動 *n.* demonstration parade
SHIH⁴ 識 *n.* experience; *v.* know, recognize
~p'o⁴ ~破 *v.* discover, detect
~t'ou⁴ ~透 *v.* see through
SHIH⁴ 適 *n.* pleasure, comfort; *v.* go to, reach, make fit; *a.* pleasant, comfortable; *adv.* sud-

163

denly, just
~feng² ~逢 v. happen
~ho² ~合 v. fit; a. suitable, fit
~i² ~宜 a. suitable
~k'ou³ ~口 a. palatable
~tu⁴ ~度 adv. moderately
~ying⁴ ~應 n. adaptation
~yung⁴ ~用 a. useful
SHIH⁴ 事 n. affair, matter
~ch'ing² ~情 n. affair, matter, business
~pien⁴ ~變 n. accident, emergency
~shih² ~實 n. fact
~wu⁴ ~務 n. affair
~wu⁴ chu³ i⁴ chia¹ ~務主義家 n. plodder**
~wu⁴ so³ ~務所 n. office
~yeh⁴ ~業 n. business, occupation
SHOU¹ 收 v. receive, collect, close
~chang⁴ ~帳 v. collect debts
~chi² ~集 v. collect; n. collection
~chü⁴ ~據 n. receipt
~huo⁴ ~獲 n. & v. harvest
~ju⁴ ~入 n. income
~liu² ~留 v. give shelter
~tao⁴ ~到 v. receive
~yin¹ chi¹ ~音機 n. radio
SHOU² 熟 a. ripe, mature, cooked
~hsi² ~悉 a. familiar, acquainted
~jen² ~人 n. acquaintance
~lien⁴ ~練 a. skillful
~shui⁴ ~睡 n. sound sleep
~t'ieh³ ~鐵 n. wrought iron
SHOU³ 手 n. hand
~chang³ ~掌 n. palm
~chih³ ~指 n. finger
~chin¹ ~巾 n. handkerchief
~ch'iang¹ ~鎗 n. pistol
~kung¹ ~工 n. handiwork, handcraft
~k'ao³ ~銬 n. handcuffs
~piao³ ~錶 n. watch device
~shih⁴ ~勢 n. gesture
~shu⁴ ~術 n. operation (med.)

164

~tuan⁴ ~段 *n.* tact, method
~t'ao⁴ ~套 *n.* glove
~ts'e⁴ ~册 *n.* manual
~wan⁴ ~腕 *n.* wrist
~yin² ~淫 *n.* masturbation, self-abuse
SHOU³ 守 *v.* watch, guard, hold, keep for defense
~chiu⁴ ~舊 *a.* conservative
~chiu⁴ p'ai⁴ ~舊派 *n.* old school
~chung¹ li⁴ ~中立 *v.* be neutral
~ping¹ ~兵 *n.* defending troops
~shih⁴ ~勢 *n.* strategic defense
~ts'ai² nu² ~財奴 *n.* miser
~wei⁴ ~衛 *v.* guard
~yeh⁴ ~夜 *v.* keep watch at night
~yüeh¹ ~約 *v.* keep a promise
SHOU³ 首 *n.* head, chief, boss; *a.* first
~hsiang⁴ ~相 *n.* premier, prime minister
~hsien¹ ~先 *adv.* first
~ling³ ~領 *n.* chief, head, leader, boss
~shih⁴ ~飾 *n.* ornaments
~tu¹ ~都 *n.* national capital
~wei³ ~尾 *n.* head and tail
SHOU⁴ 受 *v.* receive, accept
~hai⁴ ~害 *v.* damage
~hsi³ ~洗 *v.* be baptized
~k'u³ ~苦 *v.* suffer
SHOU⁴ 獸 *n.* wild animal, beast
~p'i² ~皮 *n.* animal skin
SHU¹ 書 *n.* book, handwriting
~chi⁴ ~記 *n.* clerk
~chia⁴ ~架 *n.* bookcase, bookstand
~cho¹ ~桌 *n.* desk
~fa³ ~法 *n.* handwriting
~shang¹ ~商 *n.* bookseller
~tai¹ tzu¹ ~獣子 *n.* bookworm (person)
~tien⁴ ~店 *n.* bookstore
SHU¹ 梳 *n.* & *v.* comb
SHU¹ 輸 *v.* lose, pay, transport
~ch'ien² ~錢 *v.* lose money
~ch'u¹ ~出 *v.* export
~ch'u¹ p'in³ ~出品 *n.* export goods

~ju⁴ ~入 *v.* import
~ju⁴ p'in³ ~入品 *n.* import goods
~sung⁴ ~送 *v.* transport; *n.* transportation
SHU² 叔 *n.* father's younger brother (uncle)
SHU³ 暑 *n.* summer heat
~chia⁴ ~假 *n.* summer vacation
SHU³ 署 *n.* public court, tribunal; *v.* write
~chang³ ~長 *n.* director
SHU³ 數 *v.* to count. ~⁴ *n.* number; *a.* several
~⁴ hsüeh² ~學 *n.* mathematics
~hsüeh² chia¹ ~學家 *n.* mathematician
~liang⁴ ~量 *n.* quantity
~mu⁴ ~目 *n.* number, amount, sum
SHU³ 鼠 *n.* rat, mouse
~i⁴ ~疫 *n.* plague, pest
SHU³ 屬 *n.* sort, kind, class; *v.* belong to
~ti⁴ ~地 *n.* dependency
~yü² ~於 *v.* belong to
SHU⁴ 樹 *n.* tree; *v.* plant, establish
~chiao¹ ~膠 *n.* gum
~chih¹ ~枝 *n.* tree branch
~kan⁴ ~幹 *n.* tree trunk
~ken¹ ~根 *n.* root
~lin² ~林 *n.* forest, woods
~yeh⁴ ~葉 *n.* leaf
SHU⁴ 術 *n.* path, art, plan
~yü³ ~語 *n.* terminology
SHUA¹ 刷 *n.* & *v.* brush
~hsi³ ~洗 *v.* scrub
~pai² ~白 *v.* whitewash
~tzu¹ ~子 *n.* brush
SHUA³ 耍 *v.* play
SHUAI⁴ 率 *v.* lead, follow, obey. LÜ⁴ *n.* rule, rate, ratio
~ling³ ~領 *v.* lead
SHUAN¹ 拴 *n.* pin
SHUANG¹ 雙 *a.* double, two, both; *n.* pair, couple, mate
~ch'in¹ ~親 *n.* parents
~fang¹ ~方 *a.* both
~kuan¹ yü³ ~關語 *n.* pun

~sheng¹ tzu³ ~生子 *n.* twin
~t'ai¹ ~胎 *n.* twins
SHUANG¹ 霜 *n.* frozen dew, hoar frost; *a.* crystallized
~hsüeh³ ~雪 *n.* frost and snow
SHUANG³ 爽 *a.* sunny, alert; *v.* fail
~k'uai⁴ ~快 *a.* pleasant
~yüeh¹ ~約 *v.* break a promise
SHUI² 誰 *pron.* who, whom, whose
SHUI³ 水 *n.* water, liquid, flood
~cha² ~閘 *n.* floodgate, dam
~ching¹ ~晶 *n.* crystal
~ch'an³ ~産 *n.* marine products
~ch'ih² ~池 *n.* pool
~ch'iu² ~球 *n.* water polo
~hu³ chuan⁴ ~滸傳 *n.* Water Margin (Chinese novel)
~hsien³ ~險 *n.* marine insurance
~hsing¹ ~星 *n.* Mercury (planet)
~kang¹ ~缸 *n.* cistern
~kou¹ ~溝 *n.* ditch
~kuo³ ~果 *n.* fruit
~lei² ~雷 n. torpedo
~li⁴ ~力 *n.* water power
~li⁴ pu⁴ ~利部 *n.* Ministry of Water Conservancy**
~lung² ~龍 *n.* fire engine
~men² t'ing¹ ~門汀 *n.* cement
~niu² ~牛 *n.* buffalo
~ping¹ ~兵 *n.* sailor, seaman (navy)
~p'ing² ~平 *n.* level
~shou³ ~手 *n.* sailor
~tao⁴ ~道 *n.* waterway
~t'u³ ~土 *n.* climate
~tsu² kuan³ ~族館 *n.* aquarium
~ts'ai³ hua⁴ ~彩畫 *n.* water color
~yin² ~銀 *n.* mercury
SHUI⁴ 睡 *v.* sleep
~chiao⁴ ~覺 *v.* sleep
~ch'e¹ ~車 *n.* sleeping car
~hsing³ ~醒 *v.* awaken, wake up

167

~i¹ ~衣 *n*. nightgown, nightdress, pajamas

SHUI⁴ 税 *n*. tax, taxation, duty

~kuan¹ ~關 *n*. custom house

~lü⁴ ~率 *n*. rate of tax

SHUN⁴ 順 *a*. obedient; *v*. obey, follow

~feng¹ ~風 *n*. tail wind

~hsü⁴ ~序 *n*. order

~li⁴ ~利 *n*. & *a*. prosperous

~shih² chen¹ fang¹ hsiang⁴ ~時針方向 *adv*. & *a*. clockwise

~ts'ung² ~從 *v*. obey

SHUO¹ 説 *v*. say, speak

~fu² ~服 *v*. persuade

~huang³ ~謊 *v*. tell lies

~hsiao⁴ hua⁴ ~笑話 *v*. make a joke

~ming² ~明 *v*. explain; explanation

SS

SSU¹ 思 *v*. think, consider

~hsiang³ ~想 *n*. thought

~hsiang³ kai³ tsao⁴ ~想改造 *n*. thought reform**, ideological reform**

~hsiang³ tzu⁴ yu² ~想自由 *n*. freedom of thought

~hsiang³ wen⁴ t'i² ~想問題 *n*. question of thought**

~k'ao³ ~考 *v*. think

~lü⁴ ~慮 *v*. consider

SSU¹ 私 *a*. private, personal, secret

~fa³ ~法 *n*. private law

~hsin¹ ~心 *n*. selfishness

~hsing² ~刑 *n*. illegal punishment

~jen² te¹ ~人的 *a*. personal

~li⁴ hsüeh² hsiao⁴ ~立學校 *n*. private school

~pen¹ ~奔 *n*. elopement

~sheng¹ tzu³ ~生子 *n*. bastard, illegitimate child

~t'ao² ~逃 *v*. escape

~t'ung¹ ~通 *n*. adultery

~yü³ ~語 *v.* whisper

~yün⁴ ~運 *v.* smuggle

SSU¹ 司 *v.* manage; *n.* departments under the ministry

~fa³ ~法 *a.* judicial

~fa³ hsing² cheng⁴ pu⁴ ~法行政部 *n.* Ministry of Judicial Administration*

~fa³ pu⁴ ~法部 *n.* Ministry of Justice**, Department of Justice (*U.S.*)

~fa³ yüan⁴ ~法院 *n.* Judicial Yuan*

~ling⁴ ~令 *n.* commander

~ling⁴ pu⁴ ~令部 *n.* large unit headquarters

SSU¹ 糸 *n.* silk, thread

~chih¹ p'in³ ~織品 *n.* silk goods

~wa⁴ ~襪 *n.* silk stockings

SSU¹ 斯 *n.* final particle; *pron.* this, he, they; *adv.* then

SSU³ 死 *v.* die; *a.* dead; *n.* death

~hsing² ~刑 *v.* be executed

~jen² ~人 *n.* dead person

~te¹ ~的 *a.* dead

~tsui⁴ ~罪 *n.* the penalty of death

~wang² lü⁴ ~亡率 *n.* death rate

~wang² piao³ ~亡表 *n.* obituary notice

SSU⁴ 四 *n. & a.* four

~chi⁴ ~季 *n.* four seasons

~fang¹ te¹ ~方的 *a.* square

~yüeh⁴ ~月 *n.* April

SSU⁴ 似 *a.* alike, similar, like

~hu¹ ~乎 *v.* seem, appear; *adv.* likely

~shih⁴ ~是 *adv.* plausibly

SSU⁴ 厠 *n.* privy

~so³ ~所 *n.* toilet, water closet

T

TA² 答 *v.* answer, reply

~¹ ying⁴ ~應 *v.* promise

~² an⁴ ~案 *n.* answer (solution)

~fu⁴ ~復 *v.* answer

169

~hsieh⁴ ~謝 *v.* return thanks

~pien⁴ ~辯 *v.* rebut

~tui⁴ ~對 *v.* reply

TA² 達 *v.* inform, reach

~mu³ tan⁴ ~姆彈 *n.* dumdum bullet

~tao⁴ ~到 *v.* attain

TA³ 打 *v.* beat, strike, thrash. ~² *n.* dozen

~chang⁴ ~仗 *v.* fight

~chia⁴ ~架 *v.* fight

~pai⁴ ~敗 *v.* defeat

~p'ai² ~牌 *v.* play mah-jong

~tun³ ~盹 *v.* take a nap

~t'ing¹ ~聽 *v.* detect

~tzu⁴ ~字 *v.* typewrite

~tzu⁴ chi¹ ~字機 *n.* typewriter

~tzu⁴ yüan² ~字員 *n.* typist

TA⁴ 大 *a.* big, large, great, huge, enormous; *adv.* largely, greatly, highly, extremely

~feng¹ ~風 *n.* typhoon

~hsiao³ ~小 *n.* size

~hsing² cheng⁴ ch'ü¹ ~行政區 *n.* Great Administrative Areas**

~hsüeh² ~學 *n.* university

~i¹ ~衣 *n.* overcoat

~i⁴ ~意 *n.* general idea

~kai⁴ ~概 *adv.* generally, in general

~kang¹ ~綱 *n.* outline

~li³ shih² ~理石 *n.* marble

~liang⁴ ~量 *n.* large quantity, mass; *a.* generous

~lu⁴ ~路 *n.* highroad, highway

~lu⁴ ~陸 *n.* continent, mainland

~lu⁴ kung¹ tso⁴ ch'u⁴ ~陸工作處 *n.* Mainland Operations Department*

~mai⁴ ~麥 *n.* barley

~men² ~門 *n.* front door

~pan⁴ ~半 *adv.* largely, chiefly

~pien⁴ ~便 *n.* excrement, stool

~p'ao⁴ ~砲 *n.* cannon, artillery

~she⁴ ~赦 *n.* amnesty

~shih⁴ ~使 *n.* ambassador

~tan³ ~膽 *a.* bold, daring, courageous

170

~t'ing¹ ~廳 *n.* hall
~to¹ shu⁴ ~多數 *n.* majority
~tsung³ t'ung³ ~總統 *n.* President, Executive (*U.S.*)
~t'ui³ hsi⁴ ~腿戲 *n.* burlesque
~yüeh¹ ~約 *adv.* about, probably, approximately, generally
TAI⁴ 待 *v.* wait, treat
~yü⁴ ~遇 *n.* treatment
TAI⁴ 帶 *n.* ribbon, belt, zone, bandage, region; *v.* lead, bring
~lai² ~來 *v.* bring
~lei⁴ ~累 *v.* involve (someone)
~ling³ ~領 *v.* lead
~tzu¹ ~子 *n.* belt
TAI⁴ 代 *n.* dynasty, generation; *v.* represent, replace; *prep.* instead of, in place of
~chia⁴ ~價 *n.* price
~li³ ~理 *v.* act for another
~li³ ch'u⁴ ~理處 *n.* agent
~piao³ ~表 *n.* representative; *v.* represent
~shu⁴ hsüeh² ~數學 *n.* algebra
~t'i⁴ ~替 *n.* substitution; *v.* substitute
TAI⁴ 袋 *n.* bag, pocket, purse
~shu³ ~鼠 *n.* kangaroo
TAI⁴ 貸 *v.* lend, borrow
~chin¹ ~金 *n.* loan
~ch'u¹ ~出 *v.* lend
~ju⁴ ~入 *v.* borrow
TAN¹ 單 *a.* single, alone
~fa¹ ~發 *n.* single shot
~fei¹ ~飛 *n.* solo flight
~jen² ch'uang² ~人床 *n.* single bed
~tu² ~獨 *a.* alone
~wei⁴ ~位 *n.* unit
TAN¹ 擔 *v.* carry, sustain, bear
~hsin¹ ~心 *v.* worry
~jen⁴ ~任 *v.* undertake, take part
~ko¹ ~擱 *v.* delay
~kun⁴ ~棍 *n.* crowbar
~pao³ ~保 *n.* & *v.* guarantee

171

~pao³ jen² ~保人 *n.* guarantor

~yu¹ ~憂 *v.* worry

TAN³ 膽 *n.* gall, bile, courage

~chih¹ ~汁 *n.* gall, bile

~hsiao³ ~小 *a.* cowardly

~kan³ ~敢 *v.* dare

~liang⁴ ~量 *n.* courage, bravery

~nang² ~囊 *n.* gall bladder

~shih² ~石 *n.* gall stone

~ta⁴ ~大 *a.* courageous, brave

TAN⁴ 蛋 *n.* egg

~huang² ~黃 *n.* yolk

~k'o² ~殼 *n.* eggshell

~pai² ~白 *n.* albumen

~pai² chih² ~白質 *n.* albumen

TAN⁴ 彈 *n.* bullet, shot, shell. T'AN² *v.* rebound, shoot

~chao² tien³ ~着點 *n.* point of impact

~hen² ~痕 *n.* crater, shell hole

~tao⁴ ~道 *n.* trajectory

~tao⁴ hsüeh² ~道學 *n.* ballistics

~tzu¹ fang² ~子房 *n.* billiard room

~tzu¹ hsi⁴ ~子戲 *n.* billiards

~yao⁴ ~藥 *n.* ammunition

t'an² ch'ang⁴ ~唱 *v.* play and sing

~ch'in² ~琴 *v.* play an instrument

~ho² ~劾 *v.* impeach (accuse)

~hsing⁴ ~性 *n.* elasticity

~ya¹ ~壓 *v.* repress (put down)

TAN⁴ 但 *conj.* but, yet

~shih⁴ ~是 *conj.* but

TAN⁴ 淡 *a.* insipid, tasteless, weak

~ch'i⁴ ~氣 *n.* nitrogen

~po² ~薄 *a.* dilute, thin

~te¹ ~的 *a.* fresh (food)

TANG¹ 當 *v.* act, bear; *conj.* when, while; *prep.* during. ~⁴ *a.* suitable; *v.* pawn

~¹ chen¹ ~眞 *adv.* really

~chü² ~局 *n.* authority

~hsüan³ ~選 *v.* be elected

~jan² ~然 *adv.* certainly, surely, naturally

172

~shih² ~時 *prep.* during
~⁴ p'u⁴ ~舖 *n.* pawnshop
~shui⁴ ~稅 *n.* pawnshop tax
TANG³ 黨 *n.* party, cabal
 ~kuo² yao⁴ jen² ~國要人 *n.* important figures in the party and government
 ~p'ai⁴ ~派 *n.* political party
 ~shou³ ~首 *n.* party leader
 ~yüan² ~員 *n.* party member
TAO¹ 刀 *n.* knife, sword
 ~ch'iao⁴ ~鞘 *n.* scabbard, sheath
 ~feng¹ ~鋒 *n.* point of a knife
 ~pei⁴ ~背 *n.* back of a knife
 ~p'ien⁴ ~片 *n.* blade
TAO³ 島 *n.* island, isle
 ~min² ~民 *n.* islander
 ~yü³ ~嶼 *n.* isle, islet
TAO³ 導 *v.* lead, guide
 ~huo³ hsien⁴ ~火線 *n.* explosive's fuse
 ~kuan³ ~管 *n.* pipe, fuel conductor
 ~piao¹ ~標 guidepost
 ~yen² ~言 *n.* introduction, preface
 ~yen³ ~演 *n. & v.* director
TAO⁴ 道 *v.* speak, tell; *n.* road
 ~ho⁴ ~賀 *v.* congratulate
 ~hsieh⁴ ~謝 *v.* express thanks
 ~li³ ~理 *n.* reason
 ~lu⁴ ~路 *n.* road
 ~shih⁴ ~士 *n.* taoist
 ~te² ~德 *n.* virtue
TAO⁴ 到 *v.* arrive, reach
 ~ch'i¹ ~期 *a.* due (promised to come)
 ~ch'u⁴ ~處 *adv.* everywhere
 ~jen⁴ ~任 *v.* take the post
 ~ta² ~達 *v.* arrive at; *n.* arrival
 ~ti³ ~底 *adv.* at last
TAO⁴ 倒 *a.* inverted, upset, upside-down. ~³ *v.* fall down
 ~³ ch'u¹ ~出 *v.* pour out
 ~hsia⁴ ~下 *v.* fall down
 ~mei² ~霉 *a.* unlucky

173

~pi⁴ ~閉 *v.* bankrupt
~yün⁴ ~運 *a.* unlucky
~⁴ t'ui⁴ ~退 *v.* withdraw
TAO⁴ 盜 *n.* robber; *v.* rob
~an⁴ ~案 *n.* a case of robbery
~ch'ieh⁴ ~竊 *v.* steal
~k'ou⁴ ~寇 *n.* robber
TAO⁴ 稻 *n.* rice-plant
~ts'ao³ ~草 *n.* straw
TE¹ 的 *see* **TI⁴**
TE² 德 *n.* virtue, quality, goodness
~hsing² ~行 *n.* virtue, morality
~hsing⁴ ~性 *n.* morality
~yü⁴ ~育 *n.* moral education
TE² 得 *v.* get. **TEI³** *v. aux.* must, ought
~i⁴ ~意 *a.* elated
~li⁴ ~力 *a.* helpful
~ping⁴ ~病 *v.* get sick
~sheng⁴ ~勝 *n.* victory
~tsui⁴ ~罪 *v.* offend
TEI³ 得 *see* **TE²**
TENG¹ 燈 *n.* light
~hsin¹ ~心 *n.* wick
~kuang¹ ~光 *n.* light (lamp)
~lung² ~籠 *n.* lantern
~t'a³ ~塔 *n.* lighthouse
TENG¹ 登 *v.* ascend, record
~an⁴ ~岸 *v.* disembark
~chi⁴ ~記 *v.* register; *n.* registration
~lu⁴ ~陸 *v.* land (come ashore)
~lu⁴ ch'uan² chih¹ ~陸船隻 *n.* landing craft
TENG³ 等 *v.* wait; *n.* rank, grade, degree
~chi² ~級 *n.* grade
~kao¹ hsien⁴ ~高線 *n.* contour
~tai⁴ ~待 *v.* wait for
~teng³ ~等 *conj.* and so forth, etcetera
TI¹ 低 *a.* low, mean, base
~chia⁴ ~價 *a.* cheap
~chien⁴ ~賤 *a.* mean, humble
~k'ung¹ fei¹ hsing² ~空飛行 *n.* low-flying
~neng² ~能 *a.* feeble-minded

174

~shen¹ tan⁴ tao⁴~伸彈道 *n.* flat trajectory
~ti⁴ ~地 *n.* low ground
~wei¹ ~微 *a.* base, mean
~wu⁴ ~霧 *n.* low fog
TI² 敵 *n.* enemy, competitor; *v.* oppose
~chi¹ ~機 *n.* enemy aircraft
~ch'iao² ~僑 *n.* enemy alien
~ch'ing² ~情 *n.* enemy situation
~fang¹ ~方 *n.* enemy's side
~i⁴ ~意 *a.* hostile; *n.* hostility
~jen² ~人 *n.* enemy
~tui⁴ ~對 *a.* hostile
TI³ 底 *n.* base, bottom
~hsia⁴ ~下 *prep.* under, below
~kao³ ~稿 *n.* draft copy
~mien⁴ ~面 *n.* undersurface
TI³ 抵 *v.* arrive, reach, resist
~chih⁴ ~制 *n. & v.* boycott
~hsiao¹ ~消 *n.* offset
~k'ang⁴ ~抗 *v.* resist; *n.* resistance
~k'ang⁴ hsien⁴ ~抗線 *n.* line of resistance
~k'ang⁴ li⁴ ~抗力 *n.* powerful resistance
~ya¹ ~押 *n. & v.* mortgage
TI⁴ 弟 *n.* younger brother
TI⁴ 地 *n.* earth, ground, land
~chen⁴ ~震 *n.* earthquake
~chih² hsüeh² ~質學 *n.* geology
~chih² pu⁴ ~質部 *n.* Ministry of Geological Survey**
~chih³ ~址 *n.* mail address
~chu³ chieh¹ chi² ~主階級 *n.* landlord class**
~ch'an³ ~産 *n.* real estate
~ch'in² jen² yüan² ~勤人員 *n.* ground crew
~ch'iu² ~球 *n.* earth, globe
~fang¹ cheng⁴ fu³ ~方政府 *n.* local government
~fang¹ hung² chün¹ ~方紅軍 *n.* local Red Army**
~hsin¹ hsi¹ li⁴ ~心吸力 *n.* gravitation
~hsing² ~形 *n.* terrain
~lei² ~雷 *n.* land mine
~lei² chen¹ ch'a² ch'i⁴ ~雷偵察器 *n.* mine detector

175

~mao⁴ ~貌 *n.* terrain feature

~pan³ ~板 *n.* floor

~p'ing² hsien⁴ ~平線 *n.* horizon

~tai⁴ ~帶 *n.* zone

~tien³ ~點 *n.* location, locality

~t'an³ ~毯 *n.* carpet, rug

~t'u² ~圖 *n.* map

~wei³ ~委 *n.* County Group Committee of the Chinese Communist Party**

~wei⁴ ~位 *n.* position, place, site, rank

~yü⁴ ~獄 *n.* hell

TI⁴ 第 *n.* class, order, series, mansion

~erh⁴ chi¹ hsieh⁴ kung¹ yeh⁴ pu⁴ ~二機械工業部 *n.* Second Ministry of Machine Industry**

~erh⁴ tz'u⁴ shih⁴ chieh⁴ ta⁴ chan⁴ ~二次世界大戰 *n.* World War II

~i¹ chi¹ hsieh⁴ kung¹ yeh⁴ pu⁴ ~一機械工業部 *n.* First Ministry of Machine Industry**

~san¹ kuo² chi⁴ ~三國際 *n.* Third International, Communist International

~san¹ shih⁴ li⁴ ~三勢力 *n.* Third Force

~san¹ tang³ ~三黨 *n.* Third Party

~wu³ tsung¹ tui⁴ ~五縱隊 *n.* Fifth Column

TI⁴ 的 *n.* target, mark. TE¹ [a subordinate]

~² ch'üeh⁴ ~確 *adv.* really

~⁴ shih⁴ ~士 *n.* taxi

TI⁴ 帝 *n.* emperor

~hou⁴ ~后 *n.* empress, queen

~kuo² ~國 *n.* empire, kingdom

~kuo² chu³ i⁴ ~國主義 *n.* imperialism

~kuo² te¹ ~國的 *a.* imperial

~wang² ~王 *n.* emperor, king, ruler

~wei⁴ ~位 *n.* throne

TIAO⁴ 掉 *v.* move, fall, change

~huan⁴ ~換 *v.* exchange

~lao⁴ ~落 *v.* fall

~t'ou² ~頭 *v.* return, fall back

TIAO⁴ 調 *see* T'IAO²

TIEH¹ 爹 *n.* father, daddy, papa

TIEN³ 點 *n.* point, spot, speck, dot, stain, little; *v.* nod, light

~chung¹ ~鐘 *n.* o'clock
~hao⁴ ~號 *n.* period
~huo³ ~火 *v.* kindle
~hsin¹ ~心 *n.* refreshments
~ming² ~名 *v.* call the roll; *n.* roll call
~ming² ts'e⁴ ~名冊 *n.* roll (list of names)
~teng¹ ~燈 *v.* light a lamp
~t'ou² ~頭 *v.* nod
~ts'ai⁴ ~菜 *v.* order the dish
TIEN³ 典 *v.* pawn; *n.* rite, ceremony
~hsing² ~型 *n.* model, pattern, example
~ku⁴ ~故 *n.* allusion
~li³ ~禮 *n.* ceremony
~tang⁴ ~當 *v.* pawn
TIEN⁴ 店 *n.* shop, store
~chu³ ~主 *n.* storekeeper
~huo³ ~夥 *n.* employee, clerk
~p'u⁴ ~舖 *n.* store, shop
TIEN⁴ 電 *n.* electricity, telegraphy, lightning
~ch'e¹ ~車 *n.* streetcar, trolley car
~ch'i⁴ ~氣 *a.* electric
~ch'ih² ~池 *n.* electric battery
~feng¹ shan⁴ ~風扇 *n.* electric fan
~hua⁴ ~話 *n.* telephone
~hua⁴ chü² ~話局 *n.* telephone office
~hsien⁴ ~綫 *n.* electric wires
~hsin⁴ ~信 *n.* telegram
~i³ ~椅 *n.* electric chair
~li⁴ ~力 *n.* electric power
~ling² ~鈴 *n.* electric bell
~liu² ~流 *n.* electric current
~lu² ~爐 *n.* electric stove, electric furnace
~ma³ ~碼 *n.* (telegraph) code
~nao³ ~腦 *n.* electric brain
~pao⁴ ~報 *n.* telegram, telegraph
~pao⁴ chü² ~報局 *n.* telegraph office
~shih⁴ ~視 *n.* television
~shih⁴ fang⁴ sung⁴ ~視放送 *v.* telecast
~teng¹ ~燈 *n.* electric lights
~teng¹ p'ao⁴ ~燈泡 *n.* electric bulb
~tung⁴ chi¹ ~動機 *n.* electromotor

177

~t'i¹ ~梯 *n.* elevator, escalator

~tz'u² ~磁 *n.* electromagnet

~ya¹ chi⁴ ~壓計 *n.* voltmeter

~ying³ ~影 *n.* movie, moving picture

~ying³ ming² hsing¹ ~影明星 *n.* movie star

~ying³ yüan⁴ ~影院 *n.* movie theater

TING¹ 丁 *n.* adult, individual, person

~hsiang¹ ~香 *n.* clove (plant)

~tzu⁴ ch'ih³ ~字尺 *n.* T square

TING³ 頂 *n.* top; *v.* oppose

~tien³ ~點 *n.* apex

TING⁴ 定 *v.* determine, order; *a.* fixed, firm

~chia⁴ ~價 *n.* list price

~ch'i¹ ~期 *a.* periodic

~ch'i¹ ts'un² k'uan³ ~期存款 *n.* savings account

~hun¹ ~婚 *n.* engagement (promise to marry)

~huo⁴ ~貨 *v.* order goods

~i⁴ ~義 *n.* definition

~li³ ~理 *n.* theorem

~lü⁴ ~律 *n.* theorem

~tsui⁴ ~罪 *v.* sentence

TING⁴ 訂 *v.* subscribe, examine, decide

~hun¹ ~婚 *v.* engage (pledge to marry)

~huo⁴ tan¹ ~貨單 *n.* bill of order

~meng² ~盟 *v.* pledge

~yüeh¹ ~約 *v.* conclude a treaty

TIU¹ 丟 *v.* lose

~ch'ou³ ~醜 *n.* disgrace, shame

~ch'i⁴ ~棄 *v.* abandon

~lien³ ~臉 *v.* lose face

TO¹ 多 *a.* many, numerous; *n.* plenty

~hsieh⁴ ~謝 *n.* thanks

~hsin¹ ~心 *a.* suspicious

~liang⁴ ~量 *a.* a great deal

~pien⁴ ~辯 *a.* arguable

~shao³ ~少 *adv.* how many?, how much?

~shu⁴ ~數 *n.* majority

TO² 奪 *v.* snatch, strive, take by force

~ch'ü³ ~取 *v.* take by force

~hui² ~囘 *v.* recover

TO³ 朶 *n.* cluster

178

TOU¹ 都 *see* **TU¹**

TOU³ 斗 Chinese measure for 10.35 liters, bushel, peck

~p'eng² ~篷 *n.* mantle, cape

TOU⁴ 豆 *n.* bean, pea

~chia¹ ~莢 *n.* bean pod

~fu³ ~腐 *n.* bean curd

~ya² ~芽 *n.* bean sprout

~yu² ~油 *n.* bean oil

TOU⁴ 鬥 *v.* fight

~cheng¹ ~爭 *n.* & *v.* struggle

~chi¹ ~雞 *n.* cockfight

~chi¹ yen³ ~雞眼 *n.* cross-eye

~niu² ~牛 *n.* bullfight

TU¹ 都 *n.* capital, metropolis. **TOU¹** *a.* all

~hui⁴ ~會 *n.* metropolis; *a.* metropolitan

~shih⁴ ~市 *n.* capital, metropolis

TU² 讀 *v.* read, study

~che³ ~者 *n.* reader

~pen³ ~本 *n.* textbook

~shu¹ ~書 *n.* & *v.* study

TU² 毒 *n.* poison; *a.* poisonous

~ch'i⁴ ~氣 *n.* poison gas

~wa³ ssu¹ ~瓦斯 *n.* gas

~wu⁴ ~物 *n.* poison

TU² 獨 *a.* solitary, single, only

~chan⁴ ~占 *n.* monopoly

~li⁴ ~立 *n.* independence; *a.* independent

~shen¹ ~身 *n.* single life

~shen¹ chu³ i⁴ ~身主義 *n.* bachelorhood

~ts'ai² ~裁 *a.* dictatorial

~ts'ai² cheng⁴ chih⁴ ~裁政治 *n.* dictatorship

~tzu³ ~子 *n.* only son

~tzu⁴ ~自 *pron.* oneself

TU³ 賭 *v.* gamble, bet

~po² ~博 *n.* gambling

~t'u² ~徒 *n.* gambler

TU⁴ 度 *v.* spend, measure; *n.* degree (scale)

~liang⁴ ~量 *v.* measure

~liang⁴ heng² ~量衡 *n.* length, capacity and weight

179

~shu⁴ ~數 *n.* degree (scale)

TU⁴ 肚 *n.* abdomen, belly

~ch'i² ~臍 *n.* navel

~tai⁴ ~帶 *n.* girth, cinch

~t'ung⁴ ~痛 *n.* belly-ache

TUAN³ 短 *a.* short, brief

~ch'u⁴ ~處 *n.* defect

~kung¹ ~工 *n.* piece work

~lu⁴ ~路 *n.* short circuit (*elec.*)

~ming⁴ ~命 *a.* short-lived

~p'ien¹ hsiao³ shuo¹ ~篇小説 *n.* short stories

~shao³ ~少 *v.* lack

TUAN⁴ 斷 *v.* cut apart, stop, settle, judge

~ai² ~崖 *n.* cliff

~chüeh² ~絶 *v.* break off, cut off

~chüeh² ti⁴ ~絶的 *n.* broken terrain

~t'ou² chi¹ ~頭機 *n.* guillotine

TUAN⁴ 段 *n.* portion, section

~lao⁴ ~落 *n.* paragraph, stop

TUI¹ 堆 *n.* heap, pile, mass

~chan⁴ ~棧 *n.* warehouse

~chi¹ ~積 *v.* pile

TUI⁴ 對 *n.* pair, couple; *v.* pair, answer; *a.* opposite

~chao⁴ ~照 *v.* contrast

~cheng⁴ ~證 *n.* witness

~chih⁴ chuang⁴ t'ai⁴ ~峙狀態 *n.* stalemate

~hua⁴ ~話 *n.* dialogue

~huan⁴ ~換 *v.* exchange

~k'ang⁴ ~抗 *n.* antagonism; *v.* oppose

~mien⁴ ~面 *v.* confront; *n.* confrontation

~pi³ ~比 *v.* contrast

~shou³ ~手 *n.* rival

~shu⁴ ~數 *n.* logarithm

~ta² ~答 *v.* answer, reply

~te¹ ~的 *a.* right

~t'ou² ~頭 *n.* opponent

~wai⁴ mao⁴ i⁴ pu⁴ ~外貿易部 *n.* Ministry of Foreign Trade**

TUI⁴ 隊 *n.* team, group, gang, squadron

~chang³ ~長 *n.* captain

180

~hsing² ~形 *n.* formation
~wu³ ~伍 *n.* troop
TUN⁴ 頓 *v.* bow the head
TUNG¹ 東 *n.* east; *a.* east, eastern
~fang¹ ~方 *n.* east, the Orient, the East; *a.* Oriental, Eastern
~fang¹ jen² ~方人 *n.* Orientals
~pan⁴ ch'iu² ~半球 *n.* Eastern Hemisphere
~tao⁴ chu³ ~道主 *n.* host
~yang² ~洋 *n.* Japan
TUNG¹ 冬 *n.* winter
~chi⁴ ~季 *n.* & *a.* winter
~chih⁴ ~至 *n.* winter solstice
~ch'ing¹ shu⁴ ~青樹 *n.* evergreen
~mien² ~眠 *n.* hibernation
TUNG³ 懂 *v.* understand
TUNG⁴ 動 *v.* move, shake, stir, act
~chi¹ ~機 *n.* motive
~ch'an³ ~産 *n.* movable property
~i⁴ ~議 *n.* motion (suggestion)
~mo⁴ ~脈 *n.* artery
~tso⁴ ~作 *n.* action, movement (in drill)
~tz'u² ~詞 *n.* verb
~wu⁴ ~物 *n.* animal
~wu⁴ hsüeh² ~物學 *n.* zoology
~wu⁴ hsüeh² chia¹ ~物學家 *n.* zoologist
~wu⁴ yüan² ~物園 *n.* zoo
~yao² ~搖 *v.* shake
~yüan² ~員 *n.* mobilization
~yüan² chi⁴ hua⁴ ~員計劃 *n.* mobilization plan
~yüan² ling⁴ ~員令 *n.* mobilization order
TUNG⁴ 凍 *v.* freeze, congeal
~ch'uang¹ ~瘡 *n.* chilblain
~jou⁴ ~肉 *n.* cold meat
~ssu³ ~死 *v.* be frozen to death
TUNG⁴ 洞 *n.* cave, tunnel, hole
~hsi² ~悉 *v.* understand thoroughly
~hsüeh⁴ ~穴 *n.* cave

181

T'

T'A¹ 他 *pron.* he
~**ch'u⁴** ~處 *adv.* elsewhere
~**hsiang⁴** ~項 *n.* other items
~**jih⁴** ~日 *n.* another day
~**men²** ~們 *pron.* they, them
~**men² te¹** ~們的 *pron.* their, theirs
~**te¹** ~的 *a.* his
~**tzu⁴ chi³** ~自己 *pron.* himself
T'A¹ 它 *pron.* it
T'A¹ 她 *pron.* she
~**men²** ~們 *pron.* they, them
~**te¹** ~的 *a.* her
~**tzu⁴ chi³** ~自己 *pron.* herself
T'AI² 台 *n.* platform, terrace
T'AI² 抬 *v.* lift, carry
~**kao¹** ~高 *v.* raise
T'AI⁴ 太 *adv.* very, too, extremely
~**chien⁴** ~監 *n.* eunuch, a castrated man
~**hsi²** ~息 *v.* sigh
~**ku³** ~古 *n.* antiquity, early ages of history
~**p'ing²** ~平 *n.* peace
~**p'ing² t'ien¹ kuo²** ~平天國 *n.* Taiping Heaven-ly Kingdom
~**yang²** ~陽 *n.* sun
T'AI⁴ 態 *n.* manner, attitude, bearing, mien
~**tu⁴** ~度 *n.* behavior, manner, attitude
T'AN¹ 貪 *v.* covet; *a.* greedy
~**hsin¹** ~心 *a.* greedy
~**se⁴** ~色 *a.* lustful
~**ts'ai²** ~財 *a.* greedy of money
~**wu¹** ~污 *n.* graft (corruption)
T'AN² 談 *v.* talk, chat
~**hua⁴** ~話 *v.* talk; *n.* conversation
~**p'an⁴** ~判 *v.* negotiate; *n.* negotiation
T'AN² 痰 *n.* phlegm, sputum
~**yü²** ~盂 *n.* cuspidor, spittoon
T'AN² 彈 *see* TAN⁴

T'AN⁴ 探 *v.* spy, visit, explore, sound
 ~chih¹ ~知 *v.* find out
 ~ch'iu² ~求 *v.* search
 ~fang³ ~訪 *v.* visit
 ~hsien³ ~險 *v.* explore
 ~hsien³ chia¹ ~險家 *n.* explorer, adventurer
 ~hsien³ tui⁴ ~險隊 *n.* exploration party
 ~so³ ~索 *v.* search out
 ~wen⁴ ~問 *v.* ask
T'AN⁴ 炭 *n.* charcoal, carbon
T'AN⁴ 歎 *n. & v.* sigh
 ~hsi² ~息 *n. & v.* sigh
 ~hsi² ~惜 *v.* pity
 ~hsien⁴ ~羨 *v.* admire
T'ANG¹ 湯 *n.* soup, hot water
 ~ch'ih² ~匙 *n.* soup spoon
T'ANG² 堂 *n.* hall, court, church
 ~hsiung¹ ti⁴ ~兄弟 *n.* son of one's father's brother (cousin)
 ~kuan³ ~館 *n.* waiter
 ~t'ang² ~堂 *a.* stately
 ~tzu¹ ~子 *n.* brothel
 ~tzu³ mei⁴ ~姉妹 *n.* daughter of one's father's brother (cousin)
T'ANG² 糖 *n.* sugar, candy
 ~chiang¹ ~漿 *n.* syrup
 ~ching¹ ~精 *n.* saccharin
 ~chiu³ ~酒 *n.* rum
 ~kuo³ ~果 *n.* candy, sweets
 ~kuo³ tien⁴ ~果店 *n.* confectioner
 ~niao⁴ ping⁴ ~尿病 *n.* sugar diabetes
 ~shih² ~食 *n.* sweetmeats
T'AO² 逃 *v.* escape, flee
 ~nan⁴ ~難 *v.* take a refuge
 ~pi⁴ ~避 *v.* escape
 ~ping¹ ~兵 *n.* deserter
 ~shih¹ ~失 *a.* lost horse
 ~ting¹ ~丁 *n.* draft dodger
 ~t'o¹ ~脱 *v.* escape
 ~wang² ~亡 *v.* desert; *n.* desertion
T'AO² 桃 *n.* peach

183

T'AO³ 討 *v.* punish, demand, beg
~fa² ~伐 *n.* punitive expedition
~fan⁴ ~飯 *n.* beggar
~hao³ ~好 *v.* please
~jao² ~饒 *v.* seek forgiveness
~lun⁴ ~論 *v.* discuss; *n.* discussion
~yen⁴ ~厭 *a.* disgusted; *v.* dislike
T'AO⁴ 套 *n.* suit, case, envelope, covering, set
~hsieh² ~鞋 *n.* overshoe
T'E⁴ 特 *a.* special, particular; *adv.* specially, particularly
~ch'uan² ~權 *n.* priviledge
~hsing⁴ ~性 *n.* characteristic
~hsü³ ~許 *n.* patent
~pieh² ~別 *a.* special, particular
~pieh² pan¹ ~別班 *n.* special course
~pieh² shih⁴ ~別市 *n.* special municipality
~she⁴ ~赦 *n.* amnesty
~tien³ ~點 *n.* feature (distinct part), specialty
~wu⁴ ~務 *n.* secret service
~yüeh¹ ~約 *n.* special contract
T'ENG² 疼 *n.* pain, ache, pity, love
~ai⁴ ~愛 *v.* be fond of
~t'ung⁴ ~痛 *n.* pain
T'ENG² 騰 *v.* ascend, mount
~k'ung¹ ~空 *v.* soar, fly upward
~ta² ~達 *v.* become prosperous
T'I¹ 梯 *n.* ladder, stairs
T'I² 提 *v.* lift, carry, mention
~ch'ang⁴ ~倡 *v.* promote growth
~ch'iang¹ ~槍 *v.* trail arms
~ch'in² ~琴 *n.* violin
~fang² ~防 *v.* guard, watch
~hsing³ ~醒 *v.* remind
~i⁴ ~議 *v.* suggest; *n.* suggestion
T'I² 題 *n.* subject, heading; *v.* propose, name
~mu⁴ ~目 *n.* subject, title, topic
~tseng⁴ ~贈 *n.* inscription
T'I³ ~體 *n.* body, style, form, manner, substance
~chi¹ ~積 *n.* volume (measure)
~hui⁴ ~會 *v.* comprehend

184

~hsü⁴ ~恤 *v.* conserve
~ko² ~格 *n.* physique
~ko² chien³ ch'a² ~格檢查 *n.* physical examination
~li⁴ ~力 *n.* strength (vigor)
~mien⁴ ~面 *n.* honor
~t'ieh¹ ~貼 *v.* sympathize
~ts'ao¹ ~操 *n.* physical training
~yü⁴ ~育 *n.* physical culture
~yü⁴ kuan³ ~育館 *n.* gymnasium
~yü⁴ yün⁴ tung⁴ wei³ yüan² hui⁴ ~育運動委員
會 *n.* Commission of Physical Culture**
T'I⁴ 替 *v.* substitute, replace; *prep.* for, instead of
~huan⁴ ~換 *v.* alternate
~shen¹ ~身 *n.* substitute (person)
T'IAO¹ 挑 *v.* select, lift, carry
~¹ fu¹ ~夫 *n.* porter
~hsüan³ ~選 *n.* select
~³ chan⁴ ~戰 *v.* challenge
~po¹ ~撥 *v.* instigate, stir up
T'IAO² 調 *v.* stir up, mix. TIAO⁴ *v.* transfer; *n.*
tune, rhyme
~chieh³ jen² ~解人 *n.* mediator
~ho² ~和 *n.* harmony
~hsi⁴ ~戲 *v.* dally with
~hsiao⁴ ~笑 *v.* dally with
~t'ing² ~停 *v.* mediate, adjust
~wei⁴ ~味 *v.* season
~yin¹ ~音 *v.* put in tune
tiao⁴ ch'a² ~查 *v.* investigate
~ch'a² yüan² ~查員 *n.* investigator
~huan⁴ ~換 *v.* exchange
T'IAO² 條 *n.* twig, classifier, bill, article, clause
~chien⁴ ~件 *n.* conditions, terms (of agreement)
~k'uan³ ~款 *n.* article, clause
~li⁴ ~例 *n.* regulation
~wen² ~文 *n.* provision
~yüeh¹ ~約 *n.* treaty
T'IAO⁴ 跳 *v.* jump, leap; *n.* ricochet
~kao¹ ~高 *n.* high jump
~lan² ~欄 *n.* hurdle race, hurdles

185

~san³ 傘 v. bail out

~san³ t'a³ ~傘塔 n. parachute tower

~tsao³ ~蚤 n. flea

~wu³ ~舞 n. & v. dance

~wu³ hui⁴ ~舞會 n. ball (dance)

~wu³ t'ing¹ ~舞廳 n. dance hall

T'IEH¹ 貼 v. paste up, stick

~pu³ ~補 v. subsidize

T'IEH³ 帖 n. copybook, invitation card

T'IEH³ 鐵 n. iron

~chia³ ~甲 a. armored; n. armor

~chiang⁴ ~匠 n. blacksmith

~ch'ang³ ~廠 n. ironworks

~ch'i⁴ ~器 n. ironware

~lu⁴ ~路 n. railroad, railway

~mu⁴ ~幕 n. iron curtain

~ssu¹ ~糸 n. iron wire

~tao⁴ pu⁴ ~道部 n. Ministry of Railways**

~ting¹ ~釘 n. iron nail

T'IEN¹ 天 n. sky, heaven, day

~ching³ ~井 n. yard

~chu³ chiao⁴ ~主教 n. Catholicism, Catholicity

~chu³ chiao⁴ t'u² ~主教徒 n. Catholic

~ch'eng⁴ ~秤 n. balance

~ch'i⁴ ~氣 n. weather

~ch'uang¹ ~窗 n. skylight

~e² jung² ~鵝絨 n. velvet

~hua¹ ~花 n. smallpox

~hua¹ pan³ ~花板 n. ceiling

~hsing⁴ ~性 n. instinct, nature

~k'ung¹ ~空 n. sky

~liang² ~良 n. conscience

~shih³ ~使 n. angel

~ti⁴ ~地 n. heaven and earth

~t'ang² ~堂 n. heaven, paradise

~tsai¹ ~災 n. catastrophe, disaster, calamity

~ts'ai² ~才 n. talent

~tzu¹ ~資 n. endowments

~wen² ~文 n. astronomy

~wen² t'ai² ~文臺 n. observatory

~ai² ~涯 n. horizon

T'IEN¹ 添 *v.* increase, add to
T'IEN² 甜 *a.* sweet
~mi⁴ ~蜜 *a.* sweet
~shui⁴ 睡 *n.* sound sleep
~yen² ~言 *n.* sweet words
T'IEN² 田 *n.* field
~ch'an³ ~産 *n.* estate, landed property
~ti⁴ ~地 *n.* field
~tsu¹ ~租 *n.* rent for the use of fields
T'IEN² 塡 *v.* fill up, complete
~liao⁴ ~料 *n.* gasket
~shih² ~實 *v.* tamp
~t'u³ ~土 *v.* fill (*engin.*)
T'ING¹ 聽 *v.* hear, listen. ~⁴ *v.* comply
~¹ chung⁴ ~衆 *n.* audience (meet)
~chüeh² ~覺 *n.* sense of hearing
~ch'ai¹ ~差 *n.* servant
~shuo¹ ~說 *v.* hear of
~⁴ hsin⁴ ~信 *v.* believe
~jen⁴ ~任 *v.* allow
~ming⁴ ~命 *v.* accept one's fate, obey orders
~ts'ung² ~從 *v.* obey
T'ING¹ 廳 *n.* hall, parlor, court, tribunal
~chang³ ~長 *n.* department commissioner
T'ING² 停 *v.* stop, delay, cease; *a.* settled
~chan⁴ ~戰 *n.* truce, armistice
~chan⁴ hsieh² ting⁴ ~戰協定 *n.* armistice agreement
~chih³ ~止 *v.* cease, stop, halt
~chih³ ying² yeh⁴ ~止營業 *n.* cessation of business
~hsin¹ ~薪 *n.* stoppage of officers' pay
~liu² ~留 *v.* stay, remain
~po² ~泊 *v.* anchor
~po² teng¹ ~泊燈 *n.* anchor light
~pu⁴ ~步 *v.* halt
T'ING² 庭 *n.* courtyard
~yüan⁴ ~院 *n.* courtyard
T'O¹ 脫 *v.* doff, take off, remove, strip, escape
~chieh² ~節 *n.* dislocation (joint)
~li² ~離 *v.* disengage, break contact tactics, free

187

~t'ao² 逃 *v.* escape

T'O¹ 託 *v.* entrust, ask

~erh² so³ ~兒所 *n.* day nursery

~fu⁴ ~付 *v.* entrust

~ku⁴ ~故 *v.* give a pretext

~tz'u² ~辭 *n.* excuse, pretext

T'O¹ 拖 *v.* pull, drag

~ch'ien⁴ ~欠 *v.* be in debt

~ch'uan² ~船 *n.* tug-boat

~hsieh² ~鞋 *n.* slipper

~lei³ ~累 *v.* involve

~yen² ~延 *v.* delay

T'O³ 妥 *a.* safe, secure

~hsieh² ~協 *n. & v.* compromise

~tang¹ ~當 *a.* safe, settled

T'OU¹ 偷 *v.* steal; *a.* fraudulent; *n.* theft

~an¹ ~安 *a.* sedentary

~ch'ieh⁴ ~竊 *v.* steal; *n.* theft, larceny

~p'ao³ ~跑 *v.* escape

~shui⁴ ~稅 *n.* tax-evasion

~yün⁴ ~運 *v.* smuggle

T'OU² 頭 *n.* head, top, end, chief; *a.* first

~chin¹ ~巾 *n.* head scarf

~ling³ ~領 *n.* chief

~nao³ ~腦 *n.* brain

~tang⁴ ~檔 *n.* low gear

~teng³ ~等 *n.* first class

~t'ung⁴ ~痛 *n.* headache

~yün¹ ~暈 *n.* dizziness, vertigo

T'OU² 投 *v.* throw, fling, invest

~chi¹ ~機 *v.* speculate (business)

~chün¹ ~軍 *v.* enlist

~hsiang² ~降 *n. & v.* surrender

~ju⁴ sheng¹ ch'an³ ~入生產 *v.* commence production**

~kao³ ~稿 *v.* contribute (write)

~piao¹ ~標 *n.* auction bidding

~p'iao⁴ ~票 *v.* vote

~p'iao⁴ ch'üan² ~票權 *n.* suffrage

~tzu¹ ~資 *v.* invest

T'OU⁴ 透 *v.* penetrate

~chih¹ ~支 *v.* overdraw
~ch'e⁴ ~澈 *adv.* thoroughly
~feng¹ ~風 *v.* ventilate
~kuang¹ ~光 *a.* translucent
~ming² ~明 *a.* transparent; *n.* transparency
T'U² 塗 *n.* mud, dirt, mire; *v.* plaster
~kai³ ~改 *v.* alter
~mo³ ~抹 *v.* obliterate
~wu¹ ~污 *v.* daub (stain)
T'U² 途 *n.* road, path, way
~chung¹ ~中 *adv.* on the way, en route
~ch'eng² ~程 *n.* journey
T'U² 徒 *adv.* barely, only
~hsing² ~刑 *n.* penal servitude
~jan² ~然 *adv.* in vain
~pu⁴ ~步 *v.* walk on foot
~she⁴ ~涉 *v.* ford (on foot)
~shou³ ~手 *a.* unarmed
~ti⁴ ~弟 *n.* apprentice, pupil
T'U² 圖 *n.* figure, map, picture; *v.* sketch, try for
~chang¹ ~章 *n.* seal
~chieh³ ~解 *n.* & *v.* diagram
~hua⁴ ~畫 *n.* drawing, picture
~mou² ~謀 *v.* conspire
~piao³ ~表 *n.* diagram
~shu¹ ~書 *n.* books
~shu¹ kuan³ ~書館 *n.* library
~shu¹ kuan³ yüan² ~書館員 *n.* librarian
~yang⁴ ~樣 *n.* design
T'U² 屠 *v.* kill, butcher, slaughter
~ch'ang³ ~場 *n.* slaughter house
~fu¹ ~夫 *n.* butcher
~sha¹ ~殺 *v.* slaughter
~tsai³ shui⁴ ~宰稅 *n.* butchery tax
T'U³ 土 *n.* earth, ground, soil, land, territory
~ch'an³ ~產 *n.* native product
~fei³ ~匪 *n.* bandit, highwayman, robber
~hao² ~豪 *n.* local bully
~hua⁴ ~話 *n.* dialect
~hsing¹ ~星 *n.* Saturn (astronomy)
~jang³ ~壤 *n.* soil

189

~jen² ~人 *n.* native

~kai³ ~改 *n.* land reform**

~kun⁴ ~棍 *n.* local bully

~mu⁴ kung¹ ch'eng² ~木工程 *n.* civil engineering

~ti⁴ ~地 *n.* land, territory

~ti⁴ kai³ ko² ~地改革 *n.* Agrarian Reform**

~ti⁴ ko² ming⁴ chan⁴ cheng¹ ~地革命戦争 *n.* Agrarian Revolutionary War**

T'U⁴ 吐 *v.* reveal, spit, vomit

~hsüeh⁴ ~血 *v.* spit blood

~lu⁴ ~露 *v.* tell, disclose

~t'an² ~痰 *v.* spit phlegm

T'U⁴ 突 *v.* rush; *adv.* suddenly

~chi¹ ~擊 *n.* assault, shock action

~ch'i³ ~起 *n.* protuberance

~ch'u¹ ~出 *v.* protrude

~jan² ~然 *adv.* suddenly

~p'o⁴ ~破 *v.* break through, penetrate

~p'o⁴ k'ou³ ~破口 *n.* breach

~wei² ~圍 *v.* break out (from encirclement)

T'UAN² 團 *n.* regiment, lump, sphere, body

~chang³ ~長 *n.* regimental commander

~chieh² ~結 *n.* solidarity; *v.* unite

~chieh² ching¹ shen² ~結精神 *n.* esprit de corps

~t'i³ ~体 *n.* organization, body

~t'i³ kuan¹ nien⁴ ~体観念 *n.* group feeling

~t'i³ sheng¹ huo² ~体生活 *n.* group life

~yüan² ~圓 *n.* reunion

T'UI¹ 推 *v.* push, expel, decline, ram

~chin⁴ ~進 *v.* push, advance (on a place)

~chin⁴ chi¹ ~進機 *n.* pusher airplane

~chiu¹ ~究 *v.* examine

~ch'üeh⁴ ~却 *v.* refuse

~fan¹ ~翻 *v.* overthrow, upset

~hsüan³ ~選 *v.* elect

~kan³ ~桿 *n.* plunger

~kuang³ ~廣 *v.* extend

~lun⁴ ~論 *v.* deduce, infer; *n.* logical deduction

~shih⁴ ~事 *n.* judge

~t'o¹ ~託 v. make excuse
~tse⁴ ~測 v. guess, suppose
T'UI³ 腿 n. thigh, leg
T'UI⁴ 退 v. withdraw, retire, retreat
~chih² ~職 n. retirement
~ch'u¹ ~出 v. quit
~hou⁴ ~後 v. retreat
~hua⁴ ~化 v. degenerate; n. degeneration
~huan² ~還 v. send back, return
~jang⁴ ~讓 v. give up, yield
~pi⁴ ~避 v. avert
~pu⁴ ~步 a. backward (retrogressive)
~se⁴ ~色 v. fade
~so¹ ~縮 v. shrink back
~yin³ ~隱 v. retire
T'UN¹ 吞 v. swallow, gulp, engross
~chan⁴ ~佔 v. usurp
~k'uan³ ~款 v. squeeze money
~ping⁴ ~併 v. engross
~shih² ~食 v. swallow
T'UNG¹ 通 v. go through, communicate with, contact
~chih¹ ~知 v. notify
~ch'ang² ~常 a. ordinary
~hsin⁴ ~信 v. correspond; n. correspondence
~hsin⁴ ch'u⁴ ~信处 n. mail address
~hsin⁴ yüan² ~信員 n. correspondent
~hsing² ~行 a. current
~jung² ~融 v. accommodate (oblige)
~kao⁴ ~告 n. written notice
~kuo⁴ ~過 v. pass; n. passage
~li⁴ ~例 n. custom
~su² ~俗 a. common (below ordinary)
~shang¹ ~商 v. trade with foreign countries
T'UNG² 童 n. boy
~chen¹ ~眞 n. virgin
~hua⁴ ~話 n. fairy tale
~nien² ~年 n. boyhood
~tz'u³ ~子 n. boy
~tzu³ chün¹ ~子軍 n. boy scout
T'UNG² 同 *conj.* and, with; *adv.* together; *a.*

same, alike
~chih⁴ ~志 *n.* comrade
~chung³ ~種 *n.* the same race
~ch'ing² ~情 *n.* sympathy
~ch'ou² ti² k'ai⁴ ~仇敵愾 *v.* have a common enmity and hatred
~hua⁴ ~化 *n.* amalgamation
~hsiang¹ ~鄉 *n.* natives of the same province
~hsüeh² ~學 *n.* schoolmate
~i² hsing⁴ ~一性 *n.* unity
~i⁴ ~意 *v.* agree; *n.* agreement
~kan¹ k'u³ ~甘苦 *v.* share the joys and privations
~meng² ~盟 *n.* alliance
~meng² kuo² ~盟國 *n.* alliance, allies
~pan¹ t'ung² hsüeh² ~班同學 *n.* classmate
~pan⁴ ~伴 *n.* companion
~pao¹ ~胞 *n.* brothers, countryman, compatriot
~p'ao² ~袍 *n.* fellow officer
~shih² ~時 *n.* meantime
~shih⁴ ~事 *n.* colleague, fellow worker
~teng³ ~等 *n.* equality
~wen² ~文 *a.* of the same language
~yang⁴ ~樣 *a.* same, alike
T'UNG² 銅 *n.* copper, brass
~chiang⁴ ~匠 *n.* coppersmith
~k'uang⁴ ~鑛 *n.* copper mine
~pi⁴ ~幣 *n.* copper coin
T'UNG³ 統 *a.* all, whole, total
~chi⁴ hsüeh² ~計學 *n.* statistics
~chih⁴ ~治 *v.* govern, rule
~i¹ ~一 *v.* unify; *n.* unification
~i² hsing⁴ ~一性 *n.* unity
~kung⁴ ~共 *a.* total
T'UNG³ 筒 *n.* tube, pipe
T'UNG³ 桶 *n.* bucket, barrel
T'UNG⁴ 痛 *n.* pain, ache, anguish
~hen⁴ ~恨 *v.* abhor, hate
~k'u¹ ~哭 *v.* weep bitterly
~k'u³ ~苦 *n.* pain, ache, grief

192

TS

TSA² 咱 *pron.* I, me
~chia¹ ~家 *pron.* I, me
~men² ~們 *pron.* we, us
TSA² 雜 *a.* various, mixed, miscellaneous, mingled
~chi⁴ pu⁴ ~記簿 *n.* notebook
~chih⁴ ~誌 *n.* magazine
~chung³ ~種 *n.* mixed race; *a.* illegitimate
~fei⁴ ~費 *n.* miscellaneous expenses
~huo⁴ ~貨 *n.* sundries
~huo⁴ tien⁴ ~貨店 *n.* grocery
~luan⁴ ~亂 *a.* disorderly, mix-up
TSAI¹ 栽 *v.* plant, cultivate
~chung⁴ ~種 *v.* plant, cultivate
~hua¹ ~花 *v.* plant flowers
~p'ei² ~培 *v.* educate
TSAI¹ 災 *n.* calamity, misfortune, disaster
~hai⁴ ~害 *n.* calamity
~huo⁴ ~禍 *n.* disaster
~nan⁴ ~難 *n.* disaster
TSAI⁴ 再 *adv.* again, once more
~che³ ~者 *n.* postscript
~chieh¹ tsai⁴ li⁴ ~接再厲 *v.* work hard against difficulties
~fan⁴ ~犯 *n.* recommitment
~hui⁴ ~會 *int.* & *n.* good-bye, farewell
~hun¹ ~婚 *v.* marry again
~pan³ ~版 *v.* reprint
~san¹ ~三 *adv.* repeatedly
~sheng¹ ch'an³ ~生產 *n.* reproduction (goods)
TSAI⁴ 在 *v.* remain, consist in; *prep.* at, in, on, within; *adv.* present
~chih² ~職 *adv.* in office
~ch'ang³ ~場 *a.* present
~ch'ien² ~前 *prep.* before; *adv.* ahead, in front
~hou⁴ ~後 *adv.* behind, in the rear
~hsia⁴ ~下 *prep.* below, beneath, down, under
~nei⁴ ~内 *prep.* within, in, among

193

~shang⁴ ~上 *prep.* on, above
~wai⁴ ~外 *adv.* out
TSAN⁴ 贊 *v.* advise, assist
~chu⁴ ~助 *v.* assist, help
~ch'eng² ~成 *v.* second
~mei³ ~美 *v.* praise
TSANG¹ 髒 *a.* filthy, dirty, foul
TSANG⁴ 藏 *see* TS'ANG²
TSAO³ 早 *adv.* early; *a.* previous; *n.* morning, good morning
~ch'en² ~晨 *n.* morning
~ch'i³ ~起 *v.* get up early
~hun¹ ~婚 *n.* early marriage
~shou² ~熟 *a.* premature; *adv.* prematurely
~shui⁴ ~睡 *v.* sleep early
~ts'an¹ ~餐 *n.* breakfast
TSAO⁴ 造 *v.* build, construct, make
~ch'uan² ~船 *n.* shipbuilding
~ch'uan² ch'ang³ ~船廠 *n.* dockyard
~pi⁴ ch'ang³ ~幣廠 *n.* money mint
~yao² ~謠 *v.* rumor
TSE² 責 *v.* reprove, punish, rebuke, require from; *n.* duty
~fa² ~罰 *v.* punish
~jen⁴ ~任 *n.* responsibility
~ma⁴ ~罵 *v.* reprove, rebuke
TSE² 澤 *n.* marsh, swamp, bog
TSE² 則 *n.* rule, regulation; *conj.* then, so
TSEI² 賊 *n.* thief, bandit, robber
TSEN³ 怎 *adv.* how, why, what
~yang⁴ ~樣 *adv.* how, why, what
TSENG¹ 增 *v.* increase, add
~chia¹ ~加 *v.* increase
~chih² ~殖 *n.* propagation
~pu³ ~補 *v.* supplement
~ta⁴ ~大 *v.* enlarge
~ting⁴ ~訂 *v.* revise; *n.* revision
~yüan² ~援 *v.* reinforce
TSO² 昨 *n.* yesterday; *adv.* formerly
~jih⁴ ~日 *n.* yesterday
~yeh⁴ ~夜 *n.* last night

TSO³ 左 *a. & n.* left
  ~ch'ing¹ ~傾 *a.* leftist idea
  ~ch'ing¹ yu⁴ chih⁴ ping⁴ ~傾幼稚病 *n.* "Left" infantile errors**
  ~i⁴ k'ung¹ t'an² chu³ i⁴ ~翼空談主義 *n.* phrase-mongering of the "leftists"**
  ~p'ai⁴ ~派 *n.* leftist member
  ~shou³ ~手 *a.* left-hand, left-handed

TSO⁴ 作 *v.* make, do
  ~² liao⁴ ~料 *n.* stuff, material
  ~⁴ chia¹ ~家 *n.* writer, author
  ~fei⁴ ~廢 *v.* rescind, cancel
  ~kung¹ ~工 *v.* work
  ~luan⁴ ~亂 *v.* rebel; *n.* rebellion
  ~meng⁴ ~夢 *v.* dream
  ~pao³ ~保 *v.* guarantee
  ~pi⁴ ~弊 *v.* cheat
  ~wen² ~文 *n.* composition
  ~yeh⁴ ~業 *n.* work (field)
  ~yeh⁴ pan¹ ~業班 *n.* work party
  ~yung⁴ ~用 *n.* function

TSO⁴ 做 *v.* do, act, make
  ~kung¹ ~工 *v.* work
  ~mei² ~媒 *n.* matchmaking

TSO⁴ 坐 *v.* sit
  ~chien¹ ~監 *v.* imprison
  ~hsia⁴ ~下 *v.* sit down
  ~tien⁴ ~墊 *n.* cushion
  ~wei⁴ ~位 *n.* seat

TSO⁴ 座 *n.* seat, place
  ~wei⁴ ~位 *n.* seat

TSOU³ 走 *v.* walk; *n.* walking
  ~feng¹ ~風 *v.* leak out the secret
  ~kou³ ~狗 *n.* hound (person)
  ~lang² ~廊 *n.* corridor
  ~lu⁴ ~路 *v.* walk
  ~shou⁴ ~獸 *n.* beast
  ~ts'o⁴ ~錯 *n.* go astray

TSU¹ 租 *n.* tax, rent; *v.* rent, lease
  ~chia⁴ ~價 *n.* rent
  ~chieh⁴ ~界 *n.* concession, settlement

195

~chieh⁴ ti⁴ ~借地 *n.* leased territory

~chin¹ ~金 *n.* rent

~ch'i⁴ ~契 *n.* lease

~fang² ~房 *v.* rent a house

~hu⁴ ~戶 *n.* tenant

~lin⁴ ~賃 *v.* rent

~shui⁴ ~稅 *n.* tax

TSU² 足 *n.* foot; *a.* enough, sufficient

~chi¹ ~跡 *n.* trace

~chih³ ~趾 *n.* toe

~ch'iu² ~球 *n.* football

~ch'iu² ch'ang⁸ ~球場 *n.* football ground

~ch'iu² sai⁴ ~球賽 *n.* football

~hsia⁴ ~下 *n.* sir

~kou⁴ ~夠 *a.* enough

TSU² 族 *n.* family, relatives, tribe, clan; *adv.* together

TSU³ 組 *n.* section, group, part; *v.* organize

~chih¹ ~織 *v.* organize; *n.* organization

~chih¹ cheng⁴ fu³ ~織政府 *v.* organize a government

~ho² ~合 *n.* combination

TSU³ 祖 *n.* grandfather, ancestor

~fu⁴ ~父 *n.* father's father (grandfather)

~hsien¹ ~先 *n.* ancestor

~mu³ ~母 *n.* father's mother (grandmother)

TSU³ 阻 *v.* stop, prevent, hinder; *n.* prevention

~ai⁴ ~礙 *n.* hinder, stop, prevent, impede

~chih³ ~止 *v.* stop, interdict

~chüeh² ~絕 *v.* block, barricade

~li⁴ ~力 *n.* air resistance

~se⁴ ~塞 *v.* barricade

TSUI³ 嘴 *n.* mouth, bill, peak

~ch'an² ~饞 *v.* desire for food

~ch'un² ~唇 *n.* lip

TSUI⁴ 最 *adv.* very, most, extremely

~chia¹ ~佳 *a.* best

~chin⁴ ~近 *a.* nearest

~hou⁴ ~後 *a.* last

~hsiao³ ~小 *a.* smallest

~kao¹ ~高 *n.* highest

196

~kao¹ chia⁴ ~高價 *n.* maximum price

~kao¹ jen² min² chien³ ch'a² shu³ ~高人民檢察署 *n.* People's Procurator-General's Office**

~kao¹ jen² min² fa³ yüan⁴ ~高人民法院 *n.* Supreme People's Court**

~lieh⁴ ~劣 *a.* worst

~ta⁴ ~大 *a.* largest, greatest, biggest

~ti¹ ~低 *a.* lowest

~ti¹ chia⁴ ~低價 *n.* minimum price

~yüan³ ~遠 *a.* farthest

TSUI⁴ 醉 *a.* drunk, intoxicated

~han⁴ ~漢 *n.* drunkard

TSUI⁴ 罪 *n.* crime, sin, wrong

~chuang⁴ ~狀 *n.* legal charge

~e⁴ ~惡 *n.* crime, sin, evil

~fan⁴ ~犯 *n.* criminal

TSUN¹ 遵 *v.* follow, conform, obey

~shou³ ~守 *v.* obey regulations

~ts'ung² ~從 *v.* obey

TSUNG¹ 宗 *n.* clan, kind, sort; *a.* ancestral

~chiao⁴ ~教 *n.* religion

~chih³ ~旨 *n.* purpose

~miao⁴ ~廟 *n.* ancestral temple

~p'ai⁴ ~派 *n.* sect

~p'ai⁴ chu³ i⁴ ~派主義 *n.* sectarianism**

~tsu² ~族 *n.* kindred

TSUNG³ 總 *v.* unite, comprise, sum up

~chang⁴ ~帳 *n.* total account

~cheng⁴ chih⁴ pu⁴ ~政治部 *n.* General Political Department*

~chi⁴ ~計 *n.* total, sum

~chieh² sheng¹ ch'an⁴ kung¹ tso⁴ ~結生産工作 *v.* sum up production work**

~chih¹ ~之 *adv.* in short

~ching¹ li³ ~經理 *n.* general manager

~hou⁴ fang¹ chin² wu⁴ pu⁴ ~後方勤務部 *n.* General Logistics Department**

~kan⁴ pu⁴ kuan³ li³ pu⁴ ~幹部管理部 *n.* General Cadre Control Department**

~kung⁴ ~共 *n.* total, whole, all

~li³ ~理 *n.* premier, prime minister

~ling³ shih⁴ ~領事 *n.* consul general

~shang¹ hui⁴ ~商會 *n.* general chamber of commerce

~shu⁴ ~數 *n.* total, sum

~ssu¹ ling⁴ ~司令 *n.* commander-in-chief

~tai⁴ piao³ ~代表 *n.* chief delegate

~tien⁴ ~店 *n.* head office, general office

~t'ung³ ~統 *n.* President, Executive (*U.S.*)

~t'ung³ fu³ ~統府 *n.* Office of the President*

~ts'ai² ~裁 *n.* director-general

~ts'ai² wu⁴ pu⁴ ~財務部 *n.* General Finance Department**

~ts'an¹ mou² pu⁴ ~參謀部 *n.* General Staff Department**

~wu⁴ chü² ~務局 *n.* General Affairs Bureau*

TS'

TS'A¹ 擦 *v.* rub, wipe

~ch'u⁴ ~去 *v.* wipe out

~hsieh² ~鞋 *v.* polish shoes

~lien³ ~臉 *v.* clean the face

~yu² ~油 *v.* varnish, oil

TS'AI¹ 猜 *v.* guess, doubt, suspect

~chi⁴ ~忌 *a.* jealous; *n.* jealousy

~hsiang³ ~想 *v.* guess

~i² ~疑 *a.* suspicious; *n.* suspicion

TS'AI² 財 *n.* money, wealth

~cheng⁴ ~政 *n.* finance

~cheng⁴ chia¹ ~政家 *n.* financier

~cheng⁴ ching¹ chi⁴ ~政經濟 *n.* finance and economics

~cheng⁴ ching¹ chi⁴ wei³ yüan² hui⁴ ~政經濟委員會 *n.* Committee of Financial and Economic Affairs**

~cheng⁴ hsüeh² ~政學 *n.* finance

~cheng⁴ pu⁴ ~政部 *n.* Ministry of Finance

~chu³ ~主 *n.* millionaire, rich man

~ch'an³ ~產 *n.* property

~ch'an³ shui⁴ ~產稅 *n.* estate duty

198

~fa² ~閥 *n.* capitalist
~fu⁴ ~富 *n.* wealth
~huo⁴ ~貨 *n.* riches
~li⁴ ~力 *n.* resources (wealth)
~shih⁴ ~勢 *n.* wealth and influence
~t'uan² ~團 *n.* foundation fund
TS'AI² 才 *n.* ability, talent
~chih⁴ ~智 *n.* intelligence, wisdom
~hsüeh² ~學 *n.* scholarship, learning, ability
~kan⁴ ~幹 *n.* talent, ability
~neng² ~能 *n.* ability, talent
~tzu³ ~子 *n.* genius, a man of talent
TS'AI² 材 *n.* ability, material
~liao⁴ ~料 *n.* material
~mu⁴ ~木 *n.* wood, timber
TS'AI² 裁 *v.* cut, reduce, decide; *n.* cut
~feng² ~縫 *n.* tailor
~p'an⁴ ~判 *v.* judge
TS'AI³ 採 *v.* pick, gather, select
~ch'a² ~茶 *v.* pick tea
~hua¹ ~花 *v.* deflower
~kuang⁴ ~鑛 *n.* mining
~na⁴ ~納 *v.* agree to accept
~shih² ch'ang³ ~石場 *n.* quarry
~tse² ~擇 *v.* choose
~yung⁴ ~用 *v.* adopt (accept)
TS'AI⁴ 菜 *n.* vegetable
~ch'ang³ ~場 *n.* market (provisions)
~tan¹ ~單 *n.* menu, bill of fare
~tzu³ ~子 *n.* rape (plant)
~yüan² ~園 *n.* vegetable garden
TS'AN¹ 參 *v.* counsel, advise, consult
~chia¹ ~加 *v.* join, participate
~chün¹ yün⁴ tung⁴ ~軍運動 *n.* "Join the Army Movement"**
~i⁴ yüan² ~議員 *n.* senator
~i⁴ yüan⁴ ~議院 *n.* Senate (*U.S.*)
~kuan¹ ~觀 *v.* visit
~k'ao³ ~考 *n.* reference
~k'ao³ shu¹ ~考書 *n.* reference book
~mou² ~謀 *n.* staff officer

199

~mou² chang³ ~謀長 *n.* chief of staff

~mou² tsung³ chang³ ~謀總長 *n.* Chief of the General Staff*

~mou² tz'u⁴ chang³ ~謀次長 *n.* Assistant Chief of the General Staff*

~mou² yeh⁴ wu⁴ ~謀業務 *n.* staff duty

~shih⁴ ~事 *n.* councilor

~tsa² ~雜 *a.* mixed

~yü³ ~與 *v.* participate

TS'AN² 殘 *a.* maimed, cruel; *v.* injure; *n.* cruelty, leavings

~fei⁴ ~廢 *a.* maimed

~hai⁴ ~害 *v.* destroy

~jen³ ~忍 *a.* cruel

~k'u⁴ ~酷 *a.* cruel

~ping¹ ~兵 *n.* disabled soldiers, remnants

~sha¹ ~殺 *v.* slaughter

~yü² ~餘 *n.* leavings

TS'AN² 蠶 *n.* silkworm

~shih² ~食 *a.* piecemeal

TS'AN³ 慘 *a.* sad, grievous

~chuang⁴ ~狀 *a.* wretched

~lieh⁴ ~烈 *a.* bloodshed (*mil.*)

~t'ung⁴ ~痛 *a.* grievous

TS'ANG¹ 倉 *n.* barn, bin, storehouse, warehouse

~k'u⁴ ~庫 *n.* storehouse, warehouse

~ts'u⁴ ~促 *a.* hurried; *adv.* hurriedly

TS'ANG¹ 蒼 *a.* green, azure

~huang² ~黃 *a.* yellow

~pai² ~白 *a.* pale

~t'ien¹ ~天 *n.* sky

~ts'ui⁴ ~翠 *a.* green

~ying² ~蠅 *n.* fly

TS'ANG² 藏 TSANG⁴ *n.* Tibet; *v.* hide

~ni⁴ ~匿 *v.* hide

TS'AO¹ 操 *n.* exercise; *v.* practise, drill

~ch'ang³ ~場 *n.* playground

~hsin¹ ~心 *a.* anxious

~lao² ~勞 *a.* laborious (hard-working)

~lien⁴ ~練 *v.* drill, train

~tsung⁴ ~縱 *v.* control

TS'AO³ 草 *n.* grass, herb, plant, hay
~an⁴ ~案 *n.* draft, proposal
~hsieh² ~鞋 *n.* sandals
~kao³ ~稿 *n.* draft (rough copy)
~liao⁴ ~料 *n.* forage
~mei² ~莓 *n.* strawberry
~p'eng² ~棚 *n.* thatched hut
~p'ing² ~坪 *n.* lawn
~ti⁴ ~地 *n.* meadow, grassland
~yüeh¹ ~約 *n.* protocol
TS'E⁴ 策 *n.* plan, policy
~hua⁴ ~劃 *v.* plan
~lüeh⁴ ~略 *n.* stratagem
TS'ENG² 曾 *a.* past, done; *adv.* still, yet
~ching¹ ~經 *adv.* already
TS'ENG² 層 *n.* layer, story, stratum
~tieh² ~疊 *n.* stratification
~tz'u⁴ ~次 *n.* gradations
TS'O⁴ 錯 *n.* mistake, error; *a.* wrong, incorrect
~ch'u⁴ ~處 *n.* error, mistake
~luan⁴ ~亂 *a.* confused
~tsung⁴ ~綜 *n.* intricacy
~tzu⁴ ~字 *n.* erratum
~wu⁴ ~誤 *n.* mistake, error; *a.* wrong
TS'U¹ 粗 *a.* coarse, rude, rough, vulgar
~ts'ao¹ ~糙 *a.* coarse
~yü³ ~語 *n.* obscene language
TS'U⁴ 醋 *n.* vinegar
TS'UI¹ 催 *v.* urge, press, importune
~mien² ~眠 *v.* hypnotize
~mien² shu⁴ ~眠術 *n.* hypnotism (science)
~mien² yao⁴ ~眠藥 *n.* hypnotic drug
~ts'u⁴ ~促 *v.* urge, press
TS'UN¹ 村 *n.* village
~chuang¹ ~莊 *n.* village
~fu¹ ~夫 *n.* villager
TS'UN² 存 *v.* keep, preserve, store, deposit, exist; *a.* alive
~chan⁴ ~棧 *v.* keep in a warehouse
~huo⁴ ~貨 *n.* stock
~ken¹ ~根 *n.* counterpart, copy, duplicate

201

~k'uan³ ~款 *n.* & *v.* deposit
~liu² ~留 *v.* remain
~tsai⁴ ~在 *n.* existence, substance, continuance
TS'UN⁴ 寸 *n.* Chinese measure for 1.41 inches
TS'UNG¹ 聰 *a.* clever
~ming² ~明 *a.* clever, intelligent
TS'UNG² 從 *v.* follow, pursue, comply with; *prep* from, by, since
~chün¹ ~軍 *v.* join the army
~ch'ien² ~前 *adv.* formerly
~ming⁴ ~命 *v.* obey
~shih⁴ ~事 *v.* pursue
~tz'u³ ~此 *prep.* henceforth
~wei⁴ ~未 *adv.* never

TZ

TZU¹ 資 *n.* wealth, property; *v.* help
~chu⁴ ~助 *v.* help
~ch'an³ ~産 *n.* capital (money)
~ch'an³ chieh¹ chi² ~産階級 *n.* bourgeoisie**
~ko² ~格 *n.* qualification
~pen³ ~本 *n.* capital (money)
~pen³ chia¹ ~本家 *n.* capitalist
~pen³ chu³ i⁴ ~本主義 *n.* capitalism
~pen³ chu³ i⁴ kuo² chia¹ ~本主義國家 *n.* capitalistic nation**
~pen³ chu³ i⁴ she⁴ hui⁴ ~本主義社會 *n.* capitalist society**
~pen³ lun⁴ ~本論 *n.* Capital**
~wang⁴ ~望 *n.* reputation
TZU³ 子 *n.* child, son; *pron.* you. ~¹ [a suffix]
~kung¹ ~宮 *n.* womb, uterus
~nü³ ~女 *n.* child
~sun¹ ~孫 *n.* descendant
~tan⁴ ~彈 *n.* bullet
~wu³ hsien⁴ ~午線 *n.* meridian
~yin¹ ~音 *n.* consonant
TZU⁴ 自 *n.* self; *prep.* since, from
~ai⁴ ~愛 *n.* self-respect

~chi³ ~己 *n.* self
~chih⁴ ~治 *n.* self-control
~chih⁴ ~制 *n.* self-control
~chih⁴ ch'ü¹ ~治區 *n.* Autonomous Region**
~chu⁴ ~助 *n.* self-help
~chung⁴ ~重 *n.* self-esteem
~ch'i¹ ~欺 *a.* self-deceptive
~ch'ien¹ ~謙 *n.* humble
~ch'uan² ~傳 *n.* autobiography
~fa¹ ch'ü¹ shih⁴ ~發趨勢 *n.* spontaneous tendency toward capitalism**
~hsin⁴ ~信 *a.* confident; *n.* confidence
~hsing² ch'e¹ ~行車 *n.* bicycle
~hsiu¹ ~修 *a.* self-taught
~jan² ~然 *adv.* of course, naturally; *a.* natural; *n.* natural, nature
~k'ua¹ ~誇 *n.* self-conceit
~lai² shui³ ch'ang³ ~來水廠 *n.* waterworks
~li⁴ ~立 *n.* self-support; *a.* self-supporting
~sha¹ ~殺 *n.* suicide; *v.* commit suicide
~ssu¹ ~私 *a.* selfish
~tung⁴ ~動 *a.* automatic
~tung⁴ pu⁴ ch'iang¹ ~動步槍 *n.* automatic rifle
~tung⁴ shou³ ch'iang¹ ~動手槍 *n.* automatic pistol
~tsai⁴ te¹ chieh¹ chi² ~在的階級 " class in itself "**
~tsun¹ ~尊 *n.* self-respect
~wei² te¹ chieh¹ chi² ~爲的階級 " class for itself "**
~wei⁴ ~衛 *n.* self-defense
~wo³ p'i¹ p'ing² ~我批評 *n.* self-criticism**
~yu² ~由 *n.* liberty, freedom; *a.* free
TZU⁴ 字 *n.* letter, character, word
~chi⁴ ~跡 *n.* handwriting
~chih³ lou³ ~紙簍 *n.* wastebasket
~hua⁴ ~畫 *n.* stroke
~hui⁴ ~彙 *n.* glossary, terminology, vocabulary
~i⁴ ~義 *n.* the meaning of a word
~ma³ ~碼 *n.* figure
~mu³ ~母 *n.* alphabet

~tien³ ~典 *n.* dictionary
~t'ieh⁴ ~帖 *n.* copybook

TZ'

TZ'U² 辭 *n.* expression, plea; *v.* decline, resign
~chih² ~職 *v.* resign; *n.* resignation
~pieh² ~別 *v.* bid farewell
~tien³ ~典 *n.* n. dictionary
~t'ui⁴ ~退 *v.* discharge, resign
TZ'U² 磁 *n.* porcelain, magnet; *a.* magnetic
~chen¹ ~針 *n.* compass
~chi² ~極 *n.* magnetic pole
~ch'ang³ ~場 *n.* magnetic field
~ch'i⁴ ~器 *n.* porcelain, china
~hsing⁴ ~性 *n.* magnetism
~li⁴ ~力 *n.* magnetism
~shih² ~石 *n.* magnet
TZ'U³ 此 *pron. & a.* this, these; *art.* the
~hou⁴ ~後 *adv.* hereafter
~k'o⁴ ~刻 *n.* this moment
~shih² ~時 *adv.* now, at present
~ti⁴ ~地 *adv.* here
~wai⁴ ~外 *adv.* besides, moreover, further
TZ'U⁴ 次 *n.* time, occasion; *a.* second, next
~chang³ ~長 *n.* vice-minister
~hsü⁴ ~序 *n.* order, series
~teng³ ~等 *n.* second class
TZ'U⁴ 刺 *v.* stab, sting, assassinate; *n.* thorn
~chi¹ ~激 *v.* stimulate
~hsiu⁴ ~繡 *v.* embroider; *n.* embroidery
~ju⁴ ~入 *v.* bore into
~k'o⁴ ~客 *n.* assassin, murderer
~sha¹ ~殺 *v.* stab; *n.* assassination
~tao¹ ~刀 *n.* bayonet
~tzu⁴ ~字 *v.* brand (skin)

W

WA¹ 控 *v.* excavate, hollow out, dig out, scoop
~ch'ien² li⁴ ~潛力 *v.* develop hidden strength**
WA³ 瓦 *n.* tile
~chieh³ ~解 *v.* disintegrate, dismember
~ssu¹ ~斯 *n.* gas (for heating)
WA⁴ 襪 *n.* sock, stocking
WAI⁴ 外 *adv.* out, outside; *prep.* outside, beyond
~chiao¹ ~交 *n.* diplomacy; *a.* diplomatic; *adv.* diplomatically
~chiao¹ cheng⁴ ts'e⁴ ~交政策 *n.* diplomatic policy
~chiao¹ chia¹ ~交家 *n.* diplomat
~chiao¹ chieh⁴ 交界 *n.* diplomatic circle
~chiao¹ pu⁴ ~交部 *n.* Ministry of Foreign Affairs
~chiao¹ t'uan² ~交團 *n.* diplomatic corps
~hang² ~行 *a.* unskilled
~hao⁴ ~號 *n.* nickname
~hui⁴ ~匯 *n.* foreign exchange
~kuo² ~國 *n.* foreign country
~kuo² yü³ ~國語 *n.* foreign language
~k'o¹ ~科 *n.* surgery
~k'o¹ i¹ sheng¹ ~科醫生 *n.* surgeon
~mien⁴ ~面 *n.* outside
~piao³ ~表 *n.* appearance
~p'o² ~婆 *n.* mother's mother (grandmother)
~sun¹ ~孫 *n.* daughter's son (grandson)
~sun¹ nü³ ~孫女 *n.* daughter's daughter (granddaughter)
~sheng¹ ~甥 *n.* son of one's sister (nephew)
~sheng¹ nü³ ~甥女 *n.* daughter of one's sister (niece)
~t'ao⁴ ~套 *n.* overcoat
~tsu³ fu⁴ ~祖父 *n.* mother's father (grandfather)
~tsu³ mu³ ~祖母 *n.* mother's mother (grandmother)
~tzu³ ~子 *n.* husband

205

WAN¹ 灣 *n.* bay, gulf, cove

WAN² 完 *v.* complete; *adv.* entirely; *a.* complete, perfect, entire; *n.* perfection

~**chüan²** ~全 *a.* perfect; *n.* perfection

~**pei⁴** ~備 *a.* well prepared

~**pi⁴** ~畢 *a.* & *v.* complete

WAN² 玩 *v.* play; *n.* amusement

~**chü⁴** ~具 *n.* toy

~**hsiao⁴** ~笑 *v.* joke

~**shang³** ~賞 *v.* enjoy

~**shua³** ~耍 *v.* play

WAN³ 晚 *n.* evening; *a.* late; *adv.* lately

~**an¹** ~安 *n.* good evening, good night

~**fan⁴** ~飯 *n.* supper

~**nien²** ~年 *a.* aged

~**pao⁴** ~報 *n.* evening newspaper

WAN³ 碗 *n.* bowl

WAN⁴ 萬 *n.* ten thousand; *a.* numerous

~**kuo²** ~國 *a.* international

~**kuo² hung² shih² tzu⁴ hui⁴** ~國紅十字會 *n.* International Red Cross Committee

~**li³ chang² ch'eng²** ~里長城 *n.* Great Wall of China

~**neng²** ~能 *a.* almighty

~**sui⁴** ~歲 *a.* long-lived

~**shih⁴** ~事 *pron.* everything

WANG² ~亡 *v.* be lost, perish, escape, die

~**ming⁴ chih¹ t'u²** ~命之徒 *n.* desperado, fugitive

WANG² 王 *n.* king, ruler; *a.* royal

~**kung¹** ~宮 *n.* palace

~**kuo²** ~國 *n.* kingdom

~**tzu³** ~子 *n.* prince

WANG³ 往 *v.* go; *a.* past; *adv.* formerly

~**hsi²** ~昔 *adv.* formerly, before

~**lai²** ~來 *adv.* to and fro, intercourse

~**wang³** ~往 *adv.* often, frequently

~**⁴ hou⁴** ~後 *adv.* hereafter

WANG⁴ 望 *v.* look at, hope; *n.* hope

~**pu⁴ chien⁴** ~不見 *v.* be out of sight

~**yüan³ ching⁴** ~遠鏡 *n.* telescope, binoculars

WANG⁴ 忘 *v.* forget
~chi⁴ ~記 *v.* forget
~en¹ ~恩 *a.* ungrateful
WANG⁴ 旺 *a.* prosperous; *n.* prosperity
~sheng⁴ ~盛 *n.* prosperity
WEI¹ 威 *n.* awe
~ch'üan² ~權 *n.* authority
~ho⁴ ~嚇 *v.* intimidate; *n.* intimidation
~ming² ~名 *n.* prestige
~wang⁴ ~望 *n.* prestige
~wu³ ~武 *a.* majestic
~yen² ~嚴 *n.* dignity
WEI² 爲 *v.* act, do, make, perform. *conj.* for, because
~⁴ ho² ~何 *adv.* why, for what reason
WEI² 危 *n.* danger; *a.* dangerous
~chi¹ ~機 *n.* crisis
~chi² ~急 *a.* dangerous, perilous
~hsien³ ~險 *n.* danger
~nan⁴ ~難 *adv.* in danger
WEI² 違 *v.* oppose, disobey
~chin⁴ p'in³ ~禁品 *n.* contraband
~fa³ ~法 *n.* breach of law
~yüeh¹ ~約 *n.* breach of contract
WEI² 維 *n.* [an initial particle] rule, law; *v.* tie, connect
~ch'ih² ~持 *v.* maintain
~ch'ih² chih⁴ hsü⁴ ~持秩序 *v.* maintain order
WEI² 圍 *v.* surround, besiege; *n.* circumference
~chin¹ ~巾 *n.* scarf, muffler
~ch'ün² ~裙 *n.* apron
~jao⁴ ~繞 *v.* surround
~kung¹ ~攻 *v.* besiege, seige
~k'un⁴ ~困 *v.* surround
WEI³ 委 *v.* appoint, assign, trust
~ch'ü¹ ~曲 *n.* injustice
~jen⁴ ~任 *v.* commission
~jen⁴ chuang⁴ ~任狀 '*n.* commission, warrant (the document)
~p'ai⁴ ~派 *v.* appoint, assign
~t'o¹ ~託 *v.* entrust

~yüan² ~員 *n.* committeeman, council member
~yüan² chang⁵ ~員長 *n.* committee chairman
~yüan² chih⁴ ~員制 *n.* committee system
WEI³ 尾 *n.* tail, end ; *a.* last
~pa¹ ~巴 *n.* tail
~sui² ~隨 *v.* follow
WEI³ 偉 *n.* hero ; *a.* great, brave
~jen² ~人 *n.* great man
~ta⁴ ~大 *a.* great
WEI⁴ 位 *n.* seat, position
~chih⁴ 置 *n.* position, location
~chü¹ ~居 *v.* situate
WEI⁴ 味 *n.* taste, flavor
~chüeh² ~覺 *n.* sense of taste
~mei³ ~美 *a.* delicious
~tao⁴ ~道 *n.* taste
WEI⁴ 喂 *v.* feed animals ; *int.* hello
WEI⁴ 胃 *n.* stomach
~k'ou³ ~口 *n.* appetite
~k'uei⁴ yang² ~潰瘍 *n.* gastric ulcer
~ping⁴ ~病 *n.* gastropathy
~t'ung⁴ ~痛 *n.* gastrodynia, gastralgia
~yen² ~炎 *n.* gastritis
WEI⁴ 慰 *n.* comfort, console
~lao² ~勞 *v.* comfort
~wen⁴ ~問 *v.* console
~yen⁴ ~唁 *v.* condole
WEI⁴ 衛 *n.* escort, guard, protect, defend
~hsing¹ ~星 *n.* satellite
~ping¹ ~兵 *n.* guard
~ping¹ shih⁴ ~兵室 *n.* guardhouse
~sheng¹ ~生 *n.* hygiene, sanitation ; *a.* sanitary
~sheng¹ chü² ~生局 *n.* health office
~shu⁴ ~戍 *v.* garrison
~shu⁴ ssu¹ ling⁴ pu⁴ ~戍司令部 *n.* garrison
headquarters
WEI⁴ 未 *adv.* not, not yet
~chih¹ shu⁴ ~知數 *n.* unknown number
~ch'ang² ~嘗 *adv.* never, not yet
~hun¹ ch'i¹ ~婚妻 *n.* fiancee
~hun¹ fu¹ ~婚夫 *n.* fiance

208

~lai² ~來 *n.* & *a.* future
~ting⁴ ~定 *a.* uncertain, undecided
WEN¹ 温 *a.* & *v.* warm
~ch'üan² ~泉 *n.* hot spring
~ho² ~和 *a.* mild
~hsi² ~習 *n.* review
~nuan³ ~暖 *a.* warm
~shih⁴ ~室 *n.* greenhouse
~tai⁴ ~帶 *n.* temperate zone
~tu⁴ ~度 *n.* temperature
~tu⁴ piao³ ~度表 *n.* heat indicator
WEN² 聞 *v.* hear; ~⁴ *a.* noted, famous
~² hsiang¹ chiao⁴ chu³ ~香教主 *n.* Bishop Smell Incense (Chinese religion)
~hsiang¹ tui⁴ ~香隊 *n.* snooping team**
~⁴ jen² ~人 *n.* celebrity
WEN² 文 *n.* essay, literature
~chang¹ ~章 *n.* essay, composition
~chien⁴ ~件 *n.* document, papers, script, dispatch
~chü⁴ ~具 *n.* stationery
~fa³ ~法 *n.* grammar
~hua⁴ ~化 *n.* civilization, culture
~hua⁴ chiao⁴ yü⁴ wei³ yüan² hui⁴ ~化教育委員會 *n.* Committee of Cultural and Educational Affairs**
~hua⁴ pu⁴ ~化部 *n.* Ministry of Cultural Affairs**
~hsüeh² ~學 *n.* literature, letters
~jen² ~人 *n.* scholarly, literary people
~mang² ~盲 *n.* illiteracy; *a.* illiterate
~ming² ~明 *n.* civilization, civility, *a.* civilized
~p'ing² ~憑 *n.* diploma
~shu¹ ~書 *n.* document, papers
~ya³ ~雅 *a.* graceful, elegant, refined, gentle
WEN² 蚊 *n.* mosquito
~chang⁴ ~帳 *n.* mosquito net
~yen¹ ~烟 *n.* mosquito incense
WEN⁴ 問 *v.* ask, inquire
~an⁴ ~案 *n.* trial
~hou⁴ ~侯 *v.* greet

209

~ta² ~答 *n.* dialogue

~t'i² ~題 *n.* question

WO³ 我 *pron.* I, me

~men² ~們 *pron.* we

~men² te¹ ~們的 *pron.* our, ours

~men² tzu⁴ chi³ ~們自己 *pron.* ourself, ourselves

~te¹ ~的 *pron.* my, mine

WO⁴ 握 *v.* grasp, shake, hold

~shou³ ~手 *v.* shake hands

WU¹ 屋 *n.* room, house

~chu³ ~主 *n.* landlord

~ting³ ~頂 *n.* roof

~ting³ hua¹ yüan² ~頂花園 *n.* roof garden

~ting³ shih⁴ t'ieh³ ssu¹ wang³ ~頂式鐵糸網 *n.* double apron fence

~yen² ~簷 *n.* eaves

~yü³ ~宇 *n.* building

WU² 無 *a.* no, none; *adv.* not; *prep.* without

~chih¹ ~知 *a.* ignorant

~ch'an³ chieh¹ chi² ~產階級 *n.* proletariat**

~ch'an³ chieh¹ chi² ko² ming⁴ ~產階級革命 *n.* proletarian revolution**

~ch'ih³ ~恥 *a.* shameless

~hsiao⁴ ~効 *a.* ineffective

~hsien⁴ chih⁴ ~限制 *n.* without limitation

~hsien⁴ kung¹ ssu¹ ~限公司 *n.* unlimited company

~hsien⁴ tien⁴ hua⁴ ~線電話 *n.* radio

~hsien⁴ tien⁴ t'ai² ~線電台 *n.* radio station

~hsin¹ ~心 *a.* unintentional

~hsing² ~形 *a.* invisible

~i⁴ ~益 *a.* disadvantageous

~ku¹ ~辜 *a.* innocent

~lai⁴ ~賴 *n.* rascal

~li³ ~理 *a.* unreasonable

~li³ ~禮 *a.* impolite

~liao² ~聊 *n.* cheerless

~lun⁴ ~論 *adv.* however

~lun⁴ ho² shih² ~論何時 *conj. & adv.* whenever

~lun⁴ shen² ma¹ ~論什麼 *pron.* whatever

~shu⁴ ~數 *n.* innumerable
~wang⁴ ~望 *a.* hopeless
~yung⁴ ~用 *a.* useless
WU³ 五 *n. & a.* five
　~chin¹ ~金 *n.* metals
　~ch'üan² hsien⁴ fa³ ~權憲法 *n.* Five Power
　　Constitution
　~fan³ yün⁴ tung⁴ ~反運動 *n.* five anti-move-
　　ments**
　~nien² chi⁴ hua⁴ ~年計劃 *n.* five-year plan
　~yüeh⁴ ~月 *n.* May
WU³ 伍 *n.* soldier's file
WU³ 午 *n.* noon, noontime, noontide
　~ch'ien² ~前 *n.* forenoon
　~hou⁴ ~後 *n. & a.* afternoon
　~shih² ~時 *n.* noontime, noontide
　~ts'an¹ ~餐 *n.* lunch
WU³ 武 *a.* military, warlike
　~chuang¹ ~裝 *a.* armed
　~chuang¹ tai⁴ ~裝帶 *n.* Sam Browne belt
　~hsia² ~俠 *n.* chivalry
　~kuan¹ ~官 *n.* military attache
　~kung¹ ~功 *n.* military merits
　~pei⁴ ~備 *n.* armament
　~shih⁴ ~士 *n.* cavalier
　~tuan⁴ ~斷 *adv.* arbitrarily
　~ch'i⁴ ~器 *n.* arms, weapon
WU³ 舞 *n. & v.* dance
　~chien⁴ ~劍 *v.* fence; *n.* fencing
　~ch'ang³ ~場 *n.* dancing hall
　~hui⁴ ~會 *n.* ball (dance)
　~nü³ ~女 *n.* dancing girl
　~pi⁴ ~弊 *v.* cheat
　~t'ai² ~臺 *n.* stage (theater)
　~yung³ chia¹ ~踊家 *n.* dancer
WU⁴ 誤 *n.* mistake, error
　~chieh³ ~解 *v.* misinterpret; *n.* misinterpreta-
　　tion
　~hui⁴ ~會 *v.* misunderstand; *n.* misunderstand-
　　ing
WU⁴ 務 *n.* affair, business

WU⁴ 悟 *v.* apprehend, awake

WU⁴ 物 *n.* substance, thing, matter

~chia⁴ ~價 *n.* price, value

~chien⁴ ~件 *n.* article, thing

~chih² ~質 *n.* matter; *a.* material

~chih² chien⁴ she⁴ ~質建設 *n.* material reconstruction

~chih² wen² ming² ~質文明 *n.* material civilization

~ch'an³ ~產 *n.* produce, product, production

~li³ hsüeh² ~理學 *n.* physics

Y

YA¹ 呀 *int.* [exclamation of pain, surprise, pity, joy] ah, aha

YA¹ 鴨 *n.* duck

~chiao⁴ ~叫 *v.* quack

~jung² pei⁴ ~羢被 *n.* feather quilt

~tan⁴ ~蛋 *n.* duck's egg

YA¹ 壓 *v.* press down, crush

~chih⁴ ~制 *v.* suppress

~fu² ~服 *v.* press down

~p'o⁴ ~迫 *v.* oppress; *n.* oppression

~so¹ ~縮 *v.* condense

~tao³ ~倒 *v.* overwhelm, overcome

YA² 牙 *n.* tooth

~ch'ien¹ ~籤 *n.* toothpick

~i¹ ~醫 *n.* dentist

~kao¹ ~膏 *n.* toothpaste

~k'o¹ ~科 *n.* dentistry

~shua¹ ~刷 *n.* toothbrush

~shui⁴ ~稅 *n.* brokerage tax

~t'ung⁴ ~痛 *n.* toothache

YA² 芽 *n.* bud, shoot, sprout

YANG¹ 央 *n.* middle, center, half; *v.* request

~ch'iu² ~求 *v.* request, beg

YANG¹ 秧 *n.* rice sprout, fried fish

~miao² ~苗 *n.* young shoot

YANG² 洋 *n.* ocean

~fu² ~服 *n.* Western suit
~hui¹ ~灰 *n.* cement
~huo³ ~火 *n.* match
~huo⁴ ~貨 *n.* foreign goods
~pu⁴ ~布 *n.* calico
~yu² ~油 *n.* kerosene
YANG² 羊 *n.* sheep
~chih¹ ~脂 *n.* sheep suet
~hsien² feng¹ ~癎瘋 *n.* epilepsy
~jou⁴ ~肉 *n.* mutton
~mao² ~毛 *n.* sheep's wool
~p'i² chih³ ~皮紙 *n.* parchment
YANG² 楊 *n.* poplar
~liu³ ~柳 *n.* willow
YANG² 陽 *a.* sunny, bright, male
~chi² ~極 *n.* anode (*elec.*)
~kuang¹ ~光 *n.* sunbeam
~li⁴ ~曆 *n.* solar calendar
~wei¹ ~萎 *a.* sexually impotent; *adj.* impotence,
    impotency; *n.* impotent
YANG² 揚 *v.* raise, spread, praise
~fan¹ ~帆 *v.* hoist a sail
~ming² ~名 *v.* make known
~tzu³ chiang¹ ~子江 *n.* Yangtze River
YANG³ 養 *v.* nourish, rear, feed
~ch'eng² ~成 *v.* educate
~ch'i⁴ ~氣 *n.* oxygen
~feng¹ fang² ~蜂房 *n.* apiary
~hua⁴ wu⁴ ~化物 *n.* oxide
~lao³ chin¹ ~老金 *n.* pension
~lao³ yüan⁴ ~老院 *n.* Old People's Home
~liao⁴ ~料 *n.* nutrition
~nü³ ~女 *n.* adopted-daughter
~tzu³ ~子 *n.* adopted-son
~yü⁴ ~育 *v.* rear, bring up
YANG⁴ 樣 *n.* sample, example, model, pattern,
    style, kind
~p'in³ ~品 *n.* sample, specimen
~shih⁴ ~式 *n.* pattern, style, fashion
YAO¹ 腰 *n.* waist
~tai⁴ ~帶 *n.* girdle

213

~t'eng² ~疼 *n.* lumbago
~tzu¹ ~子 *n.* kidney
YAO² 搖 *v.* shake, move, wave
~ch'uang² ~床 *n.* cradle
~i³ ~椅 *n.* rocking chair
YAO² 謠 *n.* rumor
~yen² ~言 n. rumor
YAO³ 咬 *v.* bite
~chüeh² ~嚼 *v.* chew
~shang¹ ~傷 *v.* bite (sting)
YAO⁴ 若 *conj.* if, as if
~shih⁴ ~是 *conj.* if
jo⁴ ho² ~何 *adv.* how
~kan¹ ~干 *a. & pron.* some (any)
YAO⁴ 要 *v.* desire. ~¹ *v.* demand; *a.* important
~¹ ch'iu² ~求 *v.* demand
~hsia² ~挾 *v.* coerce; *n.* coercion
~⁴ chin³ ~緊 *a.* important
~jen² ~人 *n.* VIP (very important person)
~sai⁴ ~塞 *n.* fort, fortification
~su⁴ ~素 *n.* element
~t'u² ~図 *n.* sketch
YAO⁴ 藥 *n.* medicine, drug
~chi⁴ shih¹ ~劑師 *n.* pharmacist
~fang¹ ~方 *n.* prescription (*med.*)
~fang² ~房 *n.* drugstore, pharmacy
~fen³ ~粉 *n.* medicinal powder
~li³ hsüeh² ~理學 *n.* pharmacology
~p'ien⁴ ~片 *n.* tablet (*med.*)
~shang¹ ~商 *n.* druggist, pharmacist
~wan² ~丸 *n.* pill
YAO⁴ 樂 *see* LE⁴
YEH² 爺 *n.* grandfather
YEH³ 也 *adv.* also; *conj.* and, also, still
~hsü³ ~許 *adv.* perhaps, maybe, possibly
~shih⁴ ~是 *adv.* also
YEH³ 野 *n.* desert, waste, wilderness; *a.* wild,
savage, rude
~chan⁴ p'ao⁴ ~戰礮 *n.* field piece
~hsin¹ ~心 *n.* ambition
~man² ~蠻 *a.* barbaric, brutal; *n.* barbarian

214

~p'ao⁴ ~砲 *n.* field gun
~p'ao⁴ ping¹ ~砲兵 *n.* field artillery
~shou⁴ ~獸 *n.* beast
~wai⁴ ~外 *n.* field
~wai⁴ yen³ hsi² ~外演習 *n.* field exercise
YEH⁴ 夜 *n.* night
  ~chien¹ hung¹ cha⁴ ~間轟炸 *n.* night bombing
  ~chien¹ kung¹ chi¹ ~間攻擊 *n.* night attack
  ~chien¹ yen³ hsi² ~間演習 *n.* night exercise
  ~fan⁴ ~飯 *n.* supper
  ~hsiao⁴ ~校 *n.* night school
  ~hsing² chün¹ ~行軍 *n.* night march
  ~li³ fu² ~禮服 *n.* evening dress
  ~mang² ~盲 *n.* night blindness
  ~pan¹ ~班 *n.* night shift
  ~pan⁴ ~半 *n.* midnight
  ~shih⁴ ~市 *n.* night market
  ~tsung³ hui⁴ ~總會 *n.* night club, night spot
  ~ying¹ ~鶯 *n.* nightingale
  ~ying¹ ~鷹 *n.* nighthawk
  ~yu² shen² ~遊神 *n.* nightwalker
YEH⁴ 業 *n.* occupation, profession, business
  ~shih¹ ~師 *n.* tutor
  ~wu⁴ ~務 *n.* task, function, job, business
YEH⁴ 葉 *n.* leaf
YEN¹ 烟 *n.* fumes, smoke, cigarette, tobacco
  ~hua¹ ~花 *n.* prostitute
  ~huo³ ~火 fireworks
  ~mei² ~煤 *n.* bituminous coal
  ~mu⁴ ~幕 *n.* smoke screen
  ~mu⁴ tan⁴ ~幕彈 *n.* smoke shell
  ~tou³ ~斗 *n.* smoking pipe
  ~ts'ao³ ~草 *n.* tobacco
  ~ts'ao³ shang¹ ~草商 *n.* tobacconist
  ~ts'ung¹ ~囪 *n.* chimney, stovepipe
  ~yeh⁴ ~葉 *n.* tobacco-leaf
YEN² 言 *v.* speak
  ~kuo⁴ ch'i² shih² ~過其實 *v.* exaggerate
  ~lun⁴ ~論 *n.* speech
  ~yü³ ~語 speech, language
YEN² 沿 *v.* follow. ~⁴ *prep.* along, by, through

215

~hai³ p'ing² yüan² ~海平原 *n.* coastal plain

YEN² 顏 *n.* color, countenance

~mien⁴ ~面 *n.* countenance

~se⁴ ~色 *n.* color

YEN² 研 *v.* grind, study

~chiu¹ ~究 *v.* study, research

~chiu¹ sheng¹ ~究生 *n.* postgraduate

YEN² 延 *v.* delay, prolong, extend, invite, spread

~ch'ang² ~長 *v.* prolong, extend; *n.* extension, prolongation

~ch'i¹ ~期 *v.* postpone

~ch'i¹ hsin⁴ kuan³ ~期信管 *n.* delay fuse

~ch'ih² ~遲 *v.* delay

~p'ing⁴ ~聘 *v.* engage (employ)

YEN² 鹽 *n.* salt

~ching³ ~井 *n.* salt well

~shui³ ~水 *n.* brine, salt water

~shui⁴ ~稅 *n.* salt revenue

YEN² 嚴 *a.* severe, stern, rigid, solemn; *adv.* very

~cheng⁴ ~正 *a.* upright (righteous)

~chung⁴ ~重 *a.* critical, serious

~han² ~寒 *n.* severe cold

~k'u⁴ ~酷 *a.* cruel, severe

~li⁴ ~厲 *a.* stern, severe

~mi⁴ ~密 *a.* close, strict

~su⁴ ~肅 *a.* austere; *n.* austerity

YEN³ 眼 *n.* eye, hole

~chao⁴ ~罩 *n.* eye-shade

~chieh⁴ ~界 *n.* field of view

~ching⁴ ~鏡 *n.* eyeglass

~k'o¹ ~科 *n.* ophthalmology

~k'o¹ i¹ sheng¹ ~科醫生 *n.* ophthalmology

~lei⁴ ~淚 *n.* tear

~lien² ~簾 *n.* eyelid

~mao² ~毛 *n.* eyelash

~mei² ~眉 *n.* eyebrow

~pei¹ ~杯 *n.* eye-cup

~t'ung² ~瞳 *n.* pupil (eye)

~yao⁴ ~藥 *n.* eye medicine

YEN³ 演 *v.* act, play, perform

~chi⁴ ~劇 *v.* act a drama

216

~chiang³ ~講 v. make a speech
~chiang³ yüan² ~講員 n. lecturer
~hsi² ~習 n. exercise, rehearsal
~pien⁴ ~變 v. develop (a situation)
~shuo¹ chia¹ ~説家 n. orator
~tsou⁴ ~奏 v. perform music
YEN⁴ 厭 v. dislike, hate
~ch'i⁴ ~棄 v. reject
~fan² ~煩 a. troublesome
~wu⁴ ~惡 v. dislike
YEN⁴ 驗 n. evidence, effect, proof; v. inspect, verify
~ming² ~明 v. verify
~shih¹ ~屍 n. autopsy, postmortem
YIN¹ 因 conj. because
~kuo³ ~果 n. cause and effect
~kuo³ lü⁴ ~果率 n. causality
~su⁴ ~素 n. factor
~tz'u³ ~此 adv. therefore
~wei⁴ ~爲 conj. because
YIN¹ 陰 a. shady, dark, secret
~ching¹ ~莖 n. penis
~kou¹ ~溝 n. sewer
~liang² ~涼 n. cool
~mao² ~毛 n. pubes
~mou² ~謀 n. conspiracy
~sen¹ ~森 a. gloomy
~tao⁴ ~道 n. vagina
~tien⁴ ~電 n. negative (elec.)
YIN¹ 音 n. tone, voice, sound
~hsin⁴ ~信 n. news, information
~tiao⁴ ~調 n. tune, pitch
~yüeh⁴ ~樂 n. music
~yüeh⁴ chia¹ ~樂家 n. musician
~yüeh⁴ hui⁴ ~樂會 n. concert, recital
~yüeh⁴ tui⁴ ~樂隊 n. band music
~yün⁴ ~韻 n. rhyme
YIN² 銀 n. silver
~ch'i⁴ ~器 n. silverware
~hang² ~行 n. bank
~hang² chia¹ ~行家 n. banker

~hang² hu⁴ t'ou² ~行戶頭 *n.* bank account

~hang² yeh⁴ ~行業 *n.* banking

~ho² ~河 *n.* Milky Way

YIN³ 引 *n.* preface, introduction; *v.* lead, introduce

~ch'ing² ~擎 *n.* engine

~hao⁴ ~號 *n.* quotation mark

~tao⁴ ~導 *v.* conduct, guide

~yu⁴ ~誘 *v.* entice, tempt, seduce, lure; *n.* attractiveness, temptation

~yung⁴ ~用 *v.* quote

YIN³ 飲 *v.* drink. ~⁴ *v.* water a horse

YIN⁴ 印 *n.* stamp, seal, mark; *v.* print, stamp

~hsiang⁴ ~象 *n.* impression

~shua¹ ~刷 *v.* print; *n.* printing

~shua¹ chi¹ ~刷機 *n.* printing press

YING¹ 應 *v. aux.* ought to. ~⁴ *n.* answer; *v.* reply, respond; *a.* suitable

~¹ tang¹ ~當 *v. aux.* ought, must

~⁴ chan⁴ ~戰 *v.* accept battle

~ch'ou² ~酬 *v.* entertain

~fu⁴ ~付 *v.* deal with

~fu⁴ ch'ing² k'uang⁴ ~付情況 *v.* meet the situation

~sheng¹ ~聲 *n.* echo

~ti² ~敵 *v.* meet the enemy

~tui⁴ ~對 *v.* answer, respond

~yung⁴ ~用 *n.* application

~yün³ ~允 *v.* promise

YING¹ 英 *a.* heroic, talented

~hsiung² ~雄 *n.* hero

~hsiung² ch'i⁴ k'ai³ ~雄氣慨 *n.* heroism

~li³ ~里 *n.* mile

~ming² ~明 *a.* clever

~ts'un⁴ ~寸 *n.* inch

~wei¹ ~威 *n.* English language

~wen² fa³ ~文法 *n.* English grammar

YING² 迎 *v.* welcome, meet

~chieh¹ ~接 *v.* meet

YING² 營 *n.* battalion, camp, business, living; *v.* manage

218

~chang³ ~長 *n.* battalion commander
~chang⁴ ~帳 *n.* camp tents
~chiu⁴ ~救 *v.* plan help
~fang² ~房 *n.* barracks
~li⁴ ~利 *n.* profit making
~tsao⁴ ~造 *v.* construct
~yang³ ~養 *n.* nourishment
~yang³ pu⁴ tsu² ~養不足 *n.* malnutrition
~yeh⁴ ~業 *n.* business
~yeh⁴ shih² chien¹ ~業時間 *n.* business hour
~yeh⁴ shui⁴ ~業稅 *n.* business tax

YING² 蠅 *n.* fly, housefly
YING³ 影 *n.* shadow, image, vestige
~hsi⁴ ~戲 *n.* movie
~hsiang³ ~響 *n.* influence
~hsing¹ ~星 *n.* movie star
~tzu¹ ~子 *n.* shadow
YING⁴ 硬 *a.* hard, obstinate, solid
~li⁴ ~力 *n.* stress
~lü³ ~鋁 duraluminum
~mei² ~煤 *n.* anthracite
YU¹ 優 *n.* clown; *a.* excellent, abundant, excessive
~hsien¹ ch'üan² ~先權 *n.* priority
~hsiu⁴ te¹ ~秀的 *a.* excellent
~sheng⁴ ~勝 *n.* victory
~shih⁴ ~勢 *n.* superiority, supremacy
~tai⁴ ~待 *v.* treat specially
~teng³ ~等 *n.* superior class
~tien³ ~點 *n.* merit
~ya³ ~雅 *a.* gracious
~yüeh⁴ ~越 *a.* superior
YU¹ 憂 *n.* melancholy; *a.* anxious, grieved
~ch'ou² ~愁 *n.* anxiety
~lü⁴ ~慮 *n.* sorrow
YU² 游 *v.* float, ramble, swim
~hsi⁴ ~戲 *n.* game
~li⁴ ~歷 *v.* travel
~min² ~民 *n.* vagrant
~tang⁴ ~蕩 *v.* wander, ramble
~yung³ ~泳 *v.* swim; *n.* swimming
~yung³ i¹ ~泳衣 *n.* swimming suit

219

~yung³ mao⁴ ~泳帽 *n.* swimming cap
~yung³ ch'ih² ~泳池 *n.* swimming pool
YU² 遊 *v.* ramble, travel
~chi⁴ ~記 *n.* travels
~hsi⁴ ~戲 *v.* play; *n.* game, play
~hsing² ~行 *v.* parade
~li⁴ ~歷 *v.* travel
~mu⁴ ~牧 *a.* nomadic
~piao¹ ~標 *n.* sight slide
~shui⁴ ~説 *v.* persuade
YU² 郵 *n.* post office, lodge
~cheng⁴ ~政 *n.* post (mail)
~cheng⁴ chü² ~政局 *n.* post office
~cheng⁴ ch'u² hsü⁴ ~政儲蓄 *n.* postal saving
~cheng⁴ hsin⁴ hsiang¹ ~政信箱 *n.* post box
~chi⁴ ~寄 *v.* mail
~chien⁴ ~件 *n.* mail
~ch'ai¹ ~差 *n.* postman, postboy, mailman
~fei⁴ ~費 *n.* postage
~hui⁴ ~匯 *n.* postal money order
~p'iao⁴ ~票 *n.* stamp
~tai⁴ ~袋 *n.* mail bag
~tien⁴ pu⁴ ~電部 *n.* Ministry of Posts and Tele-
  communications**
~t'ung³ ~筒 *n.* mailbox
YU² 油 *n.* fat, oil; *a.* oily
~chih³ ~紙 *n.* oil-paper
~ch'i¹ ~漆 *n.* oil paint, oil color
~hua⁴ ~畫 *n.* oil painting
~hsiang¹ ~箱 *n.* fuel tank
~kao¹ ~膏 *n.* ointment
~men² t'a⁴ pan³ ~門踏板 *n.* accelerator pedal
~ni⁴ ~膩 *a.* greasy
~pu⁴ ~布 *n.* oilcloth
~ts'ai⁴ ~菜 *n.* rape (plant)
~yin⁴ ~印 *v.* mimeograph
YU² 由 *n.* cause, reason; *prep.* from, by, through
~shih⁴ ~是 *adv.* therefore, hence
YU³ 有 *v.* have, hold, possess, own
~chia⁴ chih² te¹ ~價值的 *a.* valuable
~ch'an³ chieh¹ chi² ~産階級 *n.* bourgeoisie
220

~ch'ang² ~常 *n.* stability
~ch'ü⁴ ~趣 *a.* interesting
~hsi¹ wang⁴ ~希望 *a.* promising, hopeful
~hsiao⁴ ~效 *a.* effective
~hsien⁴ kung¹ ssu¹ ~限公司 *n.* limited company
~hsien⁴ te¹ ~限的 *a.* limited
~li³ ~理 *a.* reasonable
~li³ ~禮 *a.* polite
~li⁴ ~利 *a.* profitable, advantageous
~ming² te¹ ~名的 *a.* famous, well-known, noted
~neng² li⁴ te¹ ~能力的 *a.* able
~yung⁴ ~用 *a.* useful
YU³ 友 *n.* friend
~ai⁴ ~愛 *n.* amity
~i² ~誼 *n.* friendship
~jen² ~人 *n.* friend
YU⁴ 又 *adv.* again, also, too, moreover, further;
conj. and
~chi² ~及 *n.* postscript
~i¹ t'ien¹ ~一天 *adv.* another day
YU⁴ 右 *a. & n.* right (direction)
~ch'ing¹ ~傾 *a.* rightist (idea)
~p'ai⁴ ~派 *n.* rightist
~shou³ ~手 *a.* right-hand, right-handed
YUNG¹ 擁 *v.* push, crowd. ~³ *v.* embrace
~¹ chi³ ~擠 *v.* crowd
~sai¹ ~塞 *v.* block up
~³ hu⁴ ~護 *v.* support, uphold
~pao⁴ ~抱 *v.* embrace
YUNG³ 永 *a.* perpetual, eternal, permanent
~chiu³ ~久 *a.* permanent, perpetual; *adv.* permanently, perpetually
~pu⁴ ~不 *adv.* never
~sheng¹ ~生 *a.* eternal; *n.* eternity
~yüan³ ~遠 *adv.* forever, always
YUNG³ 勇 *a.* brave, courageous, daring; *n.* valor,
bravery
~ch'i⁴ ~氣 *n.* courage
~kan³ ~敢 *n.* valor, bravery
YUNG⁴ 用 *v.* use, spend; *n.* use, expense
~chi⁴ ~計 *v.* use tricks

221

~chin¹ ~金 *n.* commission (money)
~chü⁴ ~具 *n.* tool, instrument, utensil
~fei⁴ ~費 *n.* expenditure, expense
~jen² ~人 *n.* servant; *v.* employ
~kung¹ ~功 *v.* study hard
~t'u² ~途 *n.* usage
YÜ² 魚 *n.* fish, letter
YÜ² 於 *prep.* at, in, on, to, by
  ~chin¹ ~今 *adv.* at present, now
  ~hsia⁴ ~下 *adv.* below
  ~shih⁴ ~是 *adv.* therefore, hence
  ~tz'u³ ~此 *adv.* hereabout
YÜ² 餘 *n.* remainder, surplus, excess
YÜ² 娛 *v.* amuse, please, enjoy; *n.* pleasure, amusement
  ~le⁴ ~樂 *n.* entertainment
YÜ³ 語 *v.* talk, speak; *n.* language
  ~yen² ~言 *n.* language, speech
  ~yen² hsüeh² ~言學 *n.* linguistic science
  ~yen² hsüeh² chia¹ ~言學家 *n.* linguist
YÜ³ 與 *v.* give. ~⁴ *v.* share; *conj.* and
YÜ³ 雨 *n.* rain
  ~chi⁴ ~季 *n.* rainy season
  ~i¹ ~衣 *n.* raincoat
  ~liang⁴ ~量 *n.* rainfall
  ~san³ ~傘 *n.* umbrella
  ~tien³ ~點 *n.* raindrop
YÜ⁴ 遇 *v.* meet, occur
YÜ⁴ 育 *v.* nourish, foster, rear
  ~ying¹ t'ang² ~嬰堂 *n.* orphanage
YÜ⁴ 玉 *n.* jade
  ~mi³ ~米 *n.* maize
  ~shu³ shu³ ~蜀黍 *n.* Indian corn, corn
YÜ⁴ 預 *v.* prepare
  ~chao⁴ ~兆 *n.* omen
  ~chih¹ ~支 *v.* advance money
  ~fang² ~防 *v.* prevent; *n.* prevention
  ~fu⁴ ~付 *v.* pay in advance
  ~k'o¹ ~科 *n.* preparatory class
  ~pei⁴ ~備 *v.* prepare; *adv.* ready; *n.* preparation

~pei⁴ tui⁴ ~備隊 *n.* reserves (troops)
~suan⁴ ~算 *n.* budget
~suan⁴ chü² ~算局 *n.* Budget Bureau*
~ts'e⁴ ~測 *n.* forecast
~yen² ~言 *v.* foretell; *n.* prophecy
~yen² chia¹ ~言家 *n.* prophet
~yüeh¹ ~約 *v.* subscribe to
YÜAN¹ 宛 *v.* have a grudge, injure, oppress
~chia¹ ~家 *n.* enemy, foe
~ch'ou² ~仇 *n.* enemity
~ch'ü¹ ~屈 *n.* grievance
YÜAN² 元 *n.* beginning, dollar
~ch'i⁴ ~氣 *n.* energy, vigor
~su⁴ ~素 *n.* element
~shih³ ~始 *n.* origin, source, beginning
~shou³ ~首 *n.* head, ruler, chief executive
~shuai⁴ ~帥 *n.* Army General (*U.S.*)
~tan⁴ ~旦 *n.* New Year's Day
~tzu³ ~子 *n.* atom
~yüeh⁴ ~月 *n.* January
YÜAN² 原 *n.* plain; *a.* original
~chu³ ~主 *n.* proprietor, owner
~ch'i⁴ ~氣 *n.* vitality
~kao³ ~稿 *n.* protocol
~kao⁴ ~告 *n.* plaintiff
~li³ ~理 *n.* principle
~liang⁴ ~諒 *n.* pardon
~liao⁴ ~料 *n.* raw material
~su⁴ ~素 *n.* element
~shih³ ~始 *a.* primitive
~tse² hsing⁴ ~則性 *n.* character of principle**
~tzu³ ~子 *n.* atom; *a.* atomic
~tzu³ chan⁴ cheng¹ ~子戰争 *n.* atomic warfare
~tzu³ liang⁴ ~子量 *n.* atomic weight
~tzu³ lun⁴ ~子論 *n.* atomic theory
~tzu³ neng² ~子能 *n.* atomic energy
~tzu³ shu⁴ ~子數 *n.* atomic number
~tzu³ tan⁴ ~子彈 *n.* atomic bomb
~wen² ~文 *n.* text
~yin¹ ~因 *n.* reason, cause
YÜAN² 員 *n.* member

223

YÜAN² 圓 *a.* round, circular; *n.* circle, dollar

~**cho¹** ~卓 *n.* round table

~**chou¹** ~周 *n.* circumference

~**chu⁴ t'i³** ~柱體 *n.* cylinder

~**chui¹ t'i³** ~錐體 *n.* cone

~**hsing²** ~形 *n.* sphere

~**kuei¹** ~規 *n.* compass

~**man³** ~滿 *a.* complete, satisfactory

YÜAN² 園 *n.* garden, orchard, park

~**i⁴** ~藝 *n.* gardening

~**ting¹** ~丁 *n.* gardener

~**yu² hui⁴** ~遊會 *n.* garden party

YÜAN² 援 *v.* rescue, quote, hold fast

~**chiu⁴** ~救 *v.* relieve (aid)

~**chu⁴** ~助 *v.* assist, help

~**ping¹** ~兵 *n.* reinforcement

~**tui⁴** ~隊 *n.* support troops

YÜAN³ 遠 *a.* distant. ~⁴ *v.* remove

~**cheng¹ chün¹** ~征軍 *n.* expeditionary force

~**chü⁴ li²** ~距離 *n.* long range

~**she⁴ p'ao⁴** ~射砲 *n.* long range gun

~**tan⁴** ~彈 *a.* over shoot

~**tung¹** ~東 *n.* Far East

~**tung¹ wen⁴ t'i²** ~東問題 *n.* problem of the Far East

~**tung¹ yün⁴ tung⁴ hui⁴** ~東運動會 *n.* Far East Olympic Games

YÜAN⁴ 院 *n.* courtyard

YÜAN⁴ 願 *n. & v.* wish, desire

~**i⁴** ~意 *a.* willing

~**wang⁴** ~望 *n.* wish, desire

YÜAN⁴ 怨 *v.* grumble, hate; *a.* dissatisfied

~**hen⁴** ~恨 *v.* hate

~**yen²** ~言 *a.* spiteful

YÜEH¹ 約 *v.* invite; *n.* engagement, treaty

~**hui⁴** ~會 *v.* make an appointment

~**lüeh⁴** ~略 *a.* brief, concise; *adv.* approximately

~**su⁴** ~束 *v.* restrain, control

~**shih⁴** ~誓 *v.* swear; *a.* sworn

YÜEH⁴ 月 *n.* moon, month; *adv.* monthly

224

~ching¹ ~經 *n.* menses
~fen⁴ p'ai² ~份牌 *n.* calendar
~kuang¹ ~光 *n.* moonlight, moonshine
~k'an¹ ~刊 *n.* monthly magazine
~lao³ ~老 *n.* marriage matchmaker
~liang⁴ ~亮 *n.* moon
~ping³ ~餅 *n.* moon cake (eaten at the Chinese Mid-Autumn Festival)
~shih² ~蝕 *n.* lunar eclipse
~t'ai² ~台 *n.* railroad station platform
~t'ai² p'iao⁴ ~台票 *n.* platform ticket
YÜEH⁴ 越 *v.* exceed, excel, surpass
~ch'üan² ~權 *v.* exceed one's power
~kuo⁴ ~過 *v.* pass over
~yeh³ ~野 *a.* cross-country
YÜEH⁴ 閱 *v.* read, peruse, look at
~li⁴ ~歷 *n.* experience
~ping¹ ~兵 *v.* review troops
~tu² ~讀 *v.* read
YÜEH⁴ 樂 *see* LE⁴
YÜN² 雲 *n.* cloud; *a.* cloudy
YÜN⁴ 運 *v.* move, remove, transport; *n.* fate
~ch'i⁴ ~氣 *n.* fortune, luck
~ch'u¹ ~出 *v.*export
~fei⁴ ~費 *n.* freight
~ho² ~河 *n.* canal, Grand Canal
~ju⁴ ~入 *v.* import
~shu¹ ~輸 *v.* transport; *n.* transportation
~shu¹ chi¹ ~輸機 *n.* transport airplane
~tung⁴ ~動 *n. & v.* exercise; *n.* movement
~tung⁴ hui⁴ ~動會 *n.* athletic meeting
~tung⁴ hsing⁴ ~動性 *n.* mobility

225

CPSIA information can be obtained
at www.ICGtesting.com
Printed in the USA
LVHW021138040522
717858LV00004B/129